THE ART of CYCLING

THE ART of CYCLING

Staying Safe on Urban Streets

Second Edition

ROBERT HURST

Foreword by Marla Streb

FALCONGUIDES

GUILFORD, CONNECTICUT
HELENA, MONTANA

AN IMPRINT OF GLOBE PEQUOT PRESS

FALCONGUIDES®

Copyright © 2014 by Robert Hurst

FalconGuides is an imprint of Globe Pequot Press.
Falcon, FalconGuides, and Outfit Your Mind are registered trademarks of Morris Book Publishing, LLC.

Photographs and traffic diagrams by the author. Other illustrations by Sam Turner.

Text design: Maggie Peterson
Layout artist: Mary Ballachino
Project editor: Ellen Urban

Library of Congress Cataloging-in-Publication Data is available on file.
ISBN 978-0-7627-9005-0

Printed in the United States of America
10 9 8 7 6 5 4 3 2 1

CONTENTS

Contents

FOREWORD

It's about time that this book was written.

Robert Hurst succeeds in writing about cycling the way that Rachel Carson triumphed with *Silent Spring,* the seminal work whose publication spawned Earth Day, the Environmental Protection Agency, consumer recycling, and how we look at the world. *The Art of Cycling* is a clarion call not only for cyclists and those with whom we share the road, car drivers, but also for our elected representatives and urban planners who imagine and build the communities where we live.

Hurst is illustrative and inspiring without sounding preachy or depressing, even during the passages where he is righteously angry. His insightful humor ensures that this book is more than just a droll "how-to" guide.

As a professional bike racer myself, as well as a century rider and daily bike commuter, the almost perfect utility of the bicycle is reaffirmed in my mind with each pedal stroke on every ride, whether to the finish line or to the video store. I have bombed down the Kamikaze course at 60 miles per hour. I've won a Winter X Games gold medal skidding on snow. On my downhill bike, I've flown more than 40 feet through the air and landed with a fair share of broken bones. During the last ten years, while on the pro tour, I've ridden through Tokyo at rush hour, across Paris amid a general strike, and around Rome when it seemed that every Fiat's horn was signaling in Morse code.

Yet sometimes it's more dangerous just riding across town to pick up my mail.

In this book, Hurst has expressed all the emotion and logic for cycling as a means of transportation and as a way of life, which I sadly suppress. After a day of defending my right to Mount Tam's fire roads or chasing a morning's skinny tire group ride through Marin County's dairy valleys, or when I am coasting along to the grocery store, too often there occurs a moment. A supersize SUV roars past almost clipping me with a passenger door mirror. I am speechless—too tired to reserve my right to ride a bicycle on a public street. The tailpipe speeds away, and the moment passes, even more likely to happen again tomorrow.

The sad irony is that Marin County, California, is supposed to be a "bike friendly" community. During this last off-season, I rode my bike from Fort Lauderdale to Baltimore, and I can attest that "sharing the road" is more a concept than a reality.

But it doesn't have to be this way. Robert shares his strategic and tactical lessons for riding safer and faster through the urban landscape, sometimes even skirting the edges of the law more as a practical measure than as an act of civil disobedience. And I applaud.

Robert Hurst reminds us that if we cyclists don't skillfully exercise our right to the road, we lose our right to the road. This empowering urban cycling book should come in the glove box of every new car sold.

Marla Streb

Marla Streb is a world-champion mountain bike racer, has starred in the IMAX film *Top Speed,* and is the author of *Downhill: The Life Story of a Gravity Goddess,* published by Penguin Putnam. Before she joined the World Cup mountain biking circuit, she was a research biologist at the Scripps Research Institute, devoted to finding a cure for AIDS. Marla began riding a bike on a daily basis in 1990, when she took an extra job as a bike messenger. Soon, however, it became her life's passion, and she is now one of the fastest (and bravest!) bicyclists in the world. Check her out at www.marlastreb.com.

ACKNOWLEDGMENTS

Although the gaffes and screwups in these pages are solely my responsibility, and I beg your pardon for them, the good stuff comes from many people.

Thanks to Sam Turner for his illustrations.

Heartfelt thank-yous go to the several dozen urban-cycling maniacs that I am blessed with knowing, many of whom are close friends. For years I watched them negotiate the city streets with style, grace, and intelligence. The cumulative riding experience among them is mind-boggling. The advice they give comes from millions of miles and a sprinkling of near-death experiences and does not always correspond to conventional wisdom. Especially among this group I must thank Robert Reid, Christie Martin, Mike McGranahan, Steve Campana, and Joe Dillon; their comments were instrumental in the book's completion.

I received free help smoothing out the manuscript from Kamla Hurst and Steve Campana, and gave my dad, Jerry Hurst, a fat target for his grammatical acuity. (Dad is a retired high school English teacher.)

Finally, thanks to all the cyclists out there who ride every day, snow or shine, in a way that makes it easier for others to do the same.

INTRODUCTION

While this book is technically a second edition, it is really the third version of a book that was published in 2004 under the title *The Art of Urban Cycling: Lessons from the Street.* This most recent version has been updated throughout and expanded, with some new sections here and there.

It's impressive how things have changed in the bike world since 2006, when the last edition came out. We experienced an economic crisis and an energy crisis, and the "average" American (a mythical character if there ever was one) became much, much more likely to ride a bike for transportation. Urban cycling became a topic, if not a hot topic. Bike-share systems popped up around the country, and city planning departments were reinvigorated in their attempts to attract and accommodate cyclists. All these trends persist as this new edition goes to press. It's exciting for bicyclists and people in general, although arguably a result of troubling circumstances.

One thing has not changed much at all since the first edition: the core message of the book. Those so-called lessons from the street. In fact, most of the key sections on traffic cycling remain completely unchanged. The book describes the mind-set and techniques of the most experienced riders in the world, and those things haven't changed.

Essentially, I realized after the fact, the book describes a system of defensive driving for bicyclists. Preaching the virtues of defensive driving—really a way of thinking about traffic that goes beyond mere rule following and emphasizes anticipating the mistakes of other road users—is hardly new or controversial. Defensive driving has formed the core message of safety programs and educational materials for drivers and motorcyclists since the mid-1960s. In driving and motorcycling instruction, both private and government sponsored, defensive driving still takes top billing.

For some reason we bicyclists were served a very different message. Defensive cycling has not been given proper emphasis by big bike clubs, local police departments, the Feds, or anyone. Rarely has the safety message for cyclists progressed much beyond "follow traffic laws and wear a helmet." When cycling advocacy did offer deeper advice it usually deemphasized defensive driving in favor of assertive lane positioning and rule following—as if making oneself as "visible and predictable" as possible were enough to cancel the need for defensiveness. It's a comforting notion, but obviously, and unfortunately, it's a false one. It's something to think about as you read through this book.

I don't know how much the publication of *The Art of Urban Cycling* had to do with any of this, but the game has definitely changed. Today the bike-safety crowd acknowledges defensive-driving techniques more than ever. There's still a lot of room for improvement, but we definitely took a few big pedal stomps in the right direction. If we keep rolling that way, we'll improve the situation even more for people on bikes and, by extension, everybody else.

Thanks to everyone who purchased, borrowed, or stole this book. I hope it helps.

Robert Hurst
Denver, 2014

CHAPTER 1

FRANKENSTEIN'S MONSTER

CONTINUUM

Setting out to write a book about cycling, it didn't seem likely that I would be spending too much time explaining the history of the bicycle itself. Since the book's primary concern would be the cyclist's relation to the twenty-first-century city, it figured that the old-timey stuff would provide, at best, colorful side matter . . . but then an undeniable truth was revealed: The birth of the bicycle, the rise of the auto, and the postmodern American sprawled-out city are all lined up along the same continuum.

As cyclists in the new millennium, our situation has strange and ironic roots in the time of hoop skirts, silver panics, and railroad tycoons. The bicycle craze of the late nineteenth century led seamlessly into the automobile craze of the twentieth and twenty-first. Indeed, as you will later read, a strong argument could be made—a correct one, too—that the success of autos was dependent on the prior development of the bicycle. The automobile craze, having been coaxed into existence in large measure by the fledgling bicycle community, became a chronic condition that shaped America's "built environment" as drastically as its consciousness; it poked around the edges of mainstream culture, changed it, then finally became it. The car culture is a version of Frankenstein's monster that, today, every cyclist must face.

And so, because it will do us no good to avoid the wicked truth, let's begin at the beginning . . .

BICYCLES IN THE AGE OF MANURE: LEONARDO TO STARLEY

The seemingly straightforward task of explaining the history of the bicycle became rather messy in 1974, when Italian scholar Augusto Marinoni announced that Leonardo da Vinci invented the modern bicycle in the fifteenth century. It was stunning news.

Several years before Marinoni's announcement, monks from the Grottaferra Abbey near Rome were restoring one of the Vatican's obscure Leonardo da Vinci notebooks and unwittingly revealed a blockbuster scribble that had been, according to Marinoni, locked away for several hundred years. In the restoration process, the monks separated two sheets that had been glued together since the early 1600s and found out the likely reason why those pages had been sealed up in the first place. On the revealed pages were the doodles of one of Leonardo's more restless students: a few obscene cartoons of walking penises—check for yourself if you don't believe—and a nasty, perhaps jealous, caricature of a young man named Salai, who is known to have been Leonardo's prized pupil. But there was also a crude sketch of what is, unmistakably, a bicycle, up in the corner away from the cartoons. And not just any bicycle, but a chain-driven bicycle, using technology associated with the late nineteenth century. Marinoni contended that the sketch of the bicycle was the anonymous student's rendition of a genuine Leonardo design.[1]

Marinoni's claim was met with are-you-kidding-me skepticism from some historians and other academics, for several reasons. To those who were familiar with the bicycle's slow, almost painful emergence during the nineteenth century, the sudden appearance of this chain-driven design from the 1490s simply did not fit into their worldview. Their skepticism was bolstered when Carlo Pedretti, a da Vinci scholar from UCLA, said he had examined the same pages and saw no bicycle at all, only twin circles along with the obscene cartoons, implying that the bicycle had been filled in later using the circles for wheels. The skeptics concluded that the drawing must be a forgery, a hoax—perpetrated by the monks, some unknown smart-ass, or Marinoni himself.[2]

As it stands today, there is no conclusive proof to solve this mystery in favor of either side. Although the skeptics have held sway since Marinoni's death in 1997, it remains deliciously *possible* that Leonardo conceived the bicycle. Examining illustrations from Leonardo's *Codex Madrid,* which he penned at around the same time his student allegedly copied the bicycle design, one can see that Leonardo was heavily engaged with many different kinds of chain and gear combos. On one page of the *Codex Madrid,* there is an intricate drawing of a chain that looks almost exactly like today's bike chains, complete with peanut-shaped links. He even drew designs for coaster brakes. Almost all the elements of the modern bicycle are there in Leonardo's sketches.[3]

Whether Leonardo da Vinci invented the bicycle or not is essentially irrelevant, because, either way, his version of it never caught on. There is no evidence that such an advanced bicycle was ever built or used before the 1800s. One thing we can say for sure: If Leonardo did create that design, it is one of the more interesting twists of world history that it was lost, sealed up, and hidden away, cheating perhaps a dozen generations out of the genius of the bicycle. For almost four centuries after Leonardo, road travel was restricted to the same ol' tired draft animal routine that had been used since, oh, about 3000 BC.

Whenever people start getting into discussions about inventions and historical events, there is a tendency to boil complex stories down to a manageable list of names and dates, which always turns out to be incomplete. This has been a serious problem with many of the written histories of the bicycle. You should know that there are, without a doubt, many more names involved than those found in any book, including this book, names that are long forgotten or were never known—just a word of warning as we embark on our own name-dropping survey of the bicycle's development in the nineteenth century. Unavoidably there are some names to remember, and some names to forget.

Before the Leonardo controversy, the invention of the bicycle was most often credited, quite erroneously, to a German fellow named Baron Karl von Drais de Saverbrun, or just Drais. This gentleman built a wooden, two-wheeled vehicle in 1816 and patented it as the "draisienne." There were no cranks or pedals; the rider was meant to straddle the "running machine" and propel himself with the tips of his toes. Aside from certain anatomical issues (ouch!), images from the period tend to indicate that prancing around on a draisienne looked about as ridiculous as one might imagine, with the tights and poofy shirts not helping at all.

This was no bicycle—it was a scooter with a seat. Furthermore, Drais did not even invent the scooter, as variations on scooter-like contraptions go back to ancient times. So we cannot safely bestow upon Drais the credit for giving the world its first taste of two-wheeled wonderment. Drais's chief contribution was to add a steerable front wheel to a preexisting design. While this was indeed a groundbreaking innovation, it is still a long stretch to say he invented the bicycle.

About twenty years beyond the first draisienne, around 1836, a few Scottish fellows got tired of prancing and managed to rig their scooters with various cranks and levers. The exact nature of their tinkering remains a mystery, but it is believed that their vehicles used a rear-wheel-drive treadle system, sort of like an old sewing machine. These guys (Kirkpatrick MacMillan and Gavin Dalzell) were really on to something.

The attempt at a more elegant self-propulsion was taken up by well-meaning Pierre and Ernest Michaux in the decade following 1855. This Parisian father-son team tweaked and promoted their designs for small, yet heavy, crank-driven vehicles that came to be called "velocipedes" by the hopeful and "boneshakers" by the cynical.

The Michauxs' inspiration was beautiful, but their execution was a flop—they put the cranks and pedals on the front wheel. Guys! Here the development of the bicycle took an unfortunate turn down a dead-end street. Cyclists would be shackled to this fouled-up design for the next thirty years. Because of the crank placement, their machines were more Bigwheel than bicycle. The velocipedes' top speed was about ten miles per hour. Variations on the

"BONESHAKER" CIRCA 1855

boneshaker theme nonetheless enjoyed a flash of popularity around Europe, England, and even in the United States.[4]

Putting cranks on the front hub probably seemed like a genius idea at the time, but it had several major flaws: Most important, it meant that the maximum speed was limited by the size of the front wheel. Essentially, the bike's only gear was its front wheel. This is why, in 1869, the boneshaker makers began to enlarge the front wheels of their vehicles, modestly at first. English builders were the first to make the wheels as high as possible—as high as allowed by the leg length of the rider. The rear wheels became ever smaller in a desperate attempt to save weight.

These funky high-wheelers became somewhat popular in America after they were introduced at Philadelphia's Centennial Exhibition in 1876. At first the demand was filled by imports from England. After 1878 they were manufactured stateside by Colonel Albert Pope. Pope priced his "Columbia"-brand machines for around three hundred dollars each—very expensive Bigwheels—and he had no problem selling them. The high cost of the machine meant that a troubling air of class division was destined to follow the two-wheel phenomenon from the beginning.

HIGH-WHEELER CIRCA 1878

The high-wheeler was received as more of a novelty than a serious utilitarian device. It was a toy, but it was an inspiring toy. Large numbers of affluent Americans joined cycling clubs; some even had the nerve to race these things in road and track events. They called them "bicycles," even though one could argue they hadn't quite figured out what bicycles were yet.[5]

You start to see why the drawing in Leonardo's notebook caused so much disbelief. The process of eeking out a chain drive seems to have been unduly agonizing through the 1800s.

Finally, in 1885, after the front-wheel-drive idea had run its course like a bad flu, J. K. Starley of Coventry, England, invented the "Safety Bicycle." Starley's bicycle was intended as a humble alternative to the dangerous high-wheeler, but the outright superiority of his design soon became obvious. Starley had most of the right parts in the right place. The wheels were of near-equal size, and he had the cranks at the bottom bracket with a direct-drive chain to a sprocket on the rear hub. There was a semblance of a dia-mond frame. Brakes? Who needs 'em. Starley's bike had a fixed gear, so the ineffectiveness of its primitive friction brake was a nonissue.[6]

Starley's chain drive was adopted by hundreds of different manufactur-ers, and after a few modifications the safety bicycle became the standard that survives, in the same basic form, through the present day. Sleek-looking safety bicycles were being mass-produced in America by 1887.

In a world populated by an increasing number of actual bicycles, the high-wheelers became known as "ordinaries" and were suddenly obsolete.

Maybe he was channeling Leonardo. Maybe he was just a pure, plain genius. Either way, we needed him. Forget about Drais. John Kemp Starley is the name to remember.

SAFETY BICYCLE CIRCA 1890

THE BICYCLE CRAZE OF THE 1890S

One thing Starley didn't have was the pneumatic tire. His early safety bicycles were outfitted with solid rubber tires wired to the rims, just like the high-wheelers. Imagine riding rough dirt roads and cobblestones on solid rubber tires. When an Irish veterinarian named Dunlop developed the world's first practical pneumatic tire in 1889, the modern bicycle achieved the efficient, elegant, and almost-perfect form that is still so familiar to all of us. By 1893 the new tires outfitted every new bicycle sold in America. The pneumatic tire—soon to become a critical ingredient in the emergence of auto and airplane transportation—was the catalyst that launched the bicycle craze of the 1890s.[7]

If you think bicycles are great now, imagine them back then, when the chain drive was brand-new and the very thought of balancing and cruising on two wheels was still a novelty. Riding on air-filled tires must have felt silky smooth after the boneshakers and several thousand years of wagons. Not surprisingly, hordes of people fell in love with the bicycle in the 1890s.

At the height of the craze, it is estimated that there were as many as four million cyclists in the United States alone. In 1896 America, according to James McGurn, "about 250 major cycle factories produced well over a million bicycles." Augmenting the main factories were about six hundred accessory makers. And, for the time being, there were buyers to absorb all the production.[8]

Because bicycles were still quite expensive items, beyond the reach of most Americans until market saturation caused a price collapse after 1896, the vast majority of early cyclists in America were affluent, and they were city people. This connectedness helped cyclists start molding the environment to their needs. Many of the cyclists massed together into a formidable block of nagging civic agitators. The League of American Wheelmen (LAW), formed by Colonel Pope during the high-wheeler era, swelled in membership and became a feisty bunch after the invention of the safety bicycle. Guided by the savvy industrialist Pope, who understood the connection between the condition of the nation's roads and his huge bicycle business, the LAW's earliest and most important fight was for smooth roads and pavement. The politicians eventually fell over themselves trying to gain favor with the cyclists, and a significant road improvement drive was initiated.[9]

The bike craze also spawned bike paths. Amazing as it may seem, nineteenth-century cyclists were even more excited about creating a separate infrastructure than cyclists today. Separate paths were viewed as escape routes from roads that were ragged, muddy, and populated with angry teamsters.

The 5.5-mile Coney Island bikeway was so well traveled after it opened in 1895 that its surface was in constant need of improvements and repairs. On the other coast, an audacious plan to build an elevated bicycle highway between Pasadena and Los Angeles became a symbol of the bicycle's sudden rise and fall in America. A private company built nine miles of the fully enclosed wooden bikeway, which was as high as fifty feet off the ground in some spots, before a freaked-out railroad won an injunction to stop the bikeway from crossing over its tracks. The project languished in court for years. As the auto fever engulfed Southern California, the bikeway was abandoned and forgotten. All around the country early bike paths suffered similar fates, unfinished and fading back into the landscape.[10]

It was inevitable that a machine as progressive as the bicycle would crash into some of the socially backward leftovers of American culture. At the time of the safety bicycle's arrival, the traditional role prescribed for women in Western society was oppressive and untenable. When many women started riding bikes in the 1890s, the silliness was revealed in sharp relief. Many conservatives, perhaps more women than men among them, had a visceral, emotional reaction to the very idea of a woman on a bicycle. How unladylike—to actually want to go places and do things, to move and sweat—how dare they!

Eventually folks got used to the idea of female cyclists and became obsessed with their apparel. At a time when proper ladies were expected to be in full-length skirts, corsets, and big-ass hats, many female cyclists chose to ride men's bikes in practical outfits that were also much more revealing. Stockings! The bicycling "bloomer girl" became a potent symbol of feminine independence. In 1896 Susan B. Anthony said famously, "Let me tell you what I think of bicycling . . . I think it has done more to emancipate women than anything else in the world . . ." Which is pretty sad if you think about it too hard. (See Pryor Dodge, *The Bicycle* [Paris: Flammerion, 1996], pp. 122–30.)

CHUMPS OF THE ROAD

Bicyclists, I'm sorry to report, have always been the chumps of the road in America. Those of us who would like to blame automobiles and the automobile culture for all of the problems that cyclists have ever faced should take a sober look at the situation in the 1890s, when automobiles were still science fiction and bicyclists swarmed the city streets and country lanes without ever having to worry about getting run over by a motor vehicle. Even then there was an atmosphere of conflict, distrust, and outright malice between those who cycled and those who didn't.

Then as now, much of the poisonous atmosphere was derived from traffic blowups. The general attitude of urban pedestrians concerning cyclists was sour at best—the cyclists came upon them swiftly and silently, scared the hell out of them, and were gone before the pedestrians could deliver a proper scolding. And the attitude of the wagon and coach drivers could best be described as seething hatred. Horses did not react calmly to bicycles. The sudden appearance of cyclists disrupted an already delicate, tenuous balance that existed between pedestrians and horse traffic, and the teamsters' task became much more difficult as a result. The teamsters also found themselves competing with cyclists for the smooth part of the road.

Traffic conflicts were far from the only source of animosity, however. The same affluence and gentility that endowed cyclists with their early civic influence also assured that there would be a healthy dose of urban-rural conflict and an unmistakable whiff of class conflict floating over every ride. In sharp contrast to some other countries around the world, the American rural population failed to embrace the bicycle. To the average rural American, bicycles were silly contraptions, expensive toys for city dandies who, obviously, had way too much time and money to burn. Until about 1896 or so, when the market was flooded and prices plummeted, the high price of bicycles ensured that few in the working class would be able to experience and enjoy them. The typical bicycle cost about the same as the average factory worker's salary for six months.[11]

And the riders—who were these people? Wannabe cavalrymen, with their bugle signals and "ride captains." Clearly delusional. Men in girly costumes and women in manly bloomers, scaring the horses and blocking the roads. There was so much to dislike. When the local clubmen came wheeling in quasi-military formation through a country town, the residents came out to watch, and to sneer. If the cyclists left their machines unattended, they would frequently find their tires punctured by snickering kids with needles and tacks. Individual cyclists were occasionally besieged by rock-throwing farm boys.

Anticyclist road rage was common, despite the lack of a cutesy term for it. In rural areas the raging cart drivers were usually armed. Some cyclists in late nineteenth-century America took to carrying collapsible "Bicycle Rifles," available from the Sears Roebuck Catalog, when they ventured into the farmland surrounding their cities.[12]

Of course the bicyclists themselves are not blameless and never have been. Bicyclists have always been rather poor at making friends on the roadways. Let's face it: Cyclists suck at resolving conflicts. All of the conflicts that cyclists faced in the nineteenth century are still with us today, and there are some new ones as well.

FROM BICYCLES TO AUTOMOBILES IN SIXTY SECONDS

Rolling onto the horse-dominated scene, the safety bicycle finally heralded the revolution in individualized transport that had been hinted at during the draisienne, velocipede, and high-wheeler spasms. To the chagrin of the teamsters and cart drivers, who were now being passed regularly by long lines of smug cyclists, and perhaps to the relief of the horses, the safety bicycle was an obvious improvement over the horse in terms of efficiency and speed. And unlike the rail-bound traveler, the cyclist could go wherever the roads went—basically everywhere. According to John Rae, the bicycle alone created "an awareness of the flexibility and convenience of travel by road" after a long period of myopic reliance on railroads.[13] Now here was an idea—speed without rails.

After the safety bicycle blew the mind of the world and exploded its expectations for personal mobility and freedom, it turbocharged industrial technology as well, paving the way for the motorized Putsch that would soon follow. Many of the essential elements of early automobiles were developed just a few years earlier in bicycle factories and shops. In addition to Dunlop's pneumatic tire, the bicycle engineers laid at the garage door of the automobile age many crucial advancements, including lighter and stronger metal alloys, durable bearings, a mastery of chains and gears, and the know-how to have it all produced for a commercial market; the most ambitious American bicycle manufacturers pioneered certain factory-testing and mass-production techniques before Henry Ford snagged popular credit for the whole shebang.*

Of the bicycle's monumental impact, automobile historian James Flink wrote that "no preceding technological innovation—not even the internal-combustion engine—was as important to the development of the automobile as the bicycle."[14] Pause for a second to let that one sink in.

The terms "former bicycle mechanic" and "former bicycle manufacturer" (FBM) reverberate powerfully through the halls of history. We teach our kids about the Wright brothers—former bicycle manufacturers—and the pioneering flight of their mechanical bird. But what about the FBMs who jump-started the auto industry? The list is long, as the progression to motors seemed quite natural, irresistible, to the bike makers:

> . . . among others, Opel in Germany; Clément, Darracq, and Peugeot in France; Humber, Morris, and Rover in Great Britain; Pope, Peerless, Rambler, Winton, and Willys in the United States. A substantial proportion of engineering talent as well in the early automobile industry was provided by former bicycle mechanics—including William Morris, who initiated volume production of automobiles in Great Britain; Charles E. and J. Frank Duryea, who built the first successful American gasoline car; and William S. Knudsen, production head first at Ford, then at Chevrolet, and later president of General Motors.[15]

---

*The concept of planned obsolescence is also attributed to bicycle manufacturers. See Smith, *A Social History of the Bicycle,* pp. 18–19.

And don't forget the Dodge brothers, who built and sold bicycles before starting one of the most enduring brands in automotive history. So if you're the type who must always be looking for culprits, look no further than the bicycle lovers, the bicycle riders and racers, the bicycle fixers, and the bicycle makers. They planted the seed, watered the ground, and tended to the seedling that became our unrestrained car culture.

SPEED AND GREED

Bicycle racing grew quickly to become the world's fastest, most compelling spectator sport in the late nineteenth century. In the United States, crowds in the tens of thousands flocked to the races on tight, steeply banked tracks. The racers were celebrated for their fearlessness as much as their athleticism. At that time, bicycle track racing was one of the wildest, most dangerous activities that could be attempted by a human being. Crashes were numerous and spectacular. ("I say, Mabel, this beats the hell out of lawn tennis!") American racers honed their art in the States, where the competition was most fierce, then went abroad to crush the riders from Europe and Australia. Americans A. A. Zimmerman, Major Taylor, and Iver Lawson were all crowned world champions before 1905.[16]

Even before the turn of the twentieth century, however, many of the most dynamic racers spun off, transferring their tremendous energy to the budding sport of auto racing. Auto racing was the next big thing. It's hard to imagine now, but bike racers around the world became obsessed with race cars—financing, designing, building, driving, and selling. In addition to the riders themselves, many race officials, promoters, and mechanics went over to the dark side, to a new sport they considered to be more thrilling, and more potentially lucrative. Speed and greed, not necessarily in that order.

Many of these budding motorheads hoped to follow in the footsteps of Alexander Winton. Winton was a former bicycle manufacturer from Cleveland who began producing a limited number of autos for a very high-paying clientele; he used the races to advertise his product and found great success. It was recognized that defeating Winton in a high-profile race would instantly make any new builder's reputation. With this goal in mind, Tom Cooper, a national champion track sprinter who had already made a mountain of cash from bicycle racing, teamed up with a still-struggling Henry Ford to build two overpowered race vehicles in 1902. The Ford-Cooper racers had cylinders as wide as saucers and sounded like a war. Even then they were considered primitive and crude compared to other motorcars.[17] Instead of steering wheels, there were handlebars.

Cooper intended to drive one of the cars himself; as for the other, Cooper recruited a tough bike-racing friend named Barney Oldfield to drive that one, because, it's been said, Ford was too timid, or too smart, to pilot the beast.

Marshall "Major" Taylor became the sport's first black champion in 1899—almost fifty years before Jackie Robinson's entry into pro baseball. Cyclists shouldn't feel too grand about this, as Taylor was treated poorly overall and was even physically attacked, on occasion, by his opponents. He was banned from several tracks, and some of the top riders, such as Eddie "Cannon" Bald, refused to race with him. In the 1890s many bicycle clubs were explicitly racist organizations, with whites-only membership policies. The huge and powerful League of American Wheelmen, which governed racing and lobbied legislatures on behalf of cyclists, wrote a "whites only" clause into its constitution in 1894. (Robert Hurst, *The Cyclist's Manifesto* [Helena: FalconGuides, 2009], pp. 30–49. Peter Nye, *Hearts of Lions* [New York: W. W. Norton & Company, 1988], pp. 42–54.)

THE ARENA OF DEATH

There is an exhilaration in driving fast that I cannot resist; it is like intoxication.[18]

—BARNEY OLDFIELD

On the afternoon of October 25, 1902, a high-class crowd gathered outside Detroit to watch a bizarre spectacle called an automobile race. The venue was Grosse Pointe Raceway, which was, like most of the early auto-racing tracks, a dirt horse-racing oval. If the Detroit races were like the other auto races of the era, there were probably about one hundred or so of the spectators' private automobiles parked—displayed, really—between the grandstand and the track. Many of the protomobiles would have been very expensive, exotic, and made in France, and there would have been several steamers and electrics among them, as the gasoline engine had not yet emerged as the victor among these competing technologies.[19]

The folks arriving at the track that day weren't ready for it, but they were about to be treated to an event of powerful importance.

Twenty-four-year-old Barney Oldfield found himself in the driver's seat of the Ford-Cooper 999, lined up to race in the five-mile main event against a field that included one of Winton's cars. Oldfield had turned some practice laps in the 999 before, but this was his first race. He was feeling uncharacteristic jitters. He recalled many years later:

> I hit the first turn at a rapid clip. The regular procedure on coming to a turn had always been to shut off. I knew that. So I decided not to do it. Instead, I opened my throttle as wide as it would go . . . I slid all the way around the first turn, the 999 trying to jerk away from me and go straight ahead through the outside fence. The rear wheels insisted on getting ahead of the front ones. I used to stop skids on the bicycle by turning the front wheel in the direction of the skid,

so I jerked the tiller bar of my racer so as to point the front
wheels toward the outer fence.[20]

Oldfield thus spontaneously invented the sliding turn that has been the staple of dirt-track drivers ever since. More important, the spectators were enthralled with his on-the-edge driving style and couldn't take their eyes off him. Did this guy have a death wish? Surely, the 999 would go flipping and careening off the track and explode in a ball of flame at any moment. Now this was entertainment![21]

Oldfield didn't wreck; quite the opposite: He won the five-mile race by almost a mile. He continued his automotive reign of terror into the next year, traveling from city to city, cracking his own speed record at each successive track. Amazed fans mobbed him, did the "Hip, Hip, Hooray" thing, and carried him away on their shoulders. His seventy-mile-per-hour sliding daredevil turns became the main attraction in American sports through 1903. He dumped the 999 to drive for Alexander Winton in midsummer but didn't slow down a bit (this and subsequent switches show that his success had less to do with any particular car and more to do with his own talent and daring).*

Before long Oldfield found that his crazy-man image preceded him to each city. He knew how to work the crowd: "Despite the terrific speed, the absolutely fearless and reckless driver, wearing his perpetual good-natured smile, nonchalantly waved his right hand to the crowded grandstand . . ."[22] This report fails to mention the cigar that was forever clenched in his teeth during the races, even when his face was caked with mud and oil, and the whiskey flask that was probably swinging around his neck.

Oh, Barney. Such a poor example for the children.

Barney Oldfield's dream run came to a crashing halt on September 8, 1903, on his return to the Grosse Pointe track. Oldfield lost it in the turn after blowing the right-rear tire of his Winton Baby Bullet. The Bullet shot

---

*This didn't stop Ford from capitalizing immeasurably on his association with the 999 and Oldfield. Ford had actually given up on the 999 and the other Ford-Cooper before their racing debut, according to Oldfield; with the cars failing to show promise, Ford sold them to Cooper for "something like 600 or 800 dollars." Cooper, Oldfield, and an unsung hero mechanic named Spider Huff put the engines into racing shape. Ford's disowning the cars weeks earlier did not stop him from materializing on the track after the October 25 race to be photographed with the winning car and driver. He used the race to secure the cash to start the Ford Motor Company and the early reputation that kept his product in high demand. (This is Barney Oldfield's version of events, as reported to William Sturm, "Wide Open All the Way, Part One," *Saturday Evening Post,* September 19, 1925, pp. 52–54.)

through the fence and killed a spectator. Oldfield was terribly bothered by the man's death. His first reaction was to quit racing, but his need for speed prevailed and he went on. Less than one year later, in St. Louis, Oldfield crashed through another fence—"I went right into the crowd at that point"—this time killing two spectators and injuring many more.[23] Oldfield went through the fences a lot in those days. "I got so I didn't call going through the fence an accident unless I got hurt going through or hurt someone on the other side."

Oldfield was far from the only driver having trouble keeping his rig within the confines of the old horse-racing tracks. Frank Day had replaced Oldfield on the 999, only to kill himself while racing it just a few months later. In 1905 Oldfield was racing against Earl Kiser—once an internationally feared bicycle racer known as the "Match Race King"—when Kiser went through a fence and smashed his huge legs "to a pulp." Tom Cooper, Oldfield's old friend and partner, one of the greatest bicycle racers of his day, was killed while street racing in Central Park in 1906.[24]

The auto-racing circuit turned out to be pure carnage, but, through it all, Oldfield continued to race. "Drivers don't want to stop or don't seem able to stop," he said, summing up much of present-day American culture in eleven words.[25]

Moreover, unlike his friends, Barney Oldfield never died. Well, almost never. Despite all expectations to the contrary, he lived to the relatively ripe old age of sixty-eight and died of a heart attack. In the decades before his death, after a seventeen-year career as one of America's most visible daredevils, he traveled the country preaching an unlikely gospel: safe driving. (*Cough.*)

Before Barney Oldfield, automobile racing emulated horse racing as a kingly sport; the team crews were expected to be in spotless white uniforms, and car owners were given more credit than the drivers. The cars raced around the old horse tracks in a proper, orderly fashion—very civilized. Before Oldfield, the auto was exclusively a "gentleman's" toy (*gentleman* being, of course, an old-fashioned code word meaning "someone who has so much money he doesn't know what to do with himself"). Autos were such conspicuous signs of opulence that Woodrow Wilson voiced his concern that their very presence on the continent, as rare as they were, would tip the multitudes toward communism.[26]

Oldfield buried all that under a tremendous rooster tail of dirt. He was a foul-mouthed, working-class bad-ass in ratty clothes—no bleached whites for Barney. He and his mud- and blood-splattered compatriots made the aristocratic automobile attractive to tough guys, roughnecks, lowlifes, and farm boys. They made it seem cool.

It took a bunch of bike racers to do that. If your mama told you America wasn't a strange place, she lied.

A DARK WAVE COMETH

. . . the bicycle was a recreation and a fad. The automobile, while it is a recreation, is in no way a fad.[27]

—HENRY FORD, 1906

Unfortunately for us all, there turned out to be some truth in the first part of Ford's pronouncement, where he smugly waves bye-bye to the bicycle. And the second part was right on—the automobile was no fad. In the early twentieth century, ordinary Americans, when given half a chance, fell head over heels for the automobile and decided it was about as indispensable as the legs they were born with. Americans who had once laughed, cursed, and thrown rocks at the new machines, perceived to be obnoxious and unnecessary rich men's toys just a few years before, soon forgot how they ever got along without one.[28]

In 1908 Ford introduced his no-frills Model T. Ford's master plan was not original to him. There were 253 automobile companies in America at the time, and many of them had the same goal: to produce, as Ford put it, "a car for the great multitude." This industrial atmosphere in America was very different from the trend in Europe, where car makers were still handcrafting boutique, overtly pretty vehicles for an exclusive clientele. By 1914 the Euros were left completely in the dust. Factories in the United States cranked out almost five hundred thousand automobiles that year, out of a total of just more than six hundred thousand that were produced in the entire world. Clunky, black, reliable Model T's accounted for about half of new car sales as the United States entered World War I.[29]

At his new Highland Park factory, Ford demonstrated the winning formula for an industrial miracle. The famous moving assembly line allowed him to drastically reduce the price of the Model T, from $850 in 1908 to an incredible $290 in 1927 (about $4,000 today). Simultaneously doubling salaries at his factory (to $5 per day) gave his workers the purchasing power to buy the cars they made. Ford has been criticized for all kinds of things,* but he was no dummy.

By 1927 Americans owned 80 percent of the world's automobiles. The industrial miracle, however, had sown the seeds of its own demise: "Every American who could afford a car already owned one."[30] But the factory machinery ran amok and kept popping them out. Even during the Depression, Americans who owned automobiles were already so "dependent" on them that giving them up was unthinkable, destitute or not.[31]

The 1920s represented an early high point in the American love affair with the car that was diminished somewhat by the Depression, first of all, and then by the oil shortages and sacrifices of World War II, during which citizens were forced to temporarily rediscover the trains and streetcars. After the war, however, the auto reclaimed the high ground in American culture. Auto registrations doubled between 1950 and 1970.[32] In 1929 the average ratio of cars to people was 1:4.3 (California had already taken a substantial lead, with 1 car per 2.3 adults); by 1980 the nationwide ratio was very close to 1:1.[33] And today in America, according to the Department of Transportation, there are more passenger cars than available drivers, because a lot of folks out there own more than one vehicle. And the average number of adult bicycles per household has fallen below one.[34]

During the oil shocks of the 1970s, Americans rejected the giant boats (or tanks, if you prefer) that were being produced by domestic companies at

---

*Most of Ford's critics focus on his far-right political tendencies. He was one of America's most outspoken anti-Semites. He also sent goons from his "Sociological Department" on regular forays into his workers' homes to make sure they were "living properly" and weren't tempted to join any unions. The strings attached to the five-dollar day—the announcement of which caused unemployed mobs to riot outside the factory gates—proved to be too much for many of Ford's workers. (Robert Lacey, *Ford: The Men and the Machine* [Boston: Little, Brown and Company, 1986], p. 121; see also Flink, *The Automobile Age*, pp.113, 121–22.)

the time, in favor of more efficient foreign-made models. The little Volkswagen Beetle became the best-selling car of all time, passing Ford's Model T, in 1972. Toyota and Nissan soon surpassed VW to become the leading exporters to the American market,[35] and worldwide, Japanese companies became the leading suppliers of motor vehicles by 1980.[36] This time it was the American manufacturers who were left in the dust.

The American auto industry underwent a dramatic transformation in the twentieth century. Two hundred and fifty–plus independent American car companies consolidated into the very Big Three, and then, with Daimler-Benz's acquisition of Chrysler in 1998, just two behemoth car companies, General Motors and Ford. (Chrysler bounced from Daimler to an investment group named Cerberus, and is now owned by Fiat.) If not for a frenzy of bailouts, GM would have come to an end, and arguably Ford as well.

It's impossible to know for sure what would have happened if these companies had been left to "the market." Their hypothetical demise might have been as terribly dramatic and painful as we were told it would be, but perhaps it would have fertilized the ground for a brand-new type of domestic auto industry—an industry composed of innovative, young companies built to survive the conditions of a new century. But, having gone the bailout route, we'll never find out.

FAKE GAS TANKS

While bicycle track racing remained popular in America through the 1930s, cycling by ordinary adults—nonracers—evaporated into memory as the country embraced the automobile. When the auto fever was in full burn, during the 1920s, bicycles resurfaced as toys for children, styled to resemble motorcycles and airplanes. From the 1930s through the 1950s, almost every bicycle produced in America had balloon tires and a fake gas tank attached to the top tube. A fake gas tank on every bike! Doesn't that say it all?

American grown-ups shunned bicycles until the 1960s, when the European passion for cycling filtered back to the States as a trendy novelty for the style conscious. Since hardly any Americans were into it at the time, riding a bike became a badge of individuality, a quirky college professor thing to do.

America's Vietnam-era bicycle envy grew into a fad of respectable pro-portions. In 1973 American retailers enjoyed what is still called the "bike boom," selling more than fifteen million adult bikes. This number stands as the all-time yearly record.[37]

The 1970s also ushered in BMX dirt-track racing, which gave bicycles unde-niable cool status with American kids. Many of the most obsessed cyclists of today are graying adults who grew up jumping BMX bikes or BMX knockoffs on homemade plywood ramps. Their love for cycling was thus ingrained at an early age, along with a fair amount of skill. Today's little thrill seekers, on the other hand, are just as likely to choose a skateboard, skates, or one of those "razor scooters" for their wheeled transport. (Poor little bastards.)

The birth of the mountain bike, which was mass-produced and mass-purchased beginning in the early 1980s, brought cycling back into the main-stream of American culture after a short lull. Since the beginning of this movement, the majority of bikes sold have been all-terrain bikes or cheaper knockoffs of all-terrain bikes.[38] These dirt-inspired machines are worthy vehi-cles for transport, and indeed, that is how most of them are used. Which is to say, most of them are used hardly at all.

The bicycle craze of the 1890s, the Bicycle Boom of the early 1970s, and the mountain bike sales surge of the 1980s and 1990s were flare-ups in Amer-ica's long-smoldering lust for bicycles. The 120-year-old flame shrinks and flickers, has almost disappeared at times, but will not be snuffed out com-pletely. That speaks well for America, but our appreciation for bicycles has been based overwhelmingly on fun, thrill, and fitness. Too often bicycles have been placed in the category of sporting equipment, rather than serious tools for efficient transportation. It could be argued that the average American bicyclist does not fully appreciate the utilitarian value of the machine.

Even during the fuel crisis of the early 1970s, bicycling could not tran-scend its primary designation as "a recreation and a fad," as Henry Ford pre-dicted. When the mountain bikes were flying out of the shops in the 1990s, the buyers often had grandiose intentions of riding their new bikes to work and to the store, but it usually didn't turn out that way. They didn't ride bikes instead of driving, but in addition to driving, generally on the weekend.

Thankfully, Americans have started to discover the advantages of bicy-cling for transportation. From 2000 to 2010, the popularity of bike commuting doubled or more in Philadelphia, Chicago, St. Louis, Atlanta, Milwaukee, Indianapolis, Denver, Tampa, Wichita, Detroit—*Detroit!*—Kansas City, Oklahoma City, Baltimore, and Washington, DC; it tripled in Portland, Pittsburgh, Anchorage, Cleveland, Nashville, and many smaller cities.[39] The increase in utility cycling did not come at the expense of recreational cycling, which became more popular as well.

Lest you begin shuddering with excitement over the prospect of bicyclists flooding the streets, keep in mind that bicyclists still make up a very small portion of the road users in the United States. Even after the recent surge, ridership still struggles below 1 percent overall. This ain't Denmark.

Why do people choose to ride bikes anyway? Why exactly did this recent surge in cycling occur in America, a place which is, as has been firmly established, not Denmark? For that matter, why is utility cycling so huge in Denmark itself? Can anybody steer this ship, or are we all just like passengers on a roller coaster, along for the ride? For those trying to bring more cyclists onto the streets, a lot hangs on the answers to such questions.

A new generation of cycling advocates and urban planners, who had been working to bring Euro-inspired cycling facilities to North America, pointed to their own efforts as the cause of the latest increase in ridership. "Build it, and they will come," was their motto, borrowed from a baseball movie. "It," in this case, referring to copious mileage of painted bike lanes and a smattering of so-called "cycle tracks" and such. Well, they explained, we built it, and it led more people to ride. Simple, that explanation.

In communities like Boulder and Portland, the simple formula seemed to hold true. As in Europe, the cities that made the greatest investments in cycling saw the greatest increases in ridership. But we see that cycling also grew impressively in many cities where almost nothing whatsoever was done. In 2009 an op-ed writer in the *New York Times* wondered about the origins of an apparent cycling renaissance in Detroit: ". . . whether it's because of the economy or the price of gas or just because it's a nice thing to do, there are a lot more bikers out riding."[40] Well, it probably wasn't because of the new bike lanes or cycle tracks, because there weren't very many at all.

On the other hand, in some cities that have been praised for their forward-looking, bike-friendly planning departments, cycle commuting actually managed to decrease over this ten-year period, which is quite a dubious

INFRASRUCTURE INVESTMENTS ARE ASSOCIATED WITH INCREASES IN RIDERSHIP—MOST OF THE TIME.

achievement. In Mesa, Arizona, labeled a bronze-level "Bicycle-Friendly Community" by the League of American Bicyclists, signaling the city's willingness to invest in bicycle programs and infrastructure, bike commuting decreased by half.[41] Even in Portland, ridership has been edging downward in recent years.

Unfortunate though it may be for all of us, the rate of flow of new riders onto the streets depends on a complicated stew of ingredients, and infrastructure investment is just one of many. Others factors include the state of the job market and the price of crude oil, which quadrupled between 2002 and 2008, and which promises to stay uncomfortably high for the foreseeable future.* You can see the overall cycling numbers rise and dip roughly parallel with the price of gasoline. Trends and cultural pressure also seem to be among the many relevant factors. It's difficult, or maybe impossible, to determine just how important any single factor may be, or to sort out the complicated relationships among them. It's not simple at all.

So far, unfortunately, our understanding of the issue has been stifled by overly dogmatic arguments about cycling infrastructure. One faction of advocates seems to feel that cycling infrastructure can do no wrong; another group hates all infrastructure reflexively. The truth of the matter, as usual, is somewhere in between. But neither group will admit any flaw in their ideology, and they're both so loud that more reasoned, nuanced opinions are drowned out, an indication of great challenges ahead.

One thing we can say for certain: Many of the inputs that determine bicycle ridership are quite out of the control of your local "bicycle coordinator." That's not to say that planners shouldn't continue to try to mold the cityscape in positive ways, or that their efforts won't have some effect or won't be worth it. The creation, destruction, or transformation of transportation infrastructure profoundly affects the way people move in cities—and the shape and feel of the cities themselves.

TRANSPORTATION AND THE SHAPE OF CITIES

Before the advent of steam railroads in the early to mid-1800s, American cities were packed together and centralized to facilitate foot travel. Only the very rich enjoyed the use of horse-drawn carriages, so naturally people wanted to live within a few miles of where the action was so they wouldn't have to trek all day to get there. When the steam railroads came to town,

---

*Despite all the hype about a "revolution" in the oil market due to supply growth from unconventional sources like shale oil in the United States, predictions of a collapse in the current high price of oil and gasoline should be taken with a grain of salt. Hydraulic fracturing and horizontal drilling are relatively expensive methods of extracting hydrocarbons. If the price of oil falls very far, such methods will no longer be profitable and will cease before too long. Since global supply has come to depend so much on these expensive sources as the supply of cheap, conventional oil is depleted, the price of oil must remain high.

these dense cities sprouted fingers of development along the rail corridors, and many urban areas assumed pointy, starlike layouts as a result.

The first, primitive urban "mass transit" systems emerged soon after the intercity lines. Widespread use of the horse-drawn omnibus, essentially a big stagecoach for about a dozen passengers, encouraged city dwellers to move another mile or so farther away from the city centers. Almost six hundred omnibuses were rolling around New York City by 1885, on twenty-seven different routes.[42] The omnibuses caused the star-shaped cities to fill in between their points.

This filling-in process was amplified by the first intra-urban rail systems. The primal rail transit systems used horses to pull the cars—"horsecars"—then, in the 1870s, evolved into cable-car systems that used ungainly networks of continuously moving steel cables to move the coaches. Electric trolleys, drawing power from overhead wires, became standard and ubiquitous soon after Starley invented the safety bicycle.

The electric streetcar became the preferred method of urban travel for the vast majority of Americans, perhaps putting the bicycle on the back burner of utilitarian transport long before autos became popular. By the turn of the twentieth century, there were more than ten thousand miles of electric streetcar lines in America, and the mileage proliferated rapidly thereafter.[43]

The streetcars had a profound effect on the physical form of American cities, causing the dense centers to bloom outward and even stitching outlying satellite towns together with the primary areas into unbroken conurbations. On your next ride you can check out the result of the streetcar effect in your hometown. The streetcar suburbs of the late nineteenth century now form the heart of the city—rows of stately antique houses that once gave their owners the warm illusion of country living but have since been encased in layer after layer of development.

AUTOMOBILE SUBURBS

Contemporary Americans tend to use their cars for almost every trip, no matter how short or insignificant. What we see around us today, stretching from horizon to horizon, are cities shaped by this devotion to the internal combustion engine—unshaped by it, really—a process that began in earnest in the 1920s.

Travel by rail modestly expanded the cities' residential districts, but it also had a strong centralizing effect on the nation's downtowns, by virtue of the fixed nature of the rails, most of which led right into the central districts of the cities. By contrast, the almost universal use of the car by individual Americans was—and still is—incongruous with the concept of a central business district. Widespread use of cars and trucks made necessary the decentralization of American cities, while simultaneously making such decentralization possible. It was inevitable that American cities would sprout multiple centers in the Petroleum Age, and sprout they did.

The time just before World War I brought an unprecedented degree of congestion and chaos to American city centers. Automobiles and trucks joined a thick stew of horse-drawn wagons, streetcars, pedestrians, and bicycles, all competing for space on the streets. There were no parking lots, no highways, no traffic signals, and few paved roads. The cars just forced their way in there somehow, and the infrastructure, the laws, the whole cities started to morph to accommodate them—slowly at first, then massively.

Downtown was clearly the first major obstacle standing before America's automotive future. Therefore developers started to build commercial areas out in the boonies, away from the congested traffic and scarce parking of the downtowns. The first strip malls began to pop up around the nation, with Southern California, of course, leading the way. The primary characteristic of this type of outlying commercial development was the vast parking lot that surrounded it. An uncompromising new calculus flattened the city and its outskirts; for every square foot provided for the human occupants within a building, one and a half square feet had to be provided outside for parking their cars.[44]

The 1920s also saw the spread of the first automobile suburbs—suburbs built around the idea that cars would provide the primary mode of transportation to the occupants therein. These suburbs assumed a much different form than the earlier streetcar suburbs. While the streetcar suburbs were laid out in a predictable, orthogonal* fashion, many of the suburbs of the 1920s

---

*Orthogonal: characterized by right angles; streets in an orthogonal layout are parallel, perpendicular, straight, regular. This "authoritarian and legalistic" type of city design dates from ancient times. (Hugo-Brunt, *The History of City Planning*, p. 63.)

used curvilinear street layouts to emphasize the suburb's separateness from the city. The automobile allowed for a general increase in the faux pastoralism that had been a feature of suburbs from the beginning. The houses were of a new type as well. They had driveways and attached garages. That the car got its own bedroom in the family home was a striking indication that something pretty bizarre was going on.

Spurred on by government home-loan guarantees and new highways, American suburbanization went nuts after World War II and continued until the collapse of 2008. After a short hiatus the building continued at a somewhat more subdued pace.

The majority of Americans now live in Suburbia. These suburbs are maturing just as the old city centers did. With maturity comes a surprising degree of diversity—diversity of race and class, variety of commercial offerings, jobs, living situations. The suburbs have really become the new American cities, performing all the functions of the old.[45] Diverse or not, all American suburbs have one factor in common: They were all shaped by the near-universal use of the automobile.

The automobile suburbs mean different things to different people. One sees freedom, opportunity; another sees a prison.

THE GREAT STREETCAR MASSACRE

Once upon a time, every decent-size city in America, including Los Angeles, was thoroughly tracked with its own electric rail network. In a few large cities with dense and bustling centers, the old rail transit systems have been preserved, at least in part. Almost everywhere else, the systems were completely dismantled before 1960.

Where have all the streetcars and urban rail systems gone? If you smell a corporate conspiracy, join the club.

Liberal critics of urban development in America love to tell the story of the Los Angeles rail network. It goes like this: General Motors Corporation purchased the old rail company in Los Angeles with the intention of running the system into the ground or, depending on who is telling the story, replacing the electric trolleys with buses; GM's devious plan, ultimately successful, was to make sure that gas-powered buses and cars would be the only remaining transportation options available to the city's commuters. That's the lore.

In fact the conspiracy was much more widespread than that. Columbia University professor Kenneth Jackson, in his study of American suburbanization, *Crabgrass Frontier,* points out that General Motors had tried to work this same scheme in Manhattan as early as 1926. Jackson writes:

> . . . by 1950, General Motors had been involved in the replacement of more than one hundred streetcar operations—including those of Los Angeles, St. Louis, Philadelphia, Baltimore, and Salt Lake City—with GM-manufactured buses. A federal grand jury ultimately found the giant corporation guilty of criminal conspiracy for this effort [under the Sherman Antitrust Act], but the total fine—$5,000—was less than the profit returned from the conversion of a single streetcar.

The conspiracy extended well beyond Los Angeles, and many more companies besides GM were involved, including Standard Oil, Phillips Petroleum, the Firestone Tire and Rubber Company, and Mack Truck.[46]

The motorized interests, led by GM, assassinated the streetcars. No doubt about it. But it's important to remember that this deathblow was delivered to an industry already on its last legs. America's streetcar operations were down and out before the auto interests piled on, leaving nothing to chance.

Folks became sentimental about the urban rail systems after they were torn out, but they held no shortage of contempt and criticism for them while they were in place. For decades citizens loathed the overcrowded trolley cars and cursed every rate hike demanded by companies widely perceived to offer less than the minimum of service for the maximum price. And many of the traction companies were thoroughly shady and muckrakable entities, associated with greed, corruption, and the general stench of political impropriety. Before the triumph of the auto industry, streetcar companies were some of the progressives' favorite targets. The early popularity of the automobile among city dwellers was fueled largely by a grumbling dissatisfaction with the transit companies.[47]

URBAN RAIL SYSTEMS ARE BEING REINSTALLED IN MANY CITIES.

Some of the chronic failure of urban rail, and the sweeping success of the automobile, can be explained in terms of public and private investment. When the streetcar companies struggled, private investors withheld their capital, resulting in a vicious cycle. Many of these companies went bankrupt in the 1920s and 1930s. It's possible that the streetcar operations could have been made viable with a government bailout of some sort, but none was forthcoming. The streetcars, run by private companies from the beginning, were always expected to pay their own way. In sharp contrast, the auto infra-structure enjoyed a built-in source of funding—the gas tax*—and received a massive helping of regular government tax revenues as well.[48] And of course when the car companies failed in recent decades, starting in the late 1970s, they received various forms of taxpayer-funded bailouts to keep the ball rolling.

Just a few decades after the tracks were torn out, American cities were pining for their old rail systems. Predictable, eh? A 1973 federal provision allowed for a portion of the sacred federal highway funds to be diverted to mass transit, and across the nation politicians and municipal transit authori-ties proposed the building of urban rail systems as if this were a shiny new idea. Today these second-generation rail systems have been reinstalled, at great cost, in many American cities.

PRIORITIES

Amid the prosperity of the early decades of the twentieth century, there was a sense that American downtowns, built for a different era and choked with pedestrians, streetcars, and an increasing number of cars and trucks, were standing in the way of progress. A bright future was envisioned by those who were lucky enough to own an automobile. The iconic feature of this bright future was a wide, clean highway with a sprinkling of cars, each traveling zip-pily along at a previously unheard of speed.

Images of the limited-access freeway occupied the happy daydreams of many city planners of the era, most notably of Charles Edouard Jeanneret Le Corbusier, the Swiss-born architect and artist who became the most influen-tial city planner of the twentieth century. Corbu (as Le Corbusier was known to friends and innumerable disciples) created fanciful designs for entire cit-ies based on the idea that vertical density (i.e., apartment towers) should be combined with wide, green spaces on the ground. His critics called this vision

---

*Oregon was the first state to implement a gas tax, in 1919. By 1929 every state had established these "user fees," which provide the majority of highway dollars. Gas taxes are probably the most popular taxes of all time. (Rae, *The Road and the Car in American Life,* pp. 62–63.)

"WE MUST CREATE VAST AND SHELTERED PUBLIC PARKING PLACES . . ."
DONE AND DONE!

"skyscrapers in a park," but the attempt at derision paints a somewhat less than horrifying picture.

More important than his argument for vertical density, Corbu urged a wholesale transformation of old-style cities to maximize the auto's potential. In 1929 he declared, "wide avenues must be driven through the centers of our towns . . ." The visual is one of a stake driven into the heart of the nineteenth-century grid city. Conventional street layouts were conspicuously absent from his plans. Corbu wanted to kill the street and create a world consisting only of grass, buildings, highways, and walkways. Oh, and parking lots. "We must create vast and sheltered public parking places . . ." he wrote.[49] Corbu, although a thinker of large thoughts, was not a keen cyclist.

Looking around us now, in a spaghetti bowl of on-ramps and flyovers, it is tempting to pin the whole ordeal on Le Corbusier and his brethren in black spectacles, the modernist planners of the early twentieth century. Really, though, these hopeful individuals are down a bit on the list of influences on American urban development. It is always more practical to follow the money, rather than the utopians, if you want to get to the bottom of things. In this case follow the taxes on gasoline and tires that were placed in a national Highway Trust Fund. This grew into a massive pile that was doled out by the federal government in a streak of monumental appropriations, most notably the Interstate Highway Act of 1956, which allocated thirty-one and a half billion dollars over thirteen years to stitch together what was formally called the National System of Interstate and Defense Highways.* The Federal Aid Highway Act of 1973 and the Intermodal Surface Transportation Efficiency Act of 1991 are best known for their encouragement and funding of alternative transportation, but generous funding for new urban highways was also included in these packages, 18 billion dollars and 120 billion dollars, respectively. A 1998 law provided another 175 billion dollars just for highways. In 2005 Congress approved another massive transportation bill that was primarily about highway construction and maintenance.

The spending spree must continue and accelerate, just to keep the current inventory of highways in usable shape. In 2008 the Congressional Budget Office decided that "maintaining the highway system at its current performance would require $126 billion per year in capital spending by all levels of government." The federal share of that comes in at about 57 billion dollars per year—far more than Congress has allocated. Furthermore, this projection was based on conservative assumptions that have since been blown out of the water by reality. So while highway spending is currently at an astronomical level, it's also grossly inadequate even for maintaining the status quo.[50]

---

*As is evident in the name, partial support for this massive undertaking came from the belief, rational or otherwise, that a system of wide highways would be necessary in the event of a nuclear war and mass evacuation. As the specter of civil defense creeps back into the national consciousness in the post-9/11 world, we now know that the National Defense Highway System is a woefully inadequate facilitator of mass exodus.

Let's not be too quick to blame (or credit) the mysterious powers that be in government or their shadowy lobbyists and pressure groups for locking so much of the nation's treasure into asphalt slabs. Popular choice is a critical factor determining the actions of our (somewhat) representative government and the look of our new cities. Urban highway projects are popular expenditures in spite of themselves. Congress is relentlessly lambasted for unnecessary pork, but nobody bats an eyelash when it commits a quarter trillion to highways every few years.

People have plenty of love for their highways. And if they aren't loved, they are tolerated.

Ultimately the shape of the American city is the product of a complex blend of ingredients. The most important single factor, by far, has been the citizenry's inclination to motor around everywhere in private automobiles. But this reality, in turn, has been influenced in unknowable proportions by multiple inputs, mainly consumer choice, government edict, and capitalist persuasion, with a sprinkling of failed utopian fantasy thrown in.

CONGESTION

Through a spectacular confluence of interests, the urban highways have been built—lots and lots of them. The street survives, but the highway is triumphant. Every major city in the country is crisscrossed with elevated highways and ringed with beltways. In some cases small neighborhoods in forgotten parts of town were bulldozed to make way for the Paved New World, just as the early auto boosters dreamed. As legions of well-read critics are quick to point out, urban highways often cut cities into disjointed sectors and create hundred-yard-wide swaths of dead space right through the guts of the urban village. On the other hand, the defenders will remind us that the highways allowed Americans to relocate to suburbs, escape their dirty downtown digs, elevate their standard of living, and go mountain biking after work.

Strictly in terms of transportation efficiency, we can now say with some confidence that the highways' beneficial effects have not been exactly as hoped or, at least, as advertised. The cars on these urban freeways, they aren't exactly zipping along much of the time. What's this? Congestion. The very same problem the freeways were supposed to solve. Here are the proud freeways, overwhelmed from the first day they are put into service and nearly every day thereafter. One can set a watch by the rush-hour floods of motorized commuters who turn the urban highways into parking lots. Facilitating the breezy travel of the huge number of cars seen in the typical American rush hour would require the building of highways that would be, for once, unacceptable in their colossal girth.

There is another built-in difficulty that continuously frustrates those who hope a new highway, or a wider one, will make their congestion problems disappear. Just as nature abhors a vacuum, a crowded city abhors an empty highway. You can add all the lanes you want—the new, wider highway will fill up and become just as busy as the old skinny one. Even better, you can build a highway out where there is nothing, and the highway will create its own demand, sprouting developments along its length. This effect, of course, could be exactly what the developers want. The citizens who pay for the new, wider highway, however, are usually sold the project on the basis that it will alleviate congestion for the current population, and the fact it will enable more population growth and congestion is left out of the sales pitch. Even with examples of the failure of the highway ideal all around them, decades of examples, citizens tolerate still more and wider highways through and around their cities, in the vain hope that these projects will alleviate traffic congestion.

Urban planner Rem Koolhaas explains how the hopeful dreams of a fast-moving automotive future got shucked aside by the automobiles themselves: "This century has been a losing battle with the issue of quantity."[51] Who could have predicted the sweeping popularity of the automobile among a spiking population? The battle has been lost to sheer numbers of people and vehicles, but, more important, the battle has been lost to square footage. Cars are peculiar in that they take up a great deal of space. One car takes up a lot of space—something like 150 square feet—which means one person takes up a large amount of space (some might say an inordinate, unrealistic, and unsustainable amount of space) when they drive back and forth from work in their personal SUV. In the one-person-one-car society, it only takes a handful of people to create a bottleneck.

Especially to developers and their allies in cities with lots of room to expand, it's been easy to rationalize traffic congestion away as a nonproblem.

Congestion is, after all, a symptom that a city is doing a lot of business. Congestion means big numbers, and big numbers are good. In this view congestion is an unavoidable product of success, so there is little, if any, criticism of citizens' transportation choices.

American drivers remain amazingly willing to sit motionless in their automobiles for long periods of time. It seems likely that these drivers would quietly absorb even more obnoxious doses of traffic congestion than they currently endure. Commuters in the Washington, DC, area, said to be the most congested city in the country, spent about seventy hours sitting in traffic jams in 2012—is there any indication that this is anywhere near the limit of human traffic jam endurance?[52] Congestion is like an old friend to American drivers. You got your coffee, your mean-spirited morning DJs . . . it just wouldn't be the same without the traffic congestion. Without it, commuters would arrive at work too quickly.

However, a much more cynical, critical view is competing for supremacy among those with the power to do something about it. This view holds that traffic congestion is, essentially, waste. Lost time, productivity, and profits. Those in this camp point the finger of blame at the automobile, its large footprint, and its unnecessarily singular occupant.

We can't ignore the numbers forever: Each year American citizens burn over one hundred billion dollars' worth of gas and spew over fifty billion pounds of carbon dioxide while stuck in traffic jams—that's in addition to all that is burned and spewed while actually getting somewhere.[53]

Anticongestion attitudes have led to various forms of car-curbing legislation in the world's most congested cities, from Manhattan to London. While this sentiment is starkly opposed to that which led to the frenzy of highway building in decades past, there is nothing new about it—Julius Caesar was moved to ban wheeled traffic from Rome's center during peak hours. The same simple reason was given then as now: too many chariots, not enough space.[54]

The future of American highways could be interesting. There is much talk of automated highways, on which cars would move on autopilot at high speeds while the drivers attend to their morning rituals. But we should be on guard against claims that such systems will alleviate congestion rather than enable it.

On an individual basis congestion is easy to conquer: Ride a bike. Bicyclists needn't worry too much about the problems of congestion as the world grinds to a halt around them. The more congested the city gets, the more efficient the bicycle becomes in relation to motorized forms of transport, and the happier cyclists are in relation to drivers.

PEAK CAR

For the foreseeable future, traffic congestion promises to be part of the reality of the city, which only has so much area to devote to its pampered commuters. People still need to get out to places in the Internet age, and they still overwhelmingly choose a few hundred square feet of private automobile to get them there, even if that automobile happens to have an electric motor.

HAVE WE PASSED THE ALL-TIME PEAK OF THE MOTORING LIFESTYLE?

However, something very interesting happened in the history of American transportation late in 2007. As the housing bubble popped and the price of oil shot to the heavens, Americans cut back on their driving. The total mileage traveled on America's highways took a significant dive in 2008, the first real decline in several decades. While other economic indicators seem to be rising again, VMT (vehicle miles traveled) continues to trail off six years later. Domestic oil consumption is down about 15 percent from the levels of 2007. Meanwhile American teenagers are less enamored of automobiles than they've been for about a hundred years, indicating, perhaps, a "new normal" rather than a temporary reprieve.

While China and India are strikingly ramping up their motorization, the corresponding decline of personal motoring in the United States has been equally striking. At this point we can wonder if Peak Car is receding in the rearview mirror.

ENCLOSURE

There is one important thing automobiles provide that bicycles do not: enclosure.

Since the 1920s, cars have been built with closed, lockable, watertight passenger compartments. In addition to the practical benefits, like keeping occupants out of the weather, protecting them from crashes, and holding their valuables for safekeeping, this enclosure has also helped the automobile ascend to a place of surprising importance and esteem in society. Cars have become extensions of the home—living rooms, powder rooms, and bedrooms on wheels.

But the enclosure of the automobile also holds some far-reaching negative implications for the general character of American cities.

In 1961 Jane Jacobs wrote *The Death and Life of Great American Cities,* which is considered by many to be the most important critique of urban development ever written. Perhaps the most valuable point in Jacobs's work is the idea that vital, flourishing, and safe city neighborhoods owe their success to what she calls "an intensity of users."[55] Such areas within cities have people from all walks of life coming and going, on foot, at nearly all hours for a variety of reasons. This coming and going leads to face-to-face contact among strangers and neighbors. According to Jacobs, these seemingly insignificant social contacts are the basic building blocks of safe, vibrant cities.

In his book *Emergence,* Steven Johnson celebrates Jacobs's version of the city as an "emerging system" and compares it to the common anthill, in which individual ants at the bottom of the ant hierarchy exchange basic information in random nose-to-nose contacts and, unbeknownst to these individuals, form a sophisticated community that can "engage in nuanced and improvisational problem-solving."[56] The same is true of the cells in the human body, and the people on the street in the city. They all contribute intelligence, from the bottom up, to create successful self-organizing systems.

However, when everybody climbs into a car for every conceivable trip, no matter how short or insignificant, the face-to-face contact among strangers is drastically diminished. When city dwellers stay enclosed even when they leave the apartment, going from garage, to drive-thru, and back to garage in their private metal pods with blackened windows, this behavior casts a chill over neighborhoods and cities. Instead of faces, all we see is metal and glass. If Jacobs is right, then, American car culture starves the cities of their self-organizing fuel. If a city cannot organize successfully into its proper form, presumably it will organize into something different, something a bit nastier.

RAGE

We just might feel the harmful sociological effects of automobile enclosure every time we go for a ride, or drive. One noticeable effect is increased road rage and the general ramping up of bitchiness among encased drivers, who, free from the encumbrance of face-to-face contact, decide to just speed past, flipping the bird or yelling a few choice words at whomever fills them with hate at the moment, then bolt away. They figure they're never going to see that person again. Traffic is a bit like the Internet in that regard. Out on the sidewalk, where getting walloped violently is a more pressing possibility, suddenly all the road ragers are quite polite to each other.

Cyclists tend to take these hit-and-run road-rage encounters rather personally, which is unfortunate. Usually such an encounter is a simple example of motor traffic being motor traffic. Driving creates stress, which breeds tantrums. Enclosure creates anonymity, adding fuel to the fire.

If we're going to be out in it, we should not get all bent out of shape about the unshakable realities of traffic any more than we should get down on the street and bang our heads against the pavement. Doing the latter might be a little more satisfying, actually.

CYCLING THE NEW AMERICAN CITY

....

Americans are broad-minded people. They'll accept the fact that a person can be an alcoholic, a dope fiend, a wife beater, and even a newspaperman, but if a man doesn't drive there's something wrong with him.[57]

—ART BUCHWALD, 1968

....

We could argue for years about whether the postmodern, motorized metropolis is good or bad for our souls. Hundreds of books have been written about this already. Better we should tackle a question that we can really sink our teeth into: How is it for bicycling? The question is complex, and the answer, it turns out, has much to do with attitude.

Is your water bottle half empty or half full?

We bicyclists hear—and do—a lot of complaining about the car-based development of American cities and the car-dependent lifestyles of Americans. Indeed there is much to complain about. There are many dangers and special frustrations waiting for us on American streets.

In a car-dominated society, of course cyclists are marginalized, physically and socially. It sometimes feels as if the person on the bike is The Other, to be reviled. While riding a bike for transportation is a tribute to many of the basic ideas upon which this country was founded—common sense, self-reliance, and closeness with the land, to name a few—it is also, in many ways, a slap in the face to contemporary American culture.

Now wait a second. It sounds like a never-ending conflict. It sounds like war on the streets. How bad is it really?

A good bicyclist, marginalized though she or he may be, travels with ease through the modern motorized city. No doubt there are many streets to avoid out there, many hazards, many drivers with bad attitudes. But there are usually enough friendly routes available that the urban cyclist can move with incredible efficiency and reasonable safety. The best riders don't depend on drivers for much, but when they do, most drivers are still courteous and reasonably aware of their surroundings. The new city can be had.

When bad-mouthing contemporary cities, a reality check is in order. We romanticize the pre-automobile cities, forgetting that they were so overcrowded and drenched in green horse crap that the inhabitants were scrambling to evacuate. We lament the dreary sameness of the new cities, grumble about the invisible mechanism that stamps out the fast-food strips of Laramie or Cincinnati or New Haven and makes them almost indistinguishable—sometimes the only way to tell what part of the country you're in is to check the accent coming out of the speaker at the Taco Bell. But the nineteenth-century cities were all pretty much the same too (although they confined their sameness to a less ridiculous amount of surface area). No doubt our current cities will be missed and romanticized in the same way, after they are consumed by yet another form of city, based on some revolutionary form of transport that has so far escaped imagining by humankind—not likely anytime soon.

Sure you can imagine a better way to live. But we get what we get in this world. We change what we can and make the best of everything else. As bicyclists, we are in prime position to make the best of what we cannot change.

INVOCATION

The dedicated cyclist is a new kind of pioneer. Pioneers have an obligation to those who would follow in their tracks, to show them the way. Instead of highlighting the difficulties and frustrations, instead of obsessing about conflict, get out there and show the nation how easy it already is to cycle in the city. Wear "normal" clothes for short rides. Put the superiority of the bicycle on display. Be responsible, unflappable, and polite. Ride with style, grace, and intelligence. Ride with fear and joy.

CHAPTER 2

THE CITY SURFACE

PAVEMENT: GET OVER IT

Much hated, ever implicated, thought by many to be the perfect symbol for everything that is wrong in the world, it is pavement that allows us to fly home from work on flashy road bikes, or embark on six-hour rides directly from midcity apartments. Let's give pavement some credit. Pavement lets us go far and fast.

Anyway, it is a useless waste of emotion to hate pavement. Best to get over it, literally, and ride the wave.

Even before bicycle riders, makers, and mechanics sparked the auto craze, they were agitating successfully for smooth, paved roads on which to ride their beautiful machines. Your ancestral cyclists, in many ways, gave birth to the paved environment. Now go out there and claim it!

There could very well be some pavement near you right now. Crouch down low to get a good look. With a few exceptions pavement comes in two general types. These we refer to as asphalt (black) or Portland cement (white). Civil engineers and contractors call these "flexible" and "rigid," respectively, the latter being more expensive and durable. Rigid pavement, made from chalk and clay, is the material of choice for sidewalks and bike paths (although asphalt paths are still common), airport runways, and the most heavily traveled streets, highways, and intersections. It is more likely that you are looking at a flexible asphalt surface—actually a combination of black asphalt and a special gravel (aggregate), a combo known technically as "asphalt cement concrete."

Black asphaltic structures are the workhorses of earthbound transportation. They form the skeleton of America. Reach down and give it a pat. Made of rocks, it is. Little rocks of varying sizes, chosen for their angularity,* bound together with black tar. How does it feel? Depending on the budget and strategy of the road builders, the surface layer might be composed of relatively large aggregate, in which case it will be quite rough. The nicest asphalt surfaces are on freshly resurfaced streets topped with a dark, slick layer of tar and very small aggregate. These smooth surfaces are better to ride on, and better to land on.

---

*Angular, jagged aggregate, as opposed to smooth, rounded aggregate, "locks" together and helps keep the asphalt structure from sliding apart under stress.

FLEXIBLE? YEAH, RIGHT.

PORTLAND CEMENT CONCRETE

Asphalt, the black "glue" of asphaltic concrete, is strange stuff, yet another petroleum-based substance ripped from the bowels of the earth. These days we brew our own asphalt by refining certain types of crude oil. In the very early days of asphalt paving it was necessary to extract asphalt from natural deposits, the most significant of which was on the island of Trinidad. We didn't know exactly what it was, but we knew it made a nice road (while it lasted).[1]

RESPONSIBILITY AND SURFACE HAZARDS

Unlike motorists, who can just putter along worrying only about traffic signals and other vehicles, the urban cyclist must always keep an eye out for hazards fixed on the city surface as well as hazards moving across it.

First of all, American cyclists need to accept the fact that their streets will be shot with holes, cracks, grates, waves, trenches, and craters. (And that's not to mention railroad tracks, "Botts' Dots," rumble strips, and roadkill.) We must realize that some degree of road damage is considered inevitable, and even acceptable, to the planners, engineers, and bureaucrats who are responsible for the condition of street surfaces. If they see it that way, so should we. The fact that streets will degrade precipitously is built into the equation. Cost, of course, is the major factor that determines the frequency and intensity of street maintenance and the quality of the street in the first place. Street surfaces are not designed to be perfect, by any means. They are designed to hold up, just barely, and facilitate motor traffic over a certain finite life span.

Cyclists, and drivers as well, who are not clued in to the rapid aging process of pavement often experience a reflexive twinge of anger when they slam into unnoticed potholes. This is the same kind of anger felt by someone who, while stumbling through a darkened room, stubs a toe on the coffee-table leg, then must resist the urge to attack an inanimate article of furniture. Damn coffee table! You have harmed me! Of course the coffee table shouldn't be blamed for the stubbing any more than it should be praised every time someone walks past without smashing into it.

On American city streets and country roads, potholes happen. Cracks and waves are reality. Damage is the norm.

Any cyclist who overlooks a surface hazard and suffers the consequences—ranging from shocked surprise, to bent rims, to full-on yard-sale wipeouts and broken bones—has only him- or herself to blame. Even if it's not completely true, try to put yourself into that state of mind. Accepting this responsibility at the outset will go a long way toward preventing such occurrences in the future.

Of course there is a fair bit of luck involved in the cyclist's struggle against road damage. But if we focus on luck, and accept its power over our fate on the roads, we do ourselves a grave disservice. The safest cyclists do their

ROAD CREWS GENERALLY DON'T CONSIDER CYCLISTS WHEN THEY DO
THEIR WORK. AT LEAST THEY FILLED THE HOLE.

best to eliminate luck as a factor in their daily travels. They tame what seems
uncontrollable to lesser riders.

THE GREAT AMERICAN POTHOLE

In 2012 the New York City pothole crew filled 200,666 potholes. On really busy
days the crew poured ten or more tons of hot asphalt.[2] This is a job that will never
be finished. As soon as one pothole is filled and steamrolled, another opens up
somewhere else. This is the Law of Conservation of American Potholes.

Streets are generally torn up and resurfaced after about ten years of use.
In the later years of this cycle, it is expected that the streets will be buckled,
cracked, and cratered. This worn-out street, in its rickety old age, may be horrible for bicycling, but it will still be minimally usable by motor traffic, and that

is what really matters to the powers that be when it comes to streets.

Pavement structures are composed of multiple layers, each with a specific function. Unfortunately the structure is only as strong as its weakest layer. If the base layer is thin or weak, or the ground on which it is laid is rutted or uneven, the top layer will never sit quite right no matter how durable it is.[3] There are many ways for pavement layers to go wrong. Maybe the construction company was trying to skim some money and used a substandard aggregate. Maybe the crew laid down a wavy subgrade or just didn't feel motivated enough to compact the layer properly.

Even the most carefully constructed streets fight a losing battle against American traffic. From the moment it is put into service, a street is under attack from the drivers it serves, and also from the environment. Temperature changes cause the structure to expand and contract, and thus to crack and break apart. The freeze-thaw cycle is the most brutal destroyer of asphalt structures, so potholes and other forms of road damage are a more serious problem in cities that go through wet, icy winters. Freeze-thaw potholes often form first around seams in the pavement, around manholes for instance,

HOLES LIKE THIS INDICATE A MISSING SUBGRADE.

TYPICAL: A POTHOLE FORMS NEXT TO A MANHOLE

or where the asphalt meets a concrete gutter, because moisture infiltrates the structure through the seam. Any crack is a candidate to become a monster pothole if it allows water to seep in, which is why road crews stripe cracks with tar.[4]

Hydrology has further implications. Once a little chuckhole opens in the pavement, it can fill with water. Then, every time a car tire slams into it, the water is forced toward the bottom of the hole, carving it deeper and wider. With all these destructive mechanisms working at the same time, the wet and cold spring months are the worst for road damage.

To cyclists, potholes are both an annoyance and a real danger. A really bad pothole strike can pinch a tube and put a flat spot on the rim. More seriously, potholes can finish off critical components that are on the verge of failure—faulty forks, cracked steer tubes, stem bolts. A surprise pothole might cause the rider to stack painfully against the stem, fumble the bars, and just plain wipe out hard. So the specter of potholes must be taken somewhat seriously even if hitting them usually amounts to little more than a wake-up call.

Avoiding potholes is a basic test of awareness and vision. The number one way to solve the pothole problem is to keep the eyes forward, where they can scan the road surface as well as the traffic. Potholes may not be too scary by themselves, but they become so when the element of surprise is added.

Avoiding potholes is also a memory game. While it sometimes seems like a pothole has popped up overnight, it nonetheless forms in one place and stays there, growing until enough citizen complaints are lodged and the street crew comes along to fill it up. Many cyclists manage to miss the significance of this simple fact, which is the observant cyclist's ace in the hole. Consciously note, and try to remember, the location of any potholes you come across—unfortunately, actually hitting the hole is the best way to memorize its location. You might hit that sucker once, but hopefully never again. The pothole won't sneak across the street to get you on the return trip. It will be waiting in the exact same place tomorrow, a rather pathetic ambush. Memorizing pothole locations is a crucial aspect of knowing the route.

Potholes are an insidious danger while riding at night. Riding without a bright illuminating headlight in dark areas is kind of like trolling for potholes. On very dark, unknown streets, the rider needs to decrease speed and assume a sort of pothole-smashing "ready position," with the weight back, the arms and legs bent. You don't have to see the pothole to be ready for it.

CRACKS AND SEAMS

Asphalt structures crack easily and often. Cement surfaces crack as well, perhaps not so easily or so often. That's just how it goes.

Heavily stressed asphalt street sections tend to sprout a labyrinth of cracks like the bed of a dried-up river. This is called "map cracking" or "alligator crazing." Map cracking on asphalt is a warning sign for potholes. Typically, streets that have degraded in this fashion are the same streets that sport massive potholes. Often these holes are born right in the midst of a heavily cracked area, as the cracks form little islands of pavement that are knocked out one by one.

The beauty of the typical crack in pavement is its chaotic form. The crack, in other words, is crooked and irregular. By themselves, before they have a chance to evolve into potholes, crooked cracks are benign cracks. We ride across them with scarcely more than a bu-bump. Straight cracks are of much greater concern to the urban cyclist.

Certain high-traffic streets are constructed of white concrete, called Portland cement concrete (PCC). Cyclists should notice when they roll onto a Portland cement surface and should be very aware of an insidious type of surface feature that is found there: the longitudinal crack, running parallel to the path of the cyclist.

Concrete pavement structures are often built in sections with relatively large open seams between them. These seams are left open to give the slabs room to expand, contract, and move without cracking apart. Other PCC structures are laid down in one large continuous slab, but, in the absence of openings between sections, control joints are sawed in at regular intervals to dictate where the structure will crack. This is the road builder's version of fighting fire with fire. When it's all said and done, PCC pavement has no shortage of straight longitudinal seams running along it.

Expansion-contraction joints are usually no more than about half an inch wide, but this can be enough space to catch a typical road tire and throw down the rider. When the front wheel starts riding in the crack, the walls of the crack determine the path of the front wheel. This is seriously no *bueno*, as the cyclist needs freedom to adjust the front end in order to stay upright.

The rider leans slightly to the side, pulling on the wheel, which goes nowhere as it is stuck in the crack, and something very bad happens, preceded by a moment of panic. In these types of wrecks, the bike seems to be removed by a mysterious force, leaving nothing but air between the rider and the concrete. Expansion joints are implicated in some of the most violent and dangerous of the solo, non-motor-vehicle-related wrecks.

The same nasty effect results from riding up against a small ledge in the concrete, where one slab is taller than the one next to it. A ledge just an inch or so tall has the power to inflict the same punishment as a full-fledged curb.

Longitudinal cracks and ledges become much more dangerous when moisture is added to the equation. In snow, a miniscule control joint on a sidewalk can wash out the front wheel. This danger is compounded greatly by the way snow hides the cracks from view. Look for subtle indentations in the snow that correspond to indentations in the pavement below.

The dreaded parallel cracks and seams show up on asphalt surfaces as well, but not as often. Many asphalt-paved streets have parallel cracks, ruts, and lips where the pavement meets the gutter and around some manhole covers. Asphalt streets also are known to degrade in such a way that a long straight strip—not so much a crack as a groove—is worn into the top layer of aggregate, and these grooves have been known to throw down a cyclist or two.

Road-bike riders, with their skinny tires, have more to fear from straight cracks than the mountain-bike crowd, although fat tires are not immune.

WAVES

The elastic nature of asphalt structures becomes obvious when the pavement forms waves. Known as "hummocks" to transportation engineers, waves in the pavement are actual, rolling waves. They're just moving very slowly. Sometimes they rise so acutely that the pavement breaks, like a wave in the ocean. Sometimes the waves are perfectly smooth and elegant formations. They can be minor ridges, or they can be about two feet tall. Waves occur primarily around intersections, where cars apply a greater amount and variety of force to the surface through continual stops, starts, and turns.

More so than potholes, hummocks represent a small failure of the system. Somewhere along the line, somebody messed up. These street surfaces are not really doing their job to the acceptable standards. Heavily waved sections cannot be easily repaired in a piecemeal fashion like potholes and are a good argument for the superiority of Portland cement structures. Wave-prone asphalt streets become candidates for premature resurfacing, and thus they are inefficient and cost money.

Waves are particularly dangerous for a cyclist looking down, back, or anywhere other than forward. When encountered unexpectedly, waves are extremely efficient at tearing the handlebars from one's hands. If we see it coming, it is a small matter to negotiate the obstacle. Pick a good line, mindful of nearby motor traffic. Relax the arms and legs to absorb the bump, like a rider on a jumping horse, and just ride over it.

LANE MARKERS

It is not unusual for a lane line to be a good quarter inch tall, piled with multiple layers of special reflective latex paint. This is a problem for cyclists. Especially when moisture is added, this little lip can cause a displacement wreck similar to those caused by longitudinal cracks.

Even a very thin coat of lane line paint can be extremely slippery in rain or snow. Don't carve a turn on a wet line, or stand up and lean the bike from side to side while the front tire is on the line. Don't you watch the Tour day Frantz? Every few years some sucker eats it on a wet line and takes out like ten guys.

Performing the same function as the lane line—marking lanes and wrecking unsuspecting cyclists—is the Botts' Dot. Named after Dr. Elbert Dysart Botts, an engineer for the California Department of Transportation, these are the little bumps with reflectors on them, stuck into the pavement and glued with epoxy. Although they may look cute and unassuming, if a rider hits a Botts' Dot while looking away, it could be very messy. The Botts' Dot and its cousin, the rumble strip, have been at the center of a fair bit of cycling-related controversy. Some cyclists claim that Botts' Dots and rumble strips installed on center lines keep motorists from leaving a safe amount of space when passing cyclists on the right side of the road, because motorists are unwilling to bump across the markers. Truly, the center-line rumble strip could also add to the cyclist's safety in certain situations.

WET METAL

When coated with a thin layer of H_2O, metal strips, manhole covers, and grates of various kinds are probably the most treacherous—slippery—of all city surfaces. Wet metal is a real shocker to green cyclists. Ride over it, yes, but don't make any false moves while your wheels are on it.

IF YOUR BIKE DOES THIS, YOU'RE IN TROUBLE FOR SURE.

DRAINAGE

Street drainage has been a constant struggle for American cities. The use of smooth pavements meant that sizable sections of the modern city became impermeable to water—the streets were inadvertent aqueducts. An underground world of pipes, tubes, and tunnels had to be constructed to tame the runoff. To this day the makers of cities and builders of streets still fail to exhibit a solid command of the drainage problems they created. Each pool of standing water is a shimmering monument to failure.

In the interest of drainage, the modern street is "crowned," meaning it slopes downward slightly from the center to the sides. Riding on crowned streets has the effect of wearing out the tires slightly more on the left side.

More important for cyclists, the need for drainage implies the presence of various types of sewer grates embedded in the street surface. Such a grate is often recessed a good six inches below street level, so the cyclist who succumbs to it actually falls off the edge of the world for a moment before striking metal. It may not seem like it, but most of the grates you see out there today have actually been designed with a hint of concern for the humble bicyclist. Most of the grates with long, treacherous openings have been replaced with grates that have cross members across the openings, so a bike's front wheel is less likely to be stopped cold or just eaten whole. Other grates have openings that are oriented diagonally to the direction of travel, also a nod to cyclists.

Grates are much feared—and understandably so, as grate-inspired accidents can be serious and bloody—but they are no longer the reapers they are rumored to be. When ranking the most injurious surface hazards in terms of overall danger, grates are no more damaging than longitudinal cracks, ice and other slippery stuff, potholes, sand and gravel, or railroad tracks.[5] Grates are truly nasty when they are undetected. Cyclists should expect a wheel-catching grate or pothole to be concealed beneath any substantial puddle on a street they are not totally familiar with.

Grates should only be a problem on unfamiliar routes. If the bicyclist has ridden a street once or twice, any dangerous grates along the way should be detected, quickly inspected, and filed away for future reference. The next time the bicyclist is cruising that street, he or she can recall the position of the grate and start to take action to avoid it about a half block ahead of time. The same goes for potholes and as many other fixed surface hazards as can possibly be catalogued. They say we use only a small percentage of our available brain capacity. Well, here's your chance to use some more of it.

If you find yourself crashing through a catch basin on the edge of control, it's a sign you have been riding poorly up to that point, with a dangerously inadequate level of awareness. But these things happen. If you see a heinous recessed grate in your path, and can't safely get around it, one possible coping strategy is to slow way down, or even stop if possible, rather than just rolling into it. If the grate is unavoidable, size it up and actually pick a line across the metal slats. Keep your weight back somewhat—you may as well be traversing a little rock garden on a trail—relax, and visualize a successful crossing. Just don't grip the front brake and crouch stiffly over the front of the bike, or you might get bucked off. Another possible plan of attack involves speed. A skilled rider at speed should be able to lift the bike over the grate entirely for a soft landing on the other side. Riders who have mastered

CYCLISTS BECOME WELL ACQUAINTED WITH THE EDGE OF THE ROAD.

this "bunny hop" technique find occasion to use it several times per week. At slower speeds a rider can perform a sort of stunted wheelie into the hole. If you can throw the front wheel all the way over the chasm, the rear wheel will usually just clunk through without major consequence. This clumsy technique may very well damage the rim or cause a pinch flat, but it's infinitely better than pitching over the bars. Whenever encountering a major hole like this, do yourself and your bike a favor by keeping the arms and legs bent, and stay light on the bike.

RAILROAD TRACKS

Ask around among any group of experienced bicyclists, and you will find that more than a few have been felled by a railroad track. The most dangerous tracks are of two basic types: wet tracks (see Wet Metal, on page 52), and diagonal tracks. Railroad tracks that are both wet and diagonal to the cyclist's direction of travel are probably the most unforgiving of all possible forms of surface obstacles.

Like the classic "dooring," the railroad-track wreck is almost like a rite of passage among cyclists, probably because, to inexperienced riders, it just doesn't seem like crossing a railroad track could be that serious of a proposition. But one encounter with a diagonal rail is enough to remove the rider from his or her suspended state of innocence. There is nothing out there that is quite as efficient at ripping a rolling bike's front wheel to the side.

Bicyclists who wreck due to a rail report being slapped to the ground in a split second. The rider often doesn't have time to get the arms out or prepare in any way. And the landing area tends to be particularly inhospitable. Painful injuries are commonly associated with railroad track mishaps: smashed kneecaps, broken hips, broken wrists, broken collarbones, and bruised brains.

"I woke up in the ER, on the way to my CAT scan," writes one young woman of her recent streetcar-track experience in Portland, Oregon. "They say that I constantly denied even owning a bike, so how could I have had an accident? Even though I blacked out and don't remember the accident, I don't ride bikes anymore."[6] That's how diagonal tracks can cause a tragedy on top of a tragedy.

A little bit of awareness is really all it takes to neutralize common surface hazards like railroad tracks. As long as that potential danger occupies a tiny space somewhere in your brain, it will be extremely unlikely that a track will ever get the best of you. On the other hand, riders who proceed blissfully unaware through a city crisscrossed with rails are just biding their time until they hit the deck (which points to the possibility of an unacknowledged tension between urban rail projects and efforts to bring new cyclists onto the streets).

Negotiate railroad tracks by "squaring up." Cross the track at a square, ninety-degree angle. If this is not possible, cross a diagonal track by lifting the front wheel over it. This lifting of the front wheel is an important technique for smoothing over all manner of road obstacles, and it should be second nature to any bicyclist. Don't turn or lean the bike over when crossing tracks. There'll be time enough for turning when the crossing's done.

TOPPINGS

So you've chosen a flavor: asphalt (chocolate) or Portland cement (vanilla). Would you like any toppings on that?

Your choices include sand and gravel crumbles, oil sludge, water, wet leaves. Snow, ice, and even deicer. Also, upon special request, bum vomit.

Toppings make life so much more flavorful. All the toppings available here, even the deicer, ironically, serve to make streets more slippery, more difficult to ride, than they would be otherwise. Any mundane section of the city surface can be made terminally sketchy with the addition of the right topping(s). For instance, almost every experienced cyclist has slipped and crashed on a patch of sand at some point. Many have also learned the hard way that wet cement provides about half as much traction as the dry stuff.[7]

Most street toppings can be dealt with fairly easily with a modicum of caution. Simply relax—the most important word in bike handling—and ride across these problem sections without turning or using the brakes. A topping of ice, the Big Daddy of slippery street toppings, can pull the coefficient of friction down below an acceptable level even for straight rolling—the rider is just coasting along and the bottom falls out. And ice topped with water? Forget about it.

Riding in icy conditions is one of the most serious challenges a cyclist can face. It requires a very conservative, slow, upright yet super-relaxed style,

A STREET THAT IS EMPTY OF ALL OTHER TRAFFIC COULD STILL BE A PROBLEM FOR CYCLISTS.

and is not recommended for beginners. It is, however, quite possible to ride year-round even in the Great White North. Experienced winter riders adapt through the use of certain bits of winter-friendly equipment, including fixed gears, knobby tires, disc brakes, and internally geared hubs. Winter bicyclists can also buy studded tires, or rig them at home. These don't solve the ice problem, but they do help a great deal. It should be noted that winter is known to destroy bicycles as well as streets but that winter riding is good for the soul.

PLAZAS

Open plaza areas are standard equipment around buildings in American city centers. For this we can thank Charles Edouard Jeanneret, aka Le Corbusier, aka Corbu, and Ludwig Mies van der Rohe, aka Mies van der Rohe, aka Mies, and the legions of wannabes who followed along, pirating their ideas. Along with Frank Lloyd Wright, Mies and Corbu were the most-copied architects of the past century.

In a sharp departure from previous incarnations of the skyscraper, which were made of stone and so were necessarily wider at the bottom than at the top, use of reinforced concrete and steel construction allowed Le Corbusier and others to design tall buildings that appeared to be supported on pilotis (stilts). This style introduced a novel look and idea—that the land under and around the building could be left open as a park for the building's residents.

Mies used a version of Corbu's "skyscrapers in a park" vision, complete with pilotis, for his famous glass-skinned, steel-framed Seagram Building at 375 Park Avenue in Manhattan (designed with Phillip Johnson and completed in 1958).[8] The Seagram Building in itself was interesting, but the negative space of the design was the real novelty. The building was set back ninety feet from the street, and it consumed only 40 percent of the lot. With its expansive and elegant plaza, the Seagram complex became the model for corporate towers in every city center in America.

The current version of the urban plaza is generally a second-rate copy of the Seagram plaza of 1958. It is a privately owned space administered by humorless guardsmen in blue blazers, who are directed by monitor watchers in a remote nerve center. All the plazas are on camera. The primary task of the management company's rapid reaction force is to shoo panhandlers and skateboarding teens off the grounds. Second, the guards are charged with keeping cyclists from locking their bikes to any railings. The railings are shiny, and they'd like to keep them that way. Third, one hopes, they might want to set aside a moment or two after lunch to thwart any terrorists who might be planning to explode their buildings.

For cycling purposes, plazas should be treated like giant sidewalks. Pretend they belong to the pedestrians, even if they don't. Ride them only with great care and a sense of guilt, using the zero-impact style (see Sidewalks and the Law, on page 157).

Here's the deal with plazas, for those who wish to ride them. Plazas are often surfaced with granite or brick paving stones, which are then coated with slick urethane-like substances. They're slippery as heck. A small grounds crew armed with pressure washers and power blowers is charged with keeping the plaza free of snow, ice, trash, leaves, and general munge. Truthfully, they could spare themselves the work of removing the ice. When wet, plazas are often just as slick as ice and regularly claim uninitiated cyclists and even a few pedestrians in their flat-soled shoes.

CURBS

You may hear cyclists proclaim that they never, ever have to hop a curb. Nor do they want to. These nonhoppers are devoted to the idea that bicycles are vehicles, and vehicles, they'll have you know, confine themselves to roadways. When these riders decide to cross a curb, theoretically, they dismount and carry their bikes across the threshold.

As usual, the vehicularists have a point. If a rider is hopping on and off curbs all the time, it is an indication of careless, dangerous riding. Riders who pop onto the roadway in the middle of the block are often the ones who inflate the accident statistics. But—there is always a but—curb-hopping skills are undeniably useful when navigating through a three-dimensional city on a bicycle. Eventually you will find yourself looking to get off a street as quickly as possible, for safety's sake or sheer convenience. In such a situation you would not want to be limited by an inability to deal with a common obstacle, six inches high.

Curb hopping is undeniably part of the language of city cycling, and you'll help yourself quite a bit if you know how to do it reasonably well. Techniques range from smooth to crude and reveal a great deal about a rider's skill level.

The most common way to ride a bike up a curb is to pop the front wheel up with a little wheelie, then simply let momentum take care of the rear wheel. In other words, the rear wheel impacts the curb solidly, which is a less than satisfactory situation and awakens the dragons that live in the sewer. Those who employ this method may wish to graduate to a more advanced style.

Somewhat more advanced is a quick one-two combination that is potentially quite smooth. As soon as the front wheel is on the curb, shift body weight forward, unweight the rear wheel, and lift it gently onto the ledge—no impact.

Even smoother is the fluid bunny hop: The rider lifts the front wheel just before lifting the rear, sails briefly through the air, and places both tires gently on the ledge. When performed by a master, this move is completely soft and silent. This application of the bunny hop is much easier with clipless pedals, although relying on clipless pedals to hop is frowned upon by purists and is truly the junior-varsity way of doing things. Bunny hops, after all, were perfected long ago by BMXers using platform pedals. Not very many riders can pull this off one way or the other, so most of us fall back on less elegant techniques.

Curb climbing can be made easier by squaring up the angle of the approach; in fact climbing the curb dead-on at a ninety-degree angle, as we do when crossing streetcar tracks, is the method least likely to cause falls among beginners. Some riders who are really good can hop onto a curb as they ride parallel to it, but some of these same riders will tell you they have wrecked trying this move.

If the angle of approach is too small, the ledge is too high, or the timing is just plain off, use the one-foot method. Unclip the inside foot, roll to the curb, and turn almost parallel to it so your unclipped foot is close to the curb. Place your foot firmly on the step and finesse the bike up the curb using your hands as well as your outside foot, which is still clipped in.

When dropping off curbs into the street, your first and last concern should be avoiding motor traffic. If you are speeding and launching from the street to the sidewalk, or vice versa, it's a bad sign. Bicyclists need to exhibit more conservatism and patience in their curb-related freelancing. First and foremost this means checking thoroughly with all available senses for any moving traffic on the road. Patiently check, recheck, and re-recheck for traffic before entering any roadway. No more speed and launch. Drop gently off the curb, using your arms to make the front tire's touch on the street as light as possible. This light drop is becoming a lost art in the age of suspension forks. Also practice controlling the rear of the bike, easing it down to the street with a light application of the front brake. Your bicycle thanks you in advance.

Just because you have the skill to hop curbs doesn't mean you should hop curbs. The bicycle's versatility, it's potential to exploit both the vehicle and the pedestrian sectors of the city surface, and to move freely between them, becomes a liability in the wrong hands.

CHAPTER 3

IN TRAFFIC

BEYOND VEHICULAR CYCLING

> *Responsibility, n. A detachable burden easily shifted to the shoulders of God, Fate, Fortune, Luck, or one's Neighbor. In the days of astrology it was customary to unload it upon a star.*[1]
> —AMBROSE BIERCE

The bicycle is the magic carpet of the urban traffic grid. It can squeeze between lanes of cars in a traffic jam; pop onto the sidewalk and snake around pedestrians, newspaper boxes, and hot dog stands; or bust a tiny U-turn in the middle of the block. It can even go the wrong way up the middle of a one-way street, and not give a damn. This tremendous agility demands great care and discretion. In the wrong hands it can be deadly. The bicycle's magic power is also its Monkey's Paw.

Crash statistics indicate that there are many, many cyclists out there who are abusing the bicycle's go-anywhere potential. Most of the nasty car-versus-bicycle collisions in cities occur when bicyclists succumb to temptation and fail to yield at stop signs, turn suddenly into the paths of motorists, or ride against traffic. Their riding style, if it can be called that, is characterized by chaos and unpredictability. These victims can't handle the freedom that the bicycle gives them. Freedom requires responsibility. Unfortunately, freedom comes easily to American cyclists, but responsibility does not.

In 1975 John Forester wrote the first edition of a book called *Effective Cycling*. Forester implored cyclists to dispense with the anarchy and ride in a predictable, ordered fashion. The normal traffic laws governing motor-vehicle traffic, he declared, provide a ready-made framework that works just as well for bicycles as it does for motor vehicles. He boiled it down to a single statement: "Cyclists fare best when they act and are treated as drivers of vehicles."[2] This he called the "vehicular-cycling principle." Forester's ideas won over the cycling community, if not the general motoring public. Today the

BE READY, NOT SURPRISED.

vehicular-cycling principle is endorsed and taught by the League of Ameri-can Bicyclists (formerly the League of American Wheelmen).*

Next to the absentminded anarchy practiced by many novices, the vehicular-cycling principle is a stellar guideline. Vehicular cycling is a great starting point for beginners. Just by obeying traditional traffic-law principles and riding predictably, a bicyclist eliminates a large portion of the danger of cycling. However, the vehicular-cycling principle has a big hole in it: The strict vehicular cyclist who has eliminated many of his or her own mistakes by riding lawfully will still remain quite vulnerable to the mistakes of others. Statistics confirm that adult cyclists have much less reason to fear their own transgressions than the mistakes of other road users. Forester has no real answer for this. His system assumes near-perfect vision and law-compliance from everybody else on the road.

---

* In recent years the League of American Bicyclists (LAB) has found itself under attack from vehicular cyclists who once formed its core membership. The Foresterites charge that the LAB has lost its commitment to vehicular cycling education and principles.

But mistakes are common in the mix—indeed mistakes are the rule. Humans are famously unreliable in traffic. Because cyclists are especially vulnerable to the common mistakes that motorists make, riders who have spent decades and hundreds of thousands of miles in city traffic naturally adopt a style that is quieter, more conservative, and somewhat more skeptical than that of the vehicular cyclists.

Another of the big problems with the vehicular-cycling principle, or any principle of cycling for that matter, is that it fails to account adequately for the complexities, details, and chaos of city streets. Evidence of this failure is provided in the fact that few experienced cyclists, even those who are vocal proponents of vehicular-cycling dogma, apply it consistently in their everyday travels. Instead they use it whenever it suits their purpose and discard it when it doesn't. They're not above using an empty sidewalk if it happens to ease their travels. They roll through stop signs, treat red lights like yield signs, and filter past lines of stopped cars in traffic jams and at intersections. Not very vehicular of them. That's the reality of cycling today. If cyclists were to suddenly start living by the vehicular principle in all situations, disregarding the special privileges and de facto rules they have built for themselves over the decades, the advantages of riding a bike in the city would be gutted.

It's also apparent that the vehicular principle lends itself to some very questionable interpretations. Some cyclists have added a very confrontational tone to the framework of Forester's message (which was already salty enough). It is a small group, but a very visible and loud group. Through their riding habits in traffic, which are often deliberately, theatrically antagonistic, they seek to make some kind of point to their special audience of other road users. One is never quite sure exactly what that point is—something about the rights of cyclists in traffic. Their riding often seems like little more than a passive-aggressive acting out of their disdain for every person in the world, including themselves. What a waste of a good bike ride this is. These feisty neo-vehicularists claim they are standing up for their rights, asserting themselves, showing drivers that they will not be intimidated in the face of overwhelming pressure, and increasing their own safety in the process. Others claim these riders needlessly charge the air with conflict and do grave damage to all cyclists' ability to navigate safely and easily in traffic.

The vehicular-cycling principle may simply be outmatched and outdated. Indeed much has changed since the concept was formally introduced. The country's population has grown by about sixty-five million, and even more cars have been added than people. The national culture has become even more adoring of automobiles, and cities have sprawled out grotesquely to accommodate them. Traffic is much worse in just about every city in the nation. Drivers spend more time stewing in traffic jams and shaking fists at each other, and cyclists are even more unwelcome on busy streets. On the other hand, the bike lanes and paths, which drew such biting criticism from vehicular devotees for being unsafe and unfair to cyclists, have been greatly improved since the 1970s and 1980s and look more attractive to cyclists than ever before. When it suits them, even seasoned veterans of city riding abandon the traffic-packed roads in droves for separate facilities. They feel no sense of loss when doing so. A prime example is Manhattan, where all the bridges onto the island are now accessible by bicycle due to new paths, and a continuous bikeway runs beside the Hudson River.

Decades ago the vehicular-cycling ideologues had high hopes for their cause: They hoped that cyclists would be granted not only equal rights but also equal respect on America's roadways, that cyclists would be able to cruise any city thoroughfare alongside—or, to be more accurate, in front of—cars and trucks, and that the whole concept of separate facilities would wither and die from lack of usefulness. But America today is further from a vehicular-cycling utopia than it was twenty-five years ago.

In this chapter you will find a synthesis of sorts between old-fashioned vehicular cycling and the reality of modern street riding. We'll pay homage to the masters who have molded vehicular cycling to their needs, creating a more enlightened and nuanced style. Theirs is a safer style, and an easier style. Where the vehicular-cycling principle encourages cyclists to deny any off-street options and boldly stake out a position among motor traffic, flexibility will be our guide. We will use the safest, easiest, and most stress-free option available at any given time. We will exercise all our rights to cruise the busiest city streets, but also our rights and abilities to use the quiet ones and the off-street paths. We will have the best of all worlds.

While some cyclists preach assertiveness and militancy, we offer cooperation and facilitation. We will still get where we're going in a hurry, if we wish. We will recognize and respect the limitations of human nature as well as traffic law. We will recognize the basic human mistake as the salient feature of urban traffic, and we will seek to anticipate the mistakes of others. Where the vehicular-cycling principle leaves responsibility in the hands of motorists, and trusts that they will act properly, we will take back responsibility for our own safety whenever we can. We will not seek to dole out blame to anyone but ourselves. While Forester claimed that even children could ride safely on busy streets using the vehicular-cycling principle, our way is unquestionably for adults. Freedom will be our food and our poison. The streets demand from us an awareness and maturity that is very rare in a child.

We will abandon the pretension of principles and rules and will adapt to the ever-changing chaos of city life. We will find the path of least resistance. Instead of attempting to dictate the flow of traffic, we will become the flow of traffic, and it will become us.

Above all, we will have fun and get home in one piece.

The style prescribed here is nothing new. It is put to work every day in just about every city in the world. The cyclists who use it have come by it organically as individuals. They did not get together at a conference to cook it up. They did not take a course or read about it in a book. It is a natural product of their long, sometimes painful experience. It works.

Quite unfortunately for authors of books about cycling, this enlightened style is difficult to describe with words. It is born of infinite details and will not be tamed by principles or paragraphs. This brand of cycling is an art form.

BLAME VERSUS RESPONSIBILITY

The word *blame* came to the English language by way of the Latin word *blasphemare,* meaning "to blaspheme." The Old English version of the verb "to blame" had a very negative connotation. It implied dishonesty. Blame had roughly the same meaning as *malign* or *libel.* Somewhere along the line the definition of *blame* got all twisted up. *Blame* ceased to be a very bad thing and became quite respectable—not a proud or useful moment in human history.

Today's Americans spray blame around in great shotgun blasts to see what they can hit and where it might stick. They aim it everywhere except where it might actually do some good.

The proliferation of blame is rather useless for cycling. Blame is what happens when it's already too late. Obsession with blame is good for insurance purposes but not so good for safety purposes. The bicyclist should cast the twin concepts of blame and legal liability onto the scrap heap and forget about them. Thinking in terms of blame while out on the road is a perfect example of self-fulfilling prophecy. Blame is dangerous.

The most effective way for a bicyclist to stay out of trouble on city streets is to forget entirely about the possibility of blaming others and take on full responsibility for his or her own safety. This attitude will be fundamentally different from the prima donna mind-set displayed by many humans—drivers and cyclists among them—who put their safety in the hands of others, count on everything working out just right, and have a royal freak-out at the first sign of trouble. The successful cyclist counts on little other than chaos and stupidity.

Blame! Who will you blame after that floral delivery van runs a red light and pulverizes your internal organs? As you wheeze your last wheeze, will you find the breath to bitch at the driver—"Nice driving, ---hole!"? Will you be planning your suit as you lurch around on the pavement like a trout?

When you go into traffic, wear personal responsibility like a suit of armor. Think to yourself: *If some bastard breaks every law in the book and runs me over in the process, it will be my fault and nobody else's.* That is the meaning of true freedom. That is how we will keep such disasters from happening in the first place.

The delivery van example is an overdramatization, of course. To illustrate this point more clearly, let us consider a more plausible example—an example, in fact, from real life, the life of someone who shall remain nameless. A cyclist is pedaling down a relatively pleasant street in an inner-city residential area. The street has a bike lane painted on it, and because the bike lane is crowded with parked cars on the right, and this cyclist recognizes the general limitations of bike lanes, he is positioned very near the left marker of the lane, about five feet from the parked cars. He is moving along at a good clip. Suddenly (of course) a black Mercedes E320 comes ripping out of a hidden alleyway backward and the cyclist bashes into it. The rider is injured, but not seriously—a small matter involving chunks of pinky finger and road gravel in the forehead; the bike's frame, a sturdy old Columbus Battaglin, is broken. The butt end of the Mercedes is trashed. Battaglin 1–Mercedes 1.

In terms of fault, this is an open-and-shut case. The cop gives a ticket to the driver, despite her repeated unsubtle hints about being willing to "bargain." Failure to yield.

But whose fault was this wreck, really? A glance at the police report reveals that it has failed to pin down the true causes of the so-called accident. It says nothing of the cyclist becoming distracted by an attractive member of the opposite sex on a nearby porch just prior to the collision. At the critical moment, the rider wasn't even watching the road! It doesn't mention the cyclist's few miles per hour of excess speed, impatiently applied, that translated into a few tenths less available time before impact, or the sluggish action of the ill-maintained front brake, or the failure of the cyclist to respect and move away from a dangerous alley intersection hidden behind a plumber's van, even though he had ridden this same route literally thousands of times and had already experienced near misses at this same spot . . . a multitude of causes, coincidences, and consequences.

Any break in this long chain of the cyclist's failures would have neutralized the motorist's mistake and averted the final crunch. Car-versus-bike accidents require two parties: one to make a colossal mistake and another to be caught off guard by it, one to screw up and another who fails to fully respect the potential of the other road user to screw up. Any way you slice it, it's two screwups, smashing together.

Smart cyclists, for whom the stakes are inordinately high due to their notable lack of protective sheet metal, have little use for the simplistic system of classifying accidents and assigning blame after the fact. The motorist's backing blindly and illegally into the roadway is just another something that happens in the city. Drivers back out of hidden alleys, parking spots, and driveways all the time. It must be expected. It must be prepared for. The law blames the motorist for such a collision—as it should—but the safe cyclist blames him- or herself for being distracted and unprepared. It's either that or get used to eating trunks and side panels, which aren't very tasty and provide poor nutrition.

The cyclist's best chance is to gather all the responsibility that can be gathered. Hoard it from those around you. Have faith that you will do a better job with it than they will, and make it so. Don't trust your fate to the police, the planners, the pedestrians, or the paramedics. Don't leave your fate to the stars, or to luck. Definitely don't leave your fate to the drivers.

VIGILANCE

Is cycling dangerous? Sure, why not? Deadly, no, but you could go ahead and call it dangerous. Of course the question is meaningless without a precise definition of *dangerous,* one of those words that means different things to different people at different times.

There are those who bristle at any suggestion that cycling is dangerous, because they fear it will scare noncyclists away from ever ditching their cars and trying a more healthy form of transport. This is a good point, but it doesn't make cycling any less dangerous. In fact you could make the argument that downplaying the danger actually makes cycling more dangerous for unsuspecting beginners. The danger of cycling is not some urban legend that needs to be debunked. It is reality, and for the sake of our own safety, we need to embrace it.

Now, is cycling any more dangerous than driving or walking in the city? Not really. Maybe a bit more dangerous overall, depending on how vigorously you want to interpret the statistics (see Chapter Four: Bicycle Accidents and Injuries). In general, people seem to be short on respect for the dangers involved in any of their chosen modes of personal city transportation, whether driving or walking or riding a bicycle. It's dangerous out there, period. The difference with bicycling is that it brings long-term health benefits and peace of mind that the other forms of transportation can't.

Although getting killed while cycling is highly unlikely, and could honestly be labeled rare, we can't dismiss so quickly the prospect of receiving some sort of serious injury. American cyclists are admitted to hospitals—that is, they receive injuries so severe that they have to spend a few days or more in a hospital bed receiving treatment—at a rate of fifty to one hundred per day, according to government estimates. I'll dig deeper into these stats in the next section of the book. Bring an extra shovel along for that.

The cyclist's primary goal should be, first and foremost, to avoid receiving one of these serious injuries. This is the cyclist's bottom line. Do whatever it takes to achieve this goal, short of staying at home. Our other major goals as cyclists—efficiency and enjoyment—are dependent on the goal of safety. Getting packed into the back of an ambulance halfway through our commute won't help us reach our intended destination, and it probably won't be very much fun either.

The work of achieving this goal starts before you get on the bike. It's about what's floating around in your head. Instead of just hopping on the machine and pedaling, take a moment before any ride to soberly consider the dangers you are about to face and how to avoid them. Carry this serious thought into the ride and maintain it throughout, despite all the distractions of everyday life that compete for bandwidth in your skull. It is absolutely true that accidents happen when they are least expected. The old warhorses of cycling will always say their worst wrecks came at a time when their minds were wandering. They had momentarily forgotten the danger. They let themselves slip, just a little. Just enough.

The good news is that the cyclist has the potential to control his or her own destiny to a great extent. The bad news is that unpleasant things seem to happen soon after the rider drifts off into passive mode, goes on autopilot. The obvious remedy is to keep oneself from falling back into this passive mode. To always stay alert. To give the potential dangers their due respect, all the time. This is a state of mind known as vigilance.

Vigilance goes hand in hand with accepting responsibility for oneself and is the hallmark of the experienced city rider. Will it be possible, in a book, to teach beginning cyclists the value of vigilance, before the lesson is pounded into them by events? One can only hope.

In addition to constantly scanning the road surface for obstacles, vigilant cyclists keep tabs on other road users—motorists, pedestrians, and other cyclists—who have any potential to cause a collision. That's a lot of road users. Vigilant cyclists expect and prepare for serious ineptitude from strangers, and therefore are not surprised or angry when it has to be endured. Vigilant cyclists keep their heads up and eyes forward, unless it is absolutely necessary to look elsewhere, and do not assume they have been seen by other road users. Vigilant cyclists do not trust green lights or stop signs or bike lanes painted on the street or any of the other artificial trappings of traffic engineering. The vigilant cyclist is not a trusting cyclist, but makes up for this lack of trust with a load of patience.

Bicyclists may experience long intervals during which they encounter nothing but rational and lawful citizens on the road, weeks or months with everything running as smooth as silk. But the vigilant cyclist realizes this is only a setup. The vigilant cyclist will not be faked out or lulled into complacency by the semi-sadistic urban spirits and their tricks.

Luckily, maintaining a constant state of vigilance can be fun. A great trick is to meld the goal of safety with the goal of enjoying the ride. Turn your dangerous trip through the city into a kind of game. The concentration required of the bicyclist in heavy traffic is not unlike the concentration demanded of the mountain biker speeding along a singletrack trail. Constant scanning ahead, constant adjustments, unbroken focus on the task at hand. It pushes everything else out of your head when practiced correctly. It is, paradoxically, totally relaxing and fun.

As with mountain biking, the proper state of mind for riding in heavy traffic is focused but calm, almost meditative. Do not confuse vigilance with nervousness, jumpiness, or worry. Vigilance is not a kind of unfocused fear but the beginning of proactive problem solving.

ROUTE CHOICE

There are two competing philosophies about route choice in cycling. One says that cyclists should not be overly concerned with route choice at all, except to choose the fastest and most direct route to their destination. It is a corollary of this belief that all city streets and boulevards, with few exceptions, are suitable for bicycling. It's simply up to the cyclist to stake a claim to the road. Bicyclists are granted that right by law, so why not? "If we don't exercise our right to use the public roadways, they'll take that right away." Cyclists who believe this often urge others to make heavy use of busy arterial boulevards. Whether or not they actually follow their own advice on this is questionable.

Another philosophy maintains that the cyclist is better off choosing a route with as few traffic hassles along the way as possible. Cyclists who believe this prefer to avoid busy and narrow streets, whenever practical, in favor of wide, quiet streets. They are not averse to using well-designed bike paths. They will sacrifice a bit of time in exchange for a reduction in overall stress. Although these riders may be quite well versed in the methods of riding busy streets, they feel no ideological need to do so when alternative routes are available.

The second view is more realistic. In our traffic-jammed twenty-first-century urban sprawl, with its car-centric road designs, car-centric attitudes, and car-centric cops, bicyclists subject themselves to needless hassle and stress by trying to ride streets that are bad for bicycling.

Many newbies, embarking on their first commutes, simply attempt to follow the same exact routes they've been driving in their cars every day. This is ill-advised. The best routes for cars very rarely correspond to the best bike routes. Riders who attempt this are often so frazzled by the experience that they never look at their bikes again. If that's what bicycling is all about, then they want no part of it. But that is not what bicycling is all about. It's simply the consequence of a classic beginner mistake—failure to recognize or appreciate the available route options.

Know that your bicycling experience should not be marked by frequent conflict. Occasional conflict, sure. But the ride should actually be pleasant. No yelling. No fist shaking. No screaming in terror. Every commute should be a bit of a vacation. If it's not, perhaps a little creative route finding can solve the problem.

When choosing streets, try to choose a reasonably safe route, of course. But there should be an underlying recognition that all streets and bike paths will be somewhat dangerous. Danger can never be eliminated through route choice. Vigilance must be maintained, no matter what route is used. Don't be lulled to sleep by a quiet route.

Route choice has as much to do with minimizing hassle and stress as it has to do with safety. With this in mind, look to avoid lane conflicts and turning/crossing conflicts rather than simply being concerned with volume of traffic. Find streets with low intensity of traffic. Traffic intensity, an official-sounding term that I just now made up, is a function of volume, speed, frequency of turning/crossing vehicles, lane width, and a certain frantic disposition. Traffic intensity will vary on the same streets at different times of the day. Some very

SIDE PARKING COMPLICATES THE SITUATION.

well-traveled boulevards may also have relatively low traffic intensity. Some near-deserted streets cross a heinous intersection every block, and are insidiously problematic.

Really, you should be looking for streets that have a minimum of motor vehicles traveling across your line. The fewer intersections the better. Avoid—whenever possible—hectic commercial streets bordered with many parking lots and parking-lot entrances. Riding these streets will mean dealing with an inordinate amount of left- and right-turning vehicles, and therefore lots of confused and angry drivers, lots of harrowing near misses, or worse.

Wide curb lanes or wide shoulders make the ride more comfortable. The presence of an on-street bike lane is, at least, an indication of a wide curb lane. Low speed limits—thirty miles per hour or lower—are nice. High speed limits are of no use to bicyclists. Remember that a bicyclist will travel basically at the same speed on a thirty-mile-per-hour street as a seventy-five-mile-per-hour freeway, all other factors being equal. At the same time, the seventy-five-mile-per-hour freeway could be loud, uncomfortable, and potentially more dangerous for bicycling, as the severity of crashes increases with vehicle speeds.[3] The worst roads of all are high-speed streets with frequent intersections and parking lot entrances.

One is tempted to make the claim that streets with lots of on-street parking are always bad for bicycling, due to the dangers that parked vehicles imply, but in fact some parking streets are pretty nice if there is enough space. Any street on which the cyclist must block a lane of faster traffic to stay out of the Door Zone is a relatively bad bicycling street (see The Door Zone, on page 127).

There is another type of street that can be singled out for its particularly heinous traffic intensity: the street that passes schools, especially high schools. Here we have many inexperienced, distracted, and hurried drivers concentrated around one spot and swarming the surrounding neighborhood like bees around a hive. You don't have to find the high schools on a map, they make themselves obnoxiously apparent.

Traffic intensity, lane width, speed limits, and such are not the only factors to consider. Cyclists also put a premium on streets that are smooth, clean, fast, and direct. Mix and match depending on your priorities and preferences. These attributes can be competing, but not always.

Often the urban or suburban cyclist finds that the most direct route to a destination is a very narrow, high-speed roadway where the mere presence of a person on a bike causes a major disruption to motor traffic. Faced with these situations, the experienced bicyclist often chooses to chart a longer route, even a meandering route, on streets with less intensity of traffic, if any such route is available. It's not just that the busy, narrow-laned, conflict-prone street is dangerous—all streets can be dangerous. It's the continuous hassle with motorists that is the real deal breaker on such a street. It's just not worth it most of the time. Use these streets only as a last resort—when no other

KNOW THE CROSSING POINTS!

option is available, or in a serious time crunch. A cyclist may occasionally decide to subject him- or herself to a good deal of additional contention over lane space in order to take the fastest route. Already fifteen minutes late for work? You might need to jump on Suicide Parkway and fly. It happens.

Circumstantial evidence strongly suggests that bicyclists in this late-to-work mode are more likely to be involved in collisions because of the increased intensity of traffic on their chosen routes, and because of their own impatience. There's hardly anything out there that could make you quite as late for work as a side trip to the hospital (although that does provide a good excuse). Perhaps the best safety tip is to leave early enough that you don't have to hurry and can afford to take a luxuriously mellow route.

The first attempt at any unfamiliar route will consume excess time because it will naturally include some backtracking, inadvertent forays onto poor cycling roads, and other general floundering. A first attempt is always something of an adventure and is to be relished. Good times—but not when you're pressed for time. Try it first on a non-workday, when the pressure's off. Some riders like to just hop on the bike and go exploring, and others like to look at a detailed street map before embarking. Be careful with the special bike-route maps; these are good for locating the bike paths but often fail to show all the city's streets.

One of the first challenges with charting a route through the modern American city is finding a way across freeways. Freeways are like huge rivers. We can't ride on them, there are only a few places to cross, and many of the crossing points are horribly inhospitable to bicyclists. So the bicyclist's options are already, shall we say, simplified dramatically for any cross-city ride. Urban freeways, rail corridors, rivers, and other colossal barriers always seem to cause the most route-oriented delays during any ride through unknown territory. Know the crossing points. Don't neglect the possibility of pedestrian tunnels and overpasses, which can be extremely useful to bicyclists. You might have to carry your bike up and down some stairs, but try that with a Nissan.

Contrary to the insistence of some misguided souls, American cyclists are lucky that continuous, fully separated bicycle/pedestrian megapaths have been and continue to be constructed in many cities. These paths flow unbroken under (or over) freeways and major boulevards, and must be distinguished from the old-style asphalt bike paths and the "sidepaths" that are little more than glorified sidewalks. Rather than cutting down on cyclists' available options as some fear, fully separated paths make the bicycle an even more versatile and efficient tool for urban transportation. Ideally the best route would consist entirely of a wide concrete bike path cutting diagonally across the city to your destination, with not a single intersection or stop sign along its entire length. Of course such a route is rarely so perfectly placed, but you might be able to pick up a segment of a good path and insert it into your route.

THE CHERRY CREEK TRAIL IN DENVER IS A GOOD EXAMPLE OF A FULLY
SEPARATED PATH.

Experienced riders know that cruising these separate paths could involve
an increased total chance of minor collisions, something that seems counter-
intuitive to many beginners. Make no mistake, as presidents like to say. Bike
paths can be dangerous too. Cyclists have to deal with hazards on the path
that they would never see on the roads. (See On the Bike Path, page 153.) But
the complete lack of traffic stops and car interactions on separate facilities
is much appreciated and makes the new bike paths the most attractive of all
possible bicycling routes. If only they led everywhere we need to go.

Paths that follow rivers and rail corridors often cut *diagonally* through
(under) the urban street grid. Diagonal routes can be extremely valuable in

urban route finding. Last time we checked, the shortest distance between two points was still a straight line, not a zigzag or L-shaped line. Ride the hypotenuse!

Once a good route has been sniffed out, the cyclist will gain a significant amount of security by riding it consistently and repeatedly. The rider will learn every pothole and rough patch of pavement, every intersection, every hidden garage exit, every "pinch point," and will grow to understand and predict the personality of the traffic at different times. Just in terms of learning the idiosyncrasies of the road surface, route repetition is extremely valuable.

Route repetition can also be boring. To add variety, scout a few alternates and learn those as well.

ROAD POSITION AND LOCATION

First timers are often puzzled by the question of where to ride in the street. "Where should I ride in the street?" they ask, puzzled.

There are no easy answers to this question. The intricate art of positioning is downloaded into cyclists' brains by experience. They don't analyze where they ride or why they ride there, they just do it. After having been passed hundreds of thousands of times by cars and trucks, after hundreds of near misses and maybe a few nonmisses, highly experienced riders gain a feel for what is easiest and safest in different situations. They ride where they are most comfortable, and the details are based largely on personal preference.

If we were to gloss over all sorts of variables and use gross generalizations, however, we could hang the positioning art on a framework of four not-so-simple guidelines:

1. The cyclist should ride in the same direction as motor traffic.
2. Cyclists should avoid riding within about four feet from the sides of parked cars, unless speed is slow enough that collision with an immovable object called a car door would be relatively benign (see The Door Zone, page 127).
3. When approaching and exiting intersections, the bicyclist should be positioned in the appropriate sector of the appropriate lane, depending

on whether he or she is going to turn right, turn left, or continue straight through—in the right half of the far-right lane, in the rightmost left-turn lane, or in the rightmost through lane, respectively. Achieving proper position for a left turn can be extremely difficult, or even impossible, depending on traffic. For this reason left turns are a special case (see Left Turns, page 115).

These three guidelines are fairly straightforward. They are standard vehicular-cycling fare. This next one is far from straightforward. We could qualify it, question it, and pick it apart until the sun dies out.

4. Use the Buffer Zone. Now we're really getting to the heart of the matter. Choosing road position on busy streets in dense urban areas—as opposed to wide, quiet boulevards with few pedestrians and near-perfect visibility of any side streets and driveways—is a delicate art. When no cars are gaining from the rear, or approaching from the front, the cyclist should ride way out in the heart of such a street, not tucked over on the side.

How far out? That's where the art comes in. Many savvy veterans enjoy riding near the center of the right lane, on the hump between the right lane's wheel depressions, or in the right wheel depression. Others like to ride farther out toward the left of the lane. Whatever your preference, consider a central-ish position to be the default position of cycling.

There are a few very good reasons why the cyclist should take this position on streets with lots of side traffic. The rider will be more visible to motorists and pedestrians on the periphery and will be less likely to have these other road users move into his or her path. More important, the "buffer zone" created by this positioning gives the cyclist a better view of what may be coming from the wings, which translates into precious milliseconds when the inevitable intrusion occurs. If a car bolts out from a driveway, alley, or side street, or a jaywalker with a fresh set of running shoes pops out from between parked cars (see The Problem with Pedestrians, page 100), the rider wants to be as far away from the hazard as possible, while still accounting for the possibility of additional hazards. This buffer zone increases the cyclist's safety but also allows the cyclist to continue rolling at a consistent clip in an obstacle-prone world, without having to swerve harshly or slam on the brakes every ten seconds.

Increases in speed bring increases in the importance of space. The more speed carried by the artful cyclist, the closer he or she gets to the center of the street. At moderate, ho-hum cycling speeds, the rider does not have to be too concerned about maintaining a buffer zone, unless the street is lined with parked cars. Streets with clear edges, few pedestrians, a view all the way to the curb, and good lines of sight to any driveways, alleys, or intersections can be ridden safely all the way to the right if the rider wishes. Lines of parked cars seriously compromise the cyclist's vision and visibility, in addition to the other dangers they pose, and change the equation drastically.

Quick speeds that are easily attained by the bulk of riders—around twenty or more miles per hour—require the rider to maintain a serious buffer zone between the bike and any parked cars on the right side of the road—ten feet or more. This means that on a very narrow side street lined with parked cars, the fast-moving rider might take a position right down the middle of the street. When forced back to the right on such a street, the rider should respond with a decrease in speed. On wide roads with multiple lanes, the bicyclist probably won't have to drift any farther left than the left side of the outside lane.

Always ask yourself: *How much am I leaving to chance here? How dependent am I on other people?* And then adjust your location and speed in such a way that this dependence is minimized, while taking traffic law, the need for speed and efficiency, and courtesy for other road users into account. Clearly this endeavor is entirely dependent on our awareness of the position, speed, and vector of every other vehicle in the vicinity.

Leaving the comfortable default position to move closer to the curb or parked cars is often necessary for sharing the road with vehicles on a parallel path, oncomers and overtakers. When faced with oncoming vehicles in the opposite lane, the cyclist might not want to continue riding near the middle of the street. (What if the driver doesn't notice the rider and decides to crank a sudden left?) Instead, the bicyclist might drift to the right, relinquishing the default position, for the same reason he or she assumes the position in the first place: to create a buffer. Moving to the right for an overtaking vehicle—a vehicle traveling in the same direction as the cyclist—is more a matter of courtesy. How far over should we move for overtaking vehicles, if at all? More art.

Safety is the bicyclist's primary motivation for shifting position left or right—to reduce the chances of getting hit or running into a pedestrian. Cooperation is another reason to change positions. Subtle shifts of road position can send signals of goodwill to drivers. When a cyclist who has established position near midlane looks back, then shifts toward the curb as a car approaches from behind, this one-two combination sends a signal to the driver that the cyclist is aware of the vehicle's presence and passing is welcome. This accommodating move is one of the fundamental building blocks of safe, swift, and hassle-free bicycling, but many riders view it as a display of weakness.

The bicyclist's approach to road positioning should be characterized by flexibility. Accept that the best possible line will be shifting on a near-constant basis. Don't cling grimly to a favored spot in the road while the disposition of traffic shifts wildly around you. City cyclists should switch their positions, toward the curb and back out, and adjust speed quite often in dense traffic as conditions fluctuate. These movements should be smooth and subtle, not swerves or weaves or lurches, and should be informed by 360-degree awareness of surrounding traffic.

At times the rider will have to accept that position on one street should be abandoned altogether for position on another street or an off-street route.

THE INVISIBLE CYCLIST

Well out in the lane, the bicyclist may be more visible to others, especially crossing drivers, pedestrians, and oncoming drivers setting up for a left turn. *May* is the operable word here.

The cyclists' struggle for visibility has been a noble and long-fought effort. Problem is, it hasn't worked. No matter how much tinsel and ornamentation we attach to ourselves, no matter how many flashing beacons we strap to our backsides, no matter what previously unseen degree of neon insanity we manage to surpass in our jersey selection, some drivers continue to look right through us, as if we were—that's right—invisible.

The dream of visibility is a sweet siren's song that will, eventually, lead us into the rocks. Not that visibility is a bad thing, mind you; we all love visibility. It's just that an attitude of faith in visibility puts the rider on a slippery slope on the way to complacency, which is a very dangerous place for a cyclist to hang out. Resist the creeping assumption that taking a more conspicuous position will actually make you visible to all drivers. Go ahead and take measures to enhance your visibility—the orange vest, the flashers and beacons— just don't fool yourself into believing these measures will always work.

New bicyclists often feel virtually omnipotent while wearing their luminous vests and insanely powerful strobe lights. It's an insidious fantasy. It's obvious that these measures will help enhance our conspicuity. What isn't so obvious is that their effectiveness changes drastically as the background changes, which makes them inconsistent and imminently fallible.[4] Among a sea of other lights, your bike light might not register to a driver. A bright green jacket won't show up well against a wall of foliage, and so on. And when it's all said and done, the driver might not even be looking in your general direction anyway.

So we have a thin line to pedal. We want to use any visibility-enhancing measures we can get our mitts on within reason—at night we should use everything available, including flashing headlights and taillights, reflective clothing, and reflective strips on the spokes—but we can't allow ourselves to feel very comfortable about using them. We can't place so much faith in these things that using them causes us to let our guard down. It's better to stubbornly assume that we are unseen until it is made absolutely obvious that we are seen.*

Bicyclists are often overlooked, no matter what they wear or how they ride. We should accept this as reality and proceed from there. We should deal with reality as it is, not how we hope or wish it to be.

---

*This stubbornness can (and must) be tempered a bit with respect to vehicles overtaking from behind. Motorists overtaking from behind are the most likely to see a cyclist, because they are generally looking forward in the cyclist's direction and have more time in which to notice him or her. For this reason the rider can usually maintain a fair buffer zone on the right even as vehicles come up behind. Shifting position to the right in these passing situations is usually more a matter of courtesy and practicality than a safety issue. Drivers and pedestrians crossing the rider's path are much less likely to notice a cyclist. This pattern is reflected in the accident statistics.

VISION VERSUS VISIBILITY

Adjusting position on the road to maximize visibility to others is a fool's game. It should not be a guiding principle.

Much more important than adding to visibility, riding in a position away from the curb and parked cars, out in the street, enhances the *cyclist's* vision. It also gives the rider precious space should a sudden hazard emerge from the right side and maneuvering room should a hazard emerge from either side. Space becomes time, which transforms collisions into near misses.

It's interesting: Riders who position like this to maximize space and vision often find themselves riding the same line as cyclists who position to maximize visibility. Both cyclists are pedaling along in the same road position, but for completely different reasons. One cyclist rides in the default position in the hope he will be seen by others; the other rides there precisely because he understands the likelihood of being overlooked, regardless of road position. Both have maximized visibility as well as space, but the attitudes of the two are fundamentally different: One readily abdicates some responsibility and places it in the hands (or eyes) of strangers; the other cyclist assumes all responsibility for his or her own safety.

Despite their identical road positions, their experiences will not be the same. One is pedaling innocently toward disaster; the other expects it and will be ready for it.

THE MYTH OF LANE OWNERSHIP

The Master said, those whose measures are dictated by mere expediency will arouse continual discontent.[5]

—CONFUCIUS

It is a common belief among cyclists, and even among drivers, that cyclists have "the same rights and responsibilities as motorists." Many cyclists take this to mean they will be protected by the law when consuming an entire lane, even if this slows or blocks motor traffic.

While it is generally true that bicycles are classified as vehicles, and cyclists are governed by the same traffic laws as motorists, there are some crucial exceptions. In most municipal traffic codes, a cyclist is not allowed to occupy an entire lane whenever he or she wishes. In this respect bicycles are not equal to cars in the eyes of the law. Cyclists are usually required to ride as far to the right-hand side of the roadway "as practicable."* This law is not in place to increase the safety of the bicyclists but simply to facilitate traffic flow—to get slower vehicles out of the way of faster vehicles. For this reason the law is often attacked by vehicular-cycling activists.[6]

Only where the lane is too narrow for a car to pass a bicycle, where there are parked cars, grates, or piles of debris near the curb, where the bicycle is moving at the same speed or faster than motor traffic, or where the rider is maneuvering for a left turn, can the cyclist legally take charge of an entire lane. The exact conditions that would relieve the cyclist of the legal requirement to keep right are generally not specified. How narrow is too narrow? How much debris constitutes a hazard? In practice these decisions are left up to the judgment of the rider. And then it's up to the whim of individual police and judges to sanction any bicyclist who oversteps the subjective and imaginary bounds.

Many jurisdictions have passed "three-foot laws," which require motorists to leave three feet of space when passing cyclists, regardless of where the cyclist is riding. Theoretically, if a rider got hit while being passed the police would know that the driver had at least violated the three-foot law. In reality, police have often been unwilling to cite drivers for colliding with cyclists even after these laws were passed.

The ride-to-the-right rule is one of the major sources of confusion in the traffic codes. It baffles cyclists, motorists, and police alike. Faced with a rule that is arbitrarily formulated and arbitrarily applied, cyclists need to take responsibility for themselves and interpret the ride-to-the-right rule for the benefit of their personal safety first, and with consideration for other road users second. The trick is not to take this quest for personal safety so far that it does more harm than good.

---

*Many cities, New York City and Seattle among them, allow cyclists to ride on the far-left side of one-way streets. Many cities specify that the cyclist is entitled to the three- or four-foot-wide strip to the left of the right-hand edge of the roadway. Albuquerque law requires that motorists allow at least five feet when passing cyclists.

There are certainly situations where the cyclist should stake out an entire lane in front of motor vehicles, no matter what the law states. For instance, any time the cyclist is moving at the same speed as motor traffic. There are many other scenarios when lane taking will be the best temporary option; these are determined by subtle variables—the speed and personality of traffic; the proximity of curbs and parked vehicles; and the presence of grates, potholes, and debris, to name a few. Recognition of these situations comes with experience and is difficult to learn from books and pamphlets.

Often those who regularly, rather than selectively, practice deliberate lane blocking say they do it to prevent motorists coming up from behind from passing too close. On narrow streets, and in the well-used curb lanes of busy boulevards, they say, motorists will buzz right by the cyclist's elbow when given half a chance. These cyclists attempt to prevent these unwelcome and dangerous intrusions into personal space by moving well into the middle of the lane. According to them this encourages motorists to move completely into another lane to pass. Some full-time lane takers even claim that the more room they give themselves on the right, the more room passing drivers give them on their left. These claims, which are not necessarily confirmed by experience or supported by empirical evidence, betray a strong obsession with same-direction traffic.

The folks who practice full-time lane taking and extol its virtues often characterize themselves as supremely confident, while they portray those who prefer not to take the lane as unreasonably fearful of same-direction traffic. This seems to be one of those doth-protest-too-much situations. It's hard to see how anybody could be more obsessed with the vehicles behind them than the strident lane takers, who spend so much mental energy attempting to control this singular aspect of traffic.

The statistical case for constant lane taking as a safety strategy is weak. Large studies of bike-car crashes suggest that moving left in order to mitigate a possible collision caused by a misjudged pass might actually increase your overall chances of being hit. Even in broad daylight, incidents of motorists' completely failing to notice and hitting cyclists in front of them are more common than collisions resulting from misjudged passes. (In low-light situations, the frequency of hits from behind goes up drastically.) And as far as collisions go, the hit from behind is the worst there is, far more likely to cause a fatality than any other crash type. Meanwhile, collisions caused by mis-judged passes—sideswipes, generally—are among the least damaging of all. So in terms of safety, those who take lanes to minimize unsafe passing seem to be going from the frying pan into the fire.[7] These numbers do not comple-ment the belief system of lane-taking devotees. (They respond by insisting that a large number of misjudged passes must have been misidentified as motorist-failed-to-notice passes.)

No matter what the studies suggest, there will always be a delegation of riders who insist they can control motor traffic through lane taking, and who are comfortable in the assumption that they will always be visible to those approaching from behind. These beliefs are part of the cultural machinery of cycling, stronger than evidence.

Sometimes—a key word here—exaggerated lane taking is justified and proper. Sometimes you have no choice, in fact. It is my opinion, however, that total lane consumption in front of faster vehicles is necessary less often than one might think and that the benefits it brings are usually marginal enough to be canceled out by hassle and hurt feelings. For riders who find themselves blocking lanes on a regular basis, more intensive route finding will be the best medicine.

Some riders use lane taking as a crutch for shortcomings in cycling tech-nique. When riding in a normal, wide curb lane, they feel as if they are caught in the Running of the Bulls. These are often inexperienced riders who are completely twizzed out by being passed, or they have little tolerance for the normal obstacles of city riding, like sand on the road. Even the most militant lane takers will have to deal with plenty of all of this, no matter how assertive they are in their positioning, and they will find out soon enough that riding the lane is no magic force field against dangerous passes. It is recommended that these riders face their demons and shake the habit. Lane taking is a poor substitute for good route finding, and lane taking is a poor substitute for finesse, skill, and experience.

Most often, if the rider has chosen a good route, plenty of room can be given to passing drivers without any real sacrifice on the part of the cyclist. If there's enough room, find the seam that will allow cars to pass while you con-tinue swiftly and safely on your way. This is cooperation and compromise— the rider moves over a bit to the right, the driver moves over a bit to the left, and everyone coexists in harmony. If no such harmonic seam can be found on a street, and the cyclist is constantly fighting drivers for one available line, that's as good a definition as any of a street that is bad for bicycling. Find a different one if possible. Save the evil street for special occasions. If it's a simple matter of feeling uncomfortable with cars passing close, practice riding relaxed and straight in tight spaces until it becomes second nature. This will make the streets seem a lot wider. The ability to share a narrow curb lane with motorists comes with experience and handling skills, although you may still choose not to do it.

The bottom line is that lane conflicts are occasionally unavoidable—inevitable to a certain degree—but need not be a regular feature of the cycling experience. The artful bicyclist rarely needs to commandeer an entire lane in front of faster traffic, is comfortable riding in tight spaces, and rarely feels threatened—physically or psychologically—by passing vehicles. Indeed the artful bicyclist rarely affects the flow of motor traffic in any significant way, is rarely put out by it, and moves with effortlessness in heavy traffic that the habitual lane takers can only dream about.

Share the lane, if possible, and make the world a better place.

RUNNING GREEN LIGHTS

Contrary to popular opinion, when an experienced adult cyclist gets smacked by a car, it is most likely that the cyclist was riding lawfully and predictably at the time. Now consider, if you will, the common American bicycle messenger. The veterans of this nearly extinct species, when the bike delivery business was booming in the dot com era, were likely to bust through one hundred or more red lights in a workday. If anyone was in a position to find out just how dangerous it is to break the law while riding bikes in the city, it was these guys and gals; and yet evidence suggests that experienced messengers had far lower accident rates than typical adult cyclists, and almost never got hit while running red lights.[8]

This isn't a suggestion that running red lights is a good idea. But clearly, following the traffic rules alone isn't necessarily synonymous with safe riding. There must be something else, a more important ingredient that keeps riders out of trouble when they sneak through red lights, but somehow turns up missing when the light is green. That critical ingredient is the rider's own awareness.

The trick is to bring the messengers' red-light awareness to green-light intersections.

Rather than simply cruising through a green light with your eyes glazed over and your head in the proverbial clouds, begin to check all the trouble spots vigilantly and anticipate conflicts before they arise. Anticipate the mistakes of those around you. There are five distinct sources of trouble:

1. Well before reaching the intersection, direct your awareness left and behind for cars that might be preparing to turn right across your path. Bicyclists on sidewalks or sidepaths are less likely to be seen and less likely to be respected if they are seen. Even if the little green man is showing on the walk signal, be prepared to stop completely before entering the intersection to stay out of the way of furious right turners. Right-of-way means nothing. Don't roll into the intersection without first looking behind you.

2. Check quickly for red-light runners moving quickly from the right and left.

3. Check for wayward pedestrians on the loose, stepping blindly into the street. (See The Problem with Pedestrians, page 100.)

4. As early as possible, give the street ahead a thorough examination in search of left turners. Is that oncoming vehicle going to turn left? There is no reliable way to tell if a vehicle is going to turn at you until it does or doesn't, so assume it will. Be ready for it. Left turners are particularly dangerous because they often carry a great deal of speed, their turns are often not telegraphed, and in their haste they often fail to notice cyclists. To avoid one you may be forced to veer right or left, speed forward, or stop quickly.

   Watching for left turners is important even on little streets, where the only intersections are minor driveways. Whenever a car approaches, going the opposite direction on the same street, consider all the potential vectors the vehicle could reasonably take—driveways, alleys, parking spaces, streets, or straight ahead. A little alarm should go off when

THE LAST ONE THROUGH THE INTERSECTION BEFORE THE LIGHT TURNS RED IS LIKELY TO ENJOY RELATIVELY LIGHT TRAFFIC FOR THE NEXT HALF BLOCK OR SO.

you are passing by some kind of parking lot entrance or street on your right just before an oncoming vehicle goes by, because you are crossing through that vehicle's possible path. Avoid these little moments of potential disaster by watching well ahead and subtly adjusting speed and position. This probably sounds excessively cautious to those who don't have much experience riding in the city. But "driver turns left into cyclist" is an extremely common scenario, and an extremely bloody one as well. A little paranoia is warranted here. You'll notice nothing is said here about watching for turn signals, except this: turn signals—ha!

5. The cyclist has a little more time to scan the right front for possible right turners. Leave an adequate buffer zone between yourself and any vehicles as you exit the intersection on the far side. Try not to roll right across in front of any bumpers. If you are entering the intersection on a yellow light, be very aware of any overanxious light timers rolling up in the right lane of the intersecting street.

So, let's see . . . that's two different types of right turners, in addition to the left turners, light runners, and wayward pedestrians. Every busy intersection is a green garden of mistakes. Two forces need to be balanced when riding through all busy intersections: the instinct to leave space on the left and the instinct to leave space on the right. Both instincts are correct.

EYE CONTACT, STOP SIGNS, AND FAKE RIGHT TURNS

Some cyclists have so much faith in the concept of eye contact with motorists that they end up confused and bitter. It's sad to watch. They're out there, riding along, doing no harm to anyone, and duly making eye contact with all drivers who represent a direct threat to their well-being. And yet some of these drivers still pull out right in front of them. These encounters start the gears turning in the poor confused cyclist's head. *But I had eye contact! That guy must hate bicyclists! Just because he's got a big-ass Yukon he thinks he can do whatever he wants! I'm sick of this $#%*!* Other victimized riders come to the less emotional conclusion that the drivers saw them but misjudged their speed.

These explanations usually represent a fair bit of overthinking. The most likely reason for a driver to pull out in front of a cyclist is far less complex. It's just the Invisible Cyclist thing again. Here is an important newsflash that any would-be rider needs to hear: Just because a driver's eyes are pointed directly at you does not mean the driver sees you. Direction does not imply detection.

It's no surprise that cyclists are baffled by this phenomenon. The driver's eyes are pointed right at you, a pleasant expression on her face, like "Ah, look at the nice bicycle rider," but really she's looking right through you somehow, trying to remember the lyrics to Neil Diamond's "Sweet Caroline." *Sweet Caroline . . . Bop buh bah . . .* It's a creepy feeling to be that invisible. Get used to it.

To be fair, most drivers are looking for cars when they look. Cyclists can blend into the background of parked cars, trees, and pedestrians, even when riding out in the middle of the road. Motorcyclists get the same foul treatment quite often. Unfortunately for motorcyclists, they are more restricted in terms of where they can be on the road. Bicyclists have more capability and leeway to avoid the seemingly blind drivers, should they choose to utilize it.

Most phantom eye-contact incidents occur when the cyclist "has the right-of-way" (ha!) on a through street, with cars pulling up to stop signs on side streets. Drivers are known to space out at stop signs completely, but the more common danger to cyclists comes from drivers' "failure to yield" upon restarting. "Failure to yield"—these are the words that appear on the driver's summons and complaint after such a mishap, but a more accurate description of the offense would be "failure to notice." Researchers call it a "looked-but-failed-to-see error," which sums it up nicely.

When the driver comes from a stop sign on the cyclist's left, the cyclist has more time and space to avoid disaster. This extra buffer is much appreciated, as drivers at stop signs on the left are less likely to notice a bicyclist pedaling down the road, and are thus more likely to launch their vehicles in the rider's general direction.

Next time you're in the driver's seat of a car, look to your right, past your wildly gesturing passenger with his gigantic head and comically large sombrero, fight through the glare of the sun on the dirty windshield, you know, that little triangle of mud-splattered glass where the wiper doesn't reach, and imagine how hard it might be to see a fast-moving cyclist out there. And notice how the doorposts in new cars have grown plenty large enough to completely block the view of an approaching cyclist—total eclipse of the cyclist—potentially for several seconds at a time if the driver is inching the car forward. A driver on the right has a much easier time seeing an approaching rider, but an intrusion from the right is more urgent due to the proximity of the vehicle.

By the time the rider is actually passing in front of the stopped vehicle, if he or she has been able to leave a decent amount of space and is holding good speed, the danger has pretty much passed. But if the vehicle arrives at the stop just before the cyclist gets there, the cyclist becomes at least partially dependent on the driver's vision and awareness. Experienced bicyclists feel it in their bones when they pass through these "sweet spots of danger": *If that guy goes right now, I'm toast.* This is when most of the frantic attempts to establish eye contact are made. At such a late stage, looking for eye contact to save you is not a good sign, to put it mildly.

It is not practical to forever avoid passing through these zones of vulnerability. In our quest to hoard responsibility, we cannot gather it all in. Some responsibility will always escape our grasp. But we still can, and must, cut down on the danger by recognizing it, leaving healthy buffer zones, and remaining physically prepared to execute evasive maneuvers when some driver launches four thousand pounds of weaponized steel in our direction. These drivers usually don't have murderous intentions toward bicyclists; they're just bad drivers.

Next time someone pulls out in front you after seeming to look right at you, watch the driver's face while you execute a smooth turning-braking evasive move. Notice at which point, if any, the driver becomes aware of your presence. Watch his or her mouth form a wide O of surprise. Seeing this can actually be quite reassuring. The successful bicyclist sees the driver make this face from the comfort of the bicycle, not while doing a fly-by past the windshield.

One of the most useful moves a cyclist can perfect is the tiny curlicue turn-and-stop that is made in perfect anticipation of a driver pulling out into the rider's would-be path. Upon the first sign of premature movement in the vehicle, the rider brakes smoothly while turning sharply, usually to the right. This sharp turn keeps the cyclist from ever crossing in front of the vehicle. Although this is a reactive move, it is not a panic stop, because there is no panic. The rider expects the pullout all the way and is ready for it.

The Fake Right Turn is an example of a proactive technique. The controversial Fake Right Turn is an advanced—plain stupid, in the opinion of some—method of dealing with jumpy cars at stop signs on the cyclist's right. It is favored by heavily scarred, very untrusting riders, and can be executed only when there are no vehicles present other than the one in question. Here's how it works: Instead of simply continuing straight in front of the car, the cyclist who wishes to leave as little as possible to chance slows down and pretends to make a right turn onto the street with the stop sign. Usually, as soon as the rider starts the fake turn, the driver hits the accelerator and blasts across the intersection. The cyclist then veers into the space vacated by the car and continues on his or her way with a minimum of disruption. By "springing" the driver, the cyclist has made the driver's questionable grip on reality a nonissue. If there are any other vehicles or pedestrians around—or any other bicyclists—such a deceptive move would be more dangerous than crossing normally. Otherwise it can be beautifully smooth: It cancels danger in a way that the fattest buffer zone could not, and allows the rider to keep moving. Many riders use the Fake Right Turn as a more courteous way to avoid stopping at four-way stops, passing behind vehicles rather than stealing the right-of-way by crossing in front.

In general, riding in an unpredictable fashion is a stupid way to move through city traffic. The carefully applied Fake Right Turn, however, is one example of how a little bit of deception can benefit a bicyclist.

THE GAP EFFECT

Mind the gap. The gap is brutal.

Consider the condition of some of the drivers locked in the typical traffic grid. They're trying to make a left turn, but all they see is an unbroken line of fast-moving vehicles coming at them, with no end in sight. They're late. They're hopped up on four cups of coffee. They're about to pee their pants. They've been waiting to make that left turn since the Mesozoic era. Actually they've been waiting about thirty seconds or so, but to them it seems like a very long time. Like the dinosaurs of the Mesozoic era, their eyes are bigger than their brains. Suddenly a small gap opens in oncoming traffic. They're going to hit that gap if it's the last thing they do, which it may very well be. They stomp on the gas and crank the wheel. This is the Gap Effect in action.

One big problem, though: There's a cyclist in the gap, puttering along. The motorist doesn't notice or perhaps, so in love with the idea of the gap, simply denies the existence of anything that could possibly spoil this golden opportunity. In any case the cyclist is going to get hit, badly, unless he or she

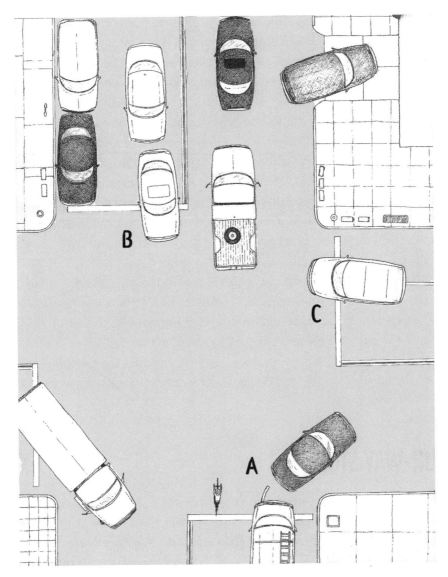

WHILE RIDING IN A PROPER POSITION IN THE STREET, TO THE LEFT OF THE RIGHT TURNERS (A), THIS CYCLIST IS NONETHELESS ENTERING THE INTERSECTION AT A DANGEROUS TIME. THE LIGHT HAS JUST TURNED YELLOW, AND AN ILLUSORY GAP HAS APPEARED IN THE TRAFFIC. AS SHE ROLLS THROUGH, THE RIDER WILL BE AT THE MERCY OF TWO IMPATIENT DRIVERS: THE LEFT TURNER (B), AND THE RIGHT TURNER (C), BOTH LOOKING TO SHOOT THE GAP.

can flash some serious evasive maneuvers. In this way the dreaded gap is often a factor in the kinds of statistically overabundant car-versus-bike incidents that claim very experienced, streetwise cyclists—the wrecks where the motorist turns left into or pulls out in front of someone on a bike.

As a bike rider in the city, it is nearly impossible to avoid riding in dangerous gaps around intersections. Too many gaps, too many intersections. The best way to avoid gap disasters is through recognition and anticipation. The Gap Effect is one of the best reasons to remain on high alert in traffic. Don't just mosey along out there. Recognize that a gap exists, your position in relation to it, and the presence of vehicles that might want to blast through it, from the left and right. If your view of any potential gap shooters is blocked, their view of you is also blocked. Assume they are there with their clodhoppers poised over the gas pedal.

Old hands who have had bad experiences in the gap develop an instinct for gaps and some very cautious techniques to solve them. Rather than occupying a gap through an intersection, the rider might jump forward to hug the space of the car in front a bit and hang about six or eight feet off its right rear, to use the car as a sort of shield against crossing traffic. Keep in mind that the blocking vehicle itself could become a hazard if its driver decides to turn or stop suddenly.

FOUR-WAY STOPS

Picture this: You're riding along and you arrive at a four-way stop five seconds after a big Buick arrives at the stop sign to your right. Being a proud lawful road user, you come to a complete stop and put your foot down, waiting for the Buick to make its move. But the Buick doesn't even flinch. Several seconds go by as you stare at the driver and he stares at you. Then you notice a flurry of activity inside the car—the driver is flapping his wrist at you in a distinctly impatient fashion. It looks almost as if a swarm of bees has been unleashed inside the passenger compartment. This is the international symbol for "Get the hell across the intersection, you *@#$* cyclist! What are you waiting for?"

The driver of the Buick, naturally, expected you to roll right through the stop. After decades of cyclists rolling through four-way stops, this behavior is now considered normal, and the general motoring public has been trained to expect it. When confronted with lawful behavior (i.e., actual stopping) from cyclists at four-way stops, drivers tend to freeze. They become indecisive and confused, and the whole system breaks down, if only for a brief moment.

Some of the drivers you encounter at four-way stops will be seething with general anticyclist resentment (like the driver of the Buick perhaps), while some have a soft spot for bicyclists and appreciate the importance of momentum in bicycling. Both types get impatient when the bicyclist doesn't fulfill expectations. Both types may recognize that the unwritten law—that which gives cyclists special leeway to roll through—actually benefits the driver too, because it means the intersection will clear sooner. Either way, the written laws have not kept up with reality on the street. The bicyclists, with the drivers as accomplices, are molding their own special laws.

Minor misunderstandings at four-way stops are a common component of the bicycling experience, and there is no easy cure for them. Luckily such annoyances are more a matter of convenience than safety. They may sap the efficiency of your commute, stop sign by stop sign, but they are unlikely to lead directly to a crash. Cyclists can minimize the hassle for all road users, while still holding onto responsibility for their own safety, by taking a realistic approach to four-way stops.

As with any stop sign or traffic light, bicyclists need to treat four-way stops with great care. But it is also true that, for an alert bicyclist moving at a walking pace, a complete stop is a mere formality. If an intersection is completely, verifiably clear, you may choose to exercise your special power to roll through. Slowly, though. Now, if you arrive at the four-way stop several seconds before a vehicle coming from another direction, first make sure that the vehicle is really going to stop; then roll through slowly, but give the driver a little wave, a goodwill gesture to display your awareness that the move is technically illegal, although convenient for both of you. That's about as lawless as we should get at four-way stops. Not exactly a capital offense.

If other vehicles have beaten you to the intersection, or arrive at the same time, or there are pedestrians present, go by the letter of the law. When the confounded drivers, bless their hearts, wave you impatiently into the intersection, you can flap your wrist back at them and get into a little wave-through war, which is always fun. Or you can accept the invitation and roll through out of turn. Be careful not to ride out in front of a driver who has given up on you. In all your dealings with stop signs, be realistic, but stay conservative.

Every now and again the rider who rolls through a four-way stop will be greeted by disapproving catcalls from drivers who observe the move from a distance: "Hey, that's a stop sign!" The hecklers are most often older males, which is not surprising, as the idea that cyclists should come to a complete stop at four-way stops is an old-fashioned one. It's nearly extinct. Like the elephants, the idea is being systematically eliminated by poachers.

MOMENTUM

Pedal cyclists, engineless by definition, have more use for momentum than drivers of motor vehicles. The quest to preserve momentum in traffic is one of the main reasons cyclists roll through stop signs and red lights, generally make a nuisance of themselves on the roadways, and get themselves hauled off to the emergency trauma centers of this fine nation. They're impressed with the thought of not having to crank back up to speed. Your grandfather might have called it laziness.

Whether you call it laziness, sneakiness, or pure stupidity, cyclists should be much more subtle and conservative about their efforts to preserve momentum than they historically have been. Cyclists should give up entirely on the unrealistic goal of holding onto high speeds through urban areas with lots of intersections. After this leap of faith is made, there will still be a few opportunities for a mature and careful rider to maintain low-speed momentum. Even at low speeds it's an art to preserve momentum while still moving in a fashion that is reasonably safe, predictable, and ethical.

The most persistent momentum sapper out there is the stop sign. An intelligent rider can deal with many stop-sign situations in a way that involves a less than strict adherence to traffic laws but also respects the right-of-way of other road users. The first step is to approach stop-signed intersections with patience as the primary emotion, at subdued speeds. Even the momentum lover needs to think safety first. Once you get a good handle on what's coming and what's not, try to time your movement through the intersection for maximum smoothness, not speed. It does no good to speed toward a stop sign, slam on the brakes, and then have to wait for some minivan to clear the intersection. Instead, slow down well in advance, triple-check the intersection for other obstacles, and roll across behind the minivan. Smooth. Even the incurable stop-sign busters should get used to the idea that walking pace is about the maximum speed a rider should ever go rolling through a stop sign, and, not only that, they will have to accept the fact that they will actually need to stop and put a foot on the tarmac more often than not.

At a stop sign, a rider who would otherwise have to stop in the literal sense might be able to make a very small, very low-speed turn within the lane to allow a driver with the right-of-way time to cross. If executed slowly and smoothly enough, this Figurative Stop seems proper to others but also allows the rider to stay in motion just a little bit—if the rider can maintain even a very slight movement, this will be greatly significant for preserving momentum. When practiced sloppily, such methods can confuse drivers and pedestrians, or even put the rider in the paths of vehicles. A small hook in either direction, for instance, applied at the wrong moment, could leave the rider staring down the business end of a right-turning vehicle. Like some other momentum-conserving techniques, the Figurative Stop is an advanced move that demands careful treatment. It should be left to experienced riders.

Not all of that lost momentum is lost at stop signs and intersections. There are plenty of little opportunities to lose or save momentum all along the route. A rider can preserve momentum simply by looking far up the road and anticipating the normal proliferation of road damage and the ill-advised movements of motorists.

A rider who looks ahead and thinks ahead can flow much more smoothly through traffic, and thus preserve energy and momentum, in addition to riding safer. But cyclists should avoid some momentum-related temptations that dangle before them like fruit ripe for the picking: Don't move at speed through traffic jams, for instance. Always slow to walking speed when passing close to any large stationary vehicle, which creates a blind corner as efficiently as any brick wall. Buses are the worst. Don't succumb to the most egregious form of pathological momentum poaching: blatant running of stop signs and lights at high speed. Cyclists don't do this nearly as often as urban myths suggest, but it's worth a mention. And resist the temptation to latch onto the perfect handhold formed by the swing arm of the spare tires of

Nissan Pathfinders and certain other SUVs, or the tailgates of pickups or the wheel wells of taxis.

Overall, preservation of some momentum is a nice bonus, especially when navigating residential streets with lots of stop signs. But momentum remains a secondary consideration, often at odds with safety concerns. As with any other hard drug, the addiction to momentum can be fatal.

THE PROBLEM WITH PEDESTRIANS

From the valley of the Euphrates to industrialized Manchester—a span of thousands of years—nobody had to look before crossing a road. Just listening was enough. If a cart or wagon was approaching, one would know without so much as a glance. *Clop clop clop clop.*

Imagine the urban pedestrian, circa 1890. All those years of *clop clop clop.* Then seemingly out of nowhere, out of some unimagined future, came the silent bicyclists, floating on air-filled tires for the first time. The wheelmen flashed into the edges of their vision, moving at bird speed, causing the same sort of involuntary reactions you might have if somebody swung a baseball bat at your head. Imagine all those hats, flying off.

With the arrival of the auto, American cities entered a relatively bike-free era that lasted about a half century. The pedestrians forgot all about us— out of sight, out of mind—while they learned to master the margins of the motorized cities. As they had in the Age of Manure, pedestrians navigated the motorized spaces largely by ear.

Until the 1970s few city dwellers realized that bicyclists, who had, for better or worse, been treated as vehicles under the law from the very early days, inherited new freedoms by default when four-wheeled vehicles ditched the horses and started burning gasoline. Previously they had been labeled "scorchers" and thrown in jail for riding faster than jogging pace, but exponential increases in speed limits gave bicyclists cover to unleash the potential of their machines. When they reappeared in the second half of the twentieth century, they were moving with traffic at car speeds, legally, but also occupying spaces in the roadway that jaywalkers had been using as safe havens, and even using the sidewalks, which had been strictly outlawed in the early days. Urban pedestrians were not excited about the new development, which is understandable.

The situation was explained by William "Holley" Whyte, *über*-pedestrian. Whyte spent much of his life staring at pedestrians in New York City. In fact he made a career out of it. With his research assistants he carefully documented the movements of people walking along the sidewalks, across the streets, and through the plazas. He paid special attention to the crowds at Grand Central Station, amazed that all those people could move in so many different directions all at the same time, without any real collisions at all. Ordinary people moved past each other deftly, instinctively it seemed, strangers communicating with strangers in an elaborate dance. It was far from chaos. More like a school of fish.

Holley, as he was known, was very impressed by the jaywalkers. "Skilled pedestrians," he called them. Far from being cowed by the heavy machinery all around, the walkers directed the drivers using subtle gestures, unsubtle gestures, and outright yelling. They crossed the roads wherever they wished. On the sidewalks, they slid past each other after silent and seamless communication, in the space of a glance. They were the masters of their domain. They owned this place.

In Whyte's view, pedestrians had it made in New York City until one day, like locusts descending from the skies, came that surge of new bicyclists, epitomized by the bicycle messengers. Suddenly the old way of moving could get you run down, or so it seemed. Pedestrians stuck in the old mode were constantly besieged by bicyclists appearing out of nowhere like ghouls in a haunted house. In the mid-1980s, Whyte noted that "instincts honed in the battle with cars ill prepares pedestrians for this newer contest." In fact the pedestrian's contest with bicycles is the older contest, but not in the perspective of Whyte or legions of old-school NYC bipeds.

Now the walker had to be aware of what might be coming through those little pockets of space that previously could be ignored—the city's *margins.* Instead of bossing the other road users, pedestrians found themselves being bossed by whistle-blowing messengers charging through the "defiles between cars." Instead of getting by with no-look street crossings, the pedestrian's privilege for millennia, now they had to look both ways even when crossing a one-way street. Whyte's reaction was representative of a large sector of the city's residents: "Walking has become much less enjoyable."[9]

That was thirty years ago, however. Have the pedestrians learned to coexist with and enjoy themselves around bicycles since then? All the vitriol accompanying the rollout of New York City's bike-sharing scheme in 2013 suggests that the conflict rages on bitterly in a new era. The pedestrians are still getting used to bicycles, some are still hopelessly lost, and many continue seething with resentment over the whole thing. However, looking at crash stats over the decades suggests that pedestrians and cyclists really are learning to work together, at least a little bit.

Recent studies show that the number of pedestrians killed in collisions with bicyclists is averaging about one per year in the North American city with the most pedestrians and the most cyclists, even as the number of cyclists has increased.[10] Meanwhile, to keep things in perspective, hundreds of pedestrians are killed by cars in NYC every year. And besides that, hundreds of drivers, passengers, and motorcyclists are killed in traffic accidents; and dozens of bicyclists are killed by cars. This should give us some rough idea of the relative deadliness posed to pedestrians by bicyclists—very, very low. Motor vehicle drivers kill about two hundred times as many pedestrians as bicyclists do.

The number of reported injuries is much higher of course, on the order of one or two per day, according to one study funded by an antibike group.[11] But the number of injuries is much lower than it was thirty years ago, according to Whyte, indicating that we may have learned a thing or two in the past quarter century. And again, about twenty times as many NYC pedestrians are injured in collisions with cars.

There is no denying that the physical harm caused by bicyclists is extremely low compared to that caused by motor vehicles. Despite this lopsided scoreboard, the pedestrians' anger and resentment has been aimed more at bicyclists than drivers.

We can't explain the poisoned bicycle-pedestrian relationship with crash statistics. The ire is not fueled by physical carnage, even though that is what people talk about most often. As in the nineteenth century, it has more to do with the pedestrian's being startled, frightened by a faceless bicyclist who approaches in relative silence and flashes suddenly through the pedestrian's comfort zone, then retreats casually down the block as the pedestrian's shock turns to anger. People hate to be frightened out of nowhere like that. No actual contact is necessary. The old-school walker takes this perceived close shave as a severe show of disrespect, not only to him- or herself but also to the (very) old way of moving in the city. The bicyclist, on the other hand, doesn't even realize what kind of psychological turmoil has been unleashed. Multiply these events by hundreds or thousands each day, and you have the essence of cyclist-pedestrian relations. Very little blood, but an overload of fear and resentment, and just maybe a touch of envy. It's a psychodrama.

In the interest of "dissonance reduction," bike-hating pedestrians play up the danger posed by bicyclists at every opportunity, to the point of absurdity. Old-school pedestrians like to portray bicyclists as sociopathic antiheroes with mysterious superpowers. Note the popular urban folktales in which scofflaw bicyclists are somehow able to bash through crowds of frail pedestrians and send them careening off in every direction like bowling pins without absorbing the slightest bit of energy themselves—all while laughing maniacally. Generally that's not how it works, for several reasons. When a bicyclist hits a pedestrian with any force, the initial collision may injure the bicyclist just as it does the pedestrian; unless he or she is able to line up the hit like an NFL defensive back, the bicyclist will be thrown forward into the handlebars and lose control. And the-person-who-had-been-bicycling is likely to hit the ground more awkwardly than the person on foot. In any case, it's something to avoid, for both parties.

Contrary to popular opinion, these unwelcome encounters, both the collisions and the near misses, have as much to do with the movements of pedestrians as the movements of bicyclists. In the experiences of veteran urban riders, the vast majority of bike-ped crashes result from a pedestrian strolling, or running, out in front of a bicyclist in the street. Yup, jaywalkers. If you hit a pedestrian, it's probably not going to be because you invaded the sidewalk, a barn dance, or any other traditional pedestrian haunt. More than likely the collision will occur out in the street, in the middle of the block, after someone pops out from between parked cars right in front of you.

This common brand of collision occurs so often because bicyclists aren't ready for it, first of all, and because pedestrians are blessed with the same perception problem that drivers have (the looked-but-failed-to-see thing).

AMAZINGLY, PEDESTRIANS MIGHT BE EVEN WORSE AT SEEING BICYCLISTS THAN DRIVERS ARE. ACT ACCORDINGLY.

In addition, pedestrians are afflicted with their own special street-crossing handicap: reliance on their sense of hearing.

How many times have you been told to look both ways before crossing a street? Quite a few, I reckon. But cars are really easy to hear when they're coming down the street, aren't they? Trucks, easier. Even a vehicle with an idling engine makes enough racket, if only from the tires ripping along the asphalt, that a person standing by the road is alerted to its approach, its general direction, and speed, without ever laying eyes on the thing. *Clop clop clop.*

Pedestrians in traffic still rely unthinkingly on their ears. No-look street crossings became part of pedestrians' instinctual behavior, so to speak. Now they—we—take silence for granted, sauntering into the street without a glance. It works great, until it doesn't.

This isn't an us-versus-them situation. We may not all be drivers or bicyclists (some of the stalwart bike-hating New Yorkers have never swung a leg over a bike in their entire lives), but we are all pedestrians, and we all cross streets like idiots. This faulty pedestrian instinct has not been repaired by 150 years of living around bicycles. Understanding it will make us much better cyclists.

Treat walkers with respect and courtesy, but do not cede to them any responsibility for your personal safety unless absolutely necessary. Pedestrians have proven themselves to be unworthy of this responsibility. So that means keeping your eyes peeled for any pedestrians around the street or path and giving them as much space as you reasonably can. It means expecting pedestrians to pop out from behind trucks and buses, or from any place you can't see. Slow down, make space. Give yourself a chance if somebody darts out. Don't assume a pedestrian will look in your direction before running across the street. And don't assume a pedestrian will see you if he or she does look in your direction.

Use some sort of audible signal to warn zombie-like pedestrians of your presence. The traditional bike bell has a pleasant ring—which may make it more suitable for the paths and suburbs than for urban cores. NYC messengers used to blow whistles like basketball referees to snap pedestrians out of their street-crossing stupors, but that's a bit much. Try using your voice to communicate with people on foot, in a way that helps you navigate safely around them but doesn't inspire additional dislike of you or other humans. "Hello. . . . Behind ya'. . . . Thanks . . ." A few loud-enough but friendly words can defuse a potential conflict before you reach the danger zone. Of course if all else fails, a forceful shout—*Yo!* or *Hey!* or *Eeeaaackk!*—is capable of stopping a running pedestrian in his or her tracks, if you do it right.

In crowded cities a bicyclist intent on giving an audible warning to every pedestrian with the potential to step into or in front of the bike may as well mount a giant 1988-vintage boom box to his or her handlebars, slap in a Motorhead tape, and turn it up to eleven. (This has what some might call an adverse effect on bike handling.) Even then some peds will not get the message. Audible signals are helpful, even legally required in some scenarios, but they are not a reliable tool for avoiding collisions.

Ultimately the unreliability of audible signals—and the convenience of not squawking at all times—leads veteran riders to rely more on their own eyes, using space and speed to create buffers, rather than the ears of strangers. That is, they ride in such a way that making noise isn't nearly as important. It all comes back to gathering up as much responsibility as you can, and not carelessly leaving any out there.

NOTES ON TRAFFIC LIGHTS

Long before the dawn of the automotive age, vehicular chaos at big city intersections led to the employment of various forms of lights, signs, and traffic cops. With the growing popularity of the automobile in America, the need for such measures became obvious, and urgent. Hundreds of different variations on the traffic signal were patented in the first decades of the twentieth century. Before too long, folks were thinking about how to link multiple signals into a coherent system. William Potts adapted railroad signals for a string of automated traffic lights in Detroit in 1920. A few years later New York City flipped the switch on its first automated traffic-control system.

From the beginning the trend has been toward greater automation and control over traffic. The dark cloud of control rolled into every American city, until one day in Los Angeles, 1925, motorists in the Shangri-La of automotive freedom began to take orders from a mechanical device for the first time.[12] With understandable reluctance, drivers began to obey. Red. Green. Stop. Go. A little of the dream died that day, and it's been downhill ever since.

The early, automated systems didn't help much, but they were nonetheless the primitive ancestors of the very impressive adaptive systems that are being used in American cities today. The modern traffic-control system gathers information from hundreds of intersections, through video cameras and buried sensors, and sends that information almost instantaneously via fiberoptic cables to a mainframe computer and to engineers in a central control room who watch the dance unfold in real time. With the aid of sophisticated hardware and algorithms, the engineers tweak the system as they see fit and, theoretically, keep traffic flowing. Sounds like fun, actually. Seen from that far up, American traffic probably looks pretty orderly and reasonable.

Computerized traffic lights can cause problems, because some motorists hold an unrealistically high opinion of their own ability to time the cycles just right. A light-timer who is just a wee bit off in his or her calculations might roll into an intersection before the green light and smash into someone who is coming through the other way after the light turns red. Being slightly slower than motor vehicles, cyclists who are late through an intersection are extremely vulnerable to the light-timing crowd. To prevent this class of wreck, traffic engineers program a substantial delay after a light turns red before the other light goes green. This period of "all red" must be subtle, or else it would be noticed—and ignored.

Lights on side streets may be coordinated with the lights on the main streets, or they may be activated by vehicles. Activated, or "actuated," lights depend on some sort of vehicle-detection system to set them off. Video cameras and radar are increasingly used to detect vehicles at intersections, but this is still relatively rare. For about half a century, the typical detection system has consisted of an electrified wire loop buried in the pavement. When a lot of metal gets parked right over the coil, it changes the frequency of the current in the wire through induction. This change of frequency causes an electronic signal to be sent to the signal box, which changes the light. Induction loops are rigged to detect beastly large metal objects and tend not to notice bicycles or even motorcycles.* The devices could be tweaked so that they always detect bicycles, but then they would be so sensitive that vehicles on other streets might also set them off. A bicyclist may be able to get some action from one of these detection systems by positioning the bike directly over one part of the coil, some visible sign of which should be apparent at the road surface, but don't bet on it. And those with carbon bikes are probably out of luck here.

New technologies are taking over for the buried loops. One wonders how long it will be before every major light is controlled by a video camera that can detect traffic while performing other important tasks, like scanning

---

*There are many different loop configurations, and some are better than others at detecting bicycles. The failure of signal systems to detect motorcycles was the rationale behind laws in several states that allow motorcyclists to ride through red lights, after coming to a complete stop and when no other vehicles are present.

license plate numbers, notifying the black helicopters, and shooting lasers at wrongdoers. The induction loop seems to be on the way out, but we are hesitant to declare it dead just yet.

WAITING AT TRAFFIC LIGHTS

When approaching a signaled intersection, the cyclist should be figuring out how to achieve proper destination positioning. This means getting to the rightmost left-turn lane, if possible, for a left turn (see Left Turns, page 115); moving to the right lane for a right turn; and establishing position in the right-most through lane to continue straight. Try not to hug the curb of a right-turn lane, as this invites right-turning drivers to pass and turn or just turn into you. If you are turning right, own the right-turn lane like a vehicle would, and if you are going straight, try to get to the left of the right turners. No big deal. Think about these things well in advance and it will greatly ease your travels.

Generally, even though they can usually sneak up the side of the road to the front of a line of vehicles at a red light, bicyclists are legally supposed to wait out the light behind any vehicles that are already waiting (unless there is a segregated bike lane or a curb lane of vast acreage). Regardless of the laws in your community, you will occasionally find yourself sneaking up front—the incurable nature of the cyclist, taking advantage of an undeniably skinny machine. In the parlance of cycle commuters, this is known as "filtering," which describes the act of riding between lanes in jammed traffic. Some riders like to filter to the very front of the line and wait about four feet to the right front of the lead vehicle, if there is enough room, where the cyclist's presence will presumably be obvious. Other riders prefer to lurk just behind and to the right of the lead vehicle. The key consideration when positioning beside a line of cars at a light is to be aware of, and out of the potential paths of, any cars that might turn right—to enhance one's visibility but to avoid becoming completely dependent on it.

Filtering to the front of the line comes with certain obligations. The ethics of sneaking up front, past vehicles that arrived at the light before you, suggest that you should allow the trailing vehicles to pass once the light turns green and traffic starts moving again. If there is not enough room for them

IN THE MIX

to pass here, then you should have stayed at the back of the line in the first place. There is really no way to justify filtering up to the front of the line and then blocking the lane after the light turns green, but some cyclists pull this one on a regular basis.

Even if you have beaten everybody to the light and are rightfully first in line, it may be a good idea to drift slightly to the right, into the void of the intersection, when the light turns green. This shows the following drivers that a pass is welcome and available. It will make your life easier to coax them into passing here, where there is usually ample space, rather than keeping them bottled up behind.

DESTINATION POSITIONING

POSITIONING FOR LEFT TURNS. WAITING TO TURN LEFT, THIS CYCLIST IS POSITIONED PROPERLY IN THE RIGHTMOST LEFT-TURN LANE. IN THE INTEREST OF COOPERATION, THE RIDER IS WAITING FAR ENOUGH TO THE RIGHT TO FACILITATE A COOPERATIVE RIGHTWARD DRIFT AT THE END OF THE TURN, BUT SHE IS NOT SO FAR OVER THAT TRAILING DRIVERS ARE ENCOURAGED TO DRIVE UP ALONGSIDE.

POSITIONING FOR RIGHT TURNS. THE RIDER SHOWN HERE HAS PUT HIMSELF INTO TROUBLE BY HUGGING THE CURB IN A RIGHT-TURN LANE. DOING SO HAS ENCOURAGED A FEW IMPATIENT AND CLUELESS DRIVERS TO ATTEMPT TO PASS THE CYCLIST BEFORE THE CORNER. SOME HIGHLY SKILLED CYCLISTS ARE COMFORTABLE TURNING IN THE TIGHT SPACE TO THE RIGHT OF A RIGHT-TURNING VEHICLE, BUT THIS GUY AIN'T ONE OF 'EM, AND HE HAS TO WAIT. IT WOULD HAVE BEEN BETTER TO KEEP THE CARS CORRALLED BY BRIEFLY OCCUPYING A CONSPICUOUSLY CENTRAL POSITION IN THE RIGHT-TURN LANE.

POSITIONING TO CONTINUE STRAIGHT. THIS RIDER IS POSITIONED ACCEPTABLY IN THE RIGHTMOST THROUGH LANE. DEPENDING ON THE SITUATION AT HAND, A STRAIGHT-THROUGH RIDER MAY FEEL THE NEED TO CONSUME MORE OF THE LANE OR, IF THE TURN LANE IS EMPTY, UTILIZE ITS LEFT EDGE IN THE INTEREST OF SHARING THE ROAD.

Often you will find yourself waiting for a light to change, positioned on the right of the vehicles going straight, with a motorist inching up behind you. Even though there is no marked turn lane, the driver hopes to make a right on red. But you're in the way. This is a needless conflict. Be mindful of the space available for right turns and try not to block it.

There is an easy way to solve the problem if you find yourself blocking an ersatz turn lane. With one foot in the pedal, and the other resting on the street, squeeze and lock the front brake, then lean forward on the locked front wheel so that the rear wheel floats in the air. Swing the backside of your bike to the left and set it down, then pick up the front end and move it over. Repeat as necessary to make enough room for the right turner to squeeze by. This courteous maneuver will be much appreciated and will foster goodwill.

Depending on the available space and other characteristics of the intersection, you may be more comfortable waiting on the sidewalk and crossing as a pedestrian.

RUNNING RED LIGHTS

Cyclists are legally required to obey all traffic lights, just like motor vehicles. We're supposed to go when it's green and stop when it's red. You knew that, right? This comes as a surprise to nobody, and yet few of us consistently obey the law when it comes to traffic lights.

As with stop-sign running and other questionable activities, red-light running by cyclists is basically expected by some motorists. But it is certainly not accepted. Red-light running engenders more bitterness in motorists than stop-sign running, maybe because the driver must stay waiting for the light to change, watching the little cyclist—often clad in tight black shorts—pedal off into the distance.

Now, y'all gather 'round. What you are about to hear is a realistic yet constructive method for dealing with traffic lights, given that many of the lights are not triggered by bicycles and will not turn green until a car comes along. It is far more conservative and careful than the method practiced by the majority of cyclists today. Still, some folks out there will get all agitated at its mere suggestion.

BENIGN BUT ANNOYING: A BICYCLIST EXPLOITS THE PEDESTRIANS' FOUR-WAY RED.

First of all, always come to a complete stop at a red light. Position yourself well and wait for the light to change.

But what if the intersection is completely deserted, and the light is clearly not being triggered by your bicycle? A rider might need to treat such a light like a stop sign in order to get anywhere in a reasonable time. If busting the light would mean crossing in front of cars on the intersecting street, don't do it, even if there is plenty of space. If there are any cars behind or across from you waiting at the same light, resist the temptation to go through. This is just good form. It sends a message of solidarity: If you gotta wait, buddy, I'll wait too.

THIS BICYCLIST SEES A CLEAR INTERSECTION AND HAS DECIDED TO RUN THE RED LIGHT. UNFORTUNATELY FOR HIM, HIDDEN PERILS AWAIT. FIRST OF ALL, THE BLACK CAR ON THE RIGHT HAS PULLED AWAY ABRUPTLY FROM A PARKING SPOT ON THE CURB, SOMETHING HE HADN'T COUNTED ON. ITS DRIVER IS LOOKING BEHIND AT VEHICLES APPROACHING IN THE RIGHT LANE, NOT TOWARD THE INTERSECTION. ON THE OTHER SIDE, BEHIND A BUS, A PEDESTRIAN LATE FOR AN APPOINTMENT HAS JUST STARTED TO SPRINT ACROSS THE STREET, NOT EVEN THINKING ABOUT THE POSSIBILITY OF CROSS TRAFFIC AS HE RUNS TOWARD THE LITTLE GREEN MAN ON THE WALK SIGNAL. MEANWHILE, PASSENGERS IN A MINI SUV AND PEDESTRIANS SEE THE BICYCLIST GOING THROUGH THE RED, AND LATER THAT AFTERNOON ONE OF THEM GIVES A LITTLE SPEECH ABOUT HOW SCOFFLAW BICYCLISTS ARE RIPPING AND TEARING THE FABRIC OF SOCIETY.

Treating the occasional red light like a stop sign is a practice for mature, adult riders only. The traffic lights are in place to keep people from thinking for themselves. When bicyclists think for themselves, they often make horrible, costly mistakes. You think you can do a better job of thinking than a traffic light? Don't be so sure.

In downtown areas the cycles of traffic lights are very often set up to give pedestrians their own special time during which motor traffic is stopped in all directions. Many cyclists cannot resist the lure of the pedestrian phase of the cycle. They come up between two lanes of stationary traffic stopped at a light, or between the right traffic lane and a line of parked cars. Moving quickly, they see that walk signal or the flashing hand and realize the intersection is in full-on pedestrian mode. So they accelerate toward the intersection. If it is done absentmindedly, this is one of the biggest mistakes in cycling. This cyclist is begging for a ped-bike collision, as a walker pops out from behind a van or sprints out at the exact wrong time, trying to get across before the light changes. A poetic bike-bike collision with some other carelessly opportunistic joker is another strong possibility. Cyclists hoping to exploit the pedestrian phase of the signal cycle often get served with instant karma.

LEFT TURNS

Because of the cyclist's usual position in the rightmost lane, making a left turn in traffic can be one of the trickiest maneuvers in urban cycling. Theoretically, the bicyclist should execute the left turn just as a car would, by changing lanes all the way over to the turn lane well in advance of reaching the intersection. When circumstances are right, this is the method of choice. Unfortunately in today's world, circumstances often conspire against the bicyclist hoping to make a left turn. On busy streets with fast movers it can be extremely tricky to get across to the turn lane. Some cyclists are used to forcing their way across on streets like this. They throw hand signals, look back, look back some more, and pull out in front of cars that are moving much quicker than themselves. The rider pedals as fast as he can and feels that should be fast enough. Meanwhile, the drivers behind step on the brakes or stare into their rearviews looking for an opportunity to change lanes. The drivers behind them hit the brakes, then the drivers behind them, and so on down the line. The rider gets to the turn lane, but at some cost to overall traffic safety and flow.

The smooth driver, by definition, does not have to force anything. There comes a point when the vehicular left turn is more trouble than it's worth, when it becomes impossible to accomplish smoothly. Even experienced riders make frequent use of a more submissive way of turning left: stay right and carefully take a place on the cross street or on the far sidewalk to cross as a pedestrian. If the road is really busy, this method, aka the "box turn," will probably not cost the rider much time at all (because you would have to wait until the end of the light cycle to make the left turn anyway). The cyclist who chooses this approach on a street with oppressive traffic displays a healthy acceptance of reality.

There's an art to this two-step turn. While it relieves the cyclist of having to cross a busy boulevard to reach a left-turn lane, it also requires a bit more thought—and a different type of thinking at that. Worming one's way into position in the traffic lane of the cross street can be a challenging and complex operation, potentially confusing other drivers as their vehicles arrive at the intersection or move forward to turn right. Like many of the freelancing moves of cycling, it can be effective and smooth, or it can lead to unwanted occurrences of various types. Left turns are tough on busy streets. Cyclists are damned if they do and damned if they don't.

There aren't any other decent options available to the left-turning cyclist. Whatever you do, don't turn left from the right side of the street.

CORNER CUTTERS

You pull up to a stop sign on what seems to be a quiet residential street. You put your foot down and wait patiently for a break in the heavy, fast traffic on the intersecting boulevard. With not a care in the world, you have placed yourself far enough forward that your front wheel is almost even with the near curb of the busy boulevard. Tucked away within five feet from the curb, you feel quite secure.

Suddenly there's a screech of tires from your right side. A car turning left from the far side of the boulevard carves directly at you. This guy's spotted a

CORNER CUTTERS

THIS DIAGRAM SHOWS HOW COMMON, MODEST CORNER CUTTING AND COMMON, REASONABLE CYCLING MIGHT LEAD TO A DISASTER FOR THE CYCLIST. BICYCLISTS SHOULD BE MINDFUL OF THIS PHENOMENON AT EVERY INTERSECTION.

minuscule gap in the oncoming traffic, and rather than wait ten seconds, has chosen to risk the health of several motorists, including himself, to shoot the gap. His line is taking him directly toward the apex of the corner, across the wrong side of the street, directly at your front wheel. Unfortunately he hasn't seen you at all, he's so focused on oncoming traffic.

Be especially wary of corner cutters upon approach to the intersection, because the offending drivers haven't even had a chance to see you yet. They may be in the process of cutting that corner just as you arrive. The corner-cutting phenomenon is a good reason to roll slowly toward intersections, to be patient, and to stay five or ten feet back from the corner, just out of the cutter's favored path. That way your well-being is not dependent on drivers who don't think twice about who or what might be waiting for them around the bend.

LOOKING BACK

Traffic cycling demands frequent look-backs. Whenever preparing for any significant lateral movement—to avoid jaywalkers, piles of glass, potholes, or parked cars, or to change lanes in preparation for a turn, to name a few examples—the rider usually needs to check behind first. And there are a multitude of scenarios where the cyclist might be maintaining a steady line but would still benefit from taking a little peek to see what's back there. Riding away from the curb, in a comfortable default position or toward it, is dependent on a 360-degree awareness of traffic.

What we have here, then, is a real dilemma, because bicycling also demands that the eyes point forward as much as possible. *Watch where you're going* is our prime directive. Every microsecond spent looking anywhere other than ahead is borrowed time. Eventually the look behind will get you. A common scenario is to hit a road crater just as the head swivels back. This type of encounter could easily lead to a crash if the rider is really overdoing the look-back—for example, sitting up and holding onto the bars with the fingertips of one hand. Another scenario involves coming in contact with the butt end of a car after looking back just in time to miss the car's brake lights coming on. Looking back robs you of precious moments. If a look-back or look-away begins a short chain of events that leads to your next accident, it wouldn't surprise anybody who has had any experience on the streets. We've all been there.

When checking behind, make it quick, but not so quick that the move is wasted. You only get so many chances to look back, so use these chances wisely. In tight traffic, where milliseconds matter and the dangers of the road surface are compounded by the dangers of motor vehicles, avoid looking back unless absolutely necessary, and then allow yourself just a lightning strike of a glance.

Here is the secret of looking back while bicycling: The first step in a safe look-back is the look-forward. Before diverting the eyes, scan the road surface well ahead for potholes, grates, manholes, and waves. Note any vehicles, currently moving or stationary, that might move into your path. Notice all driveways and other intersections from which vehicles may emerge, and scan lines of parked cars for heads, brake lights, and other signs of life (see Reading Parked Vehicles, page 130). Notice pedestrians who may step out in front of you. Calculate the time and space at your disposal assuming a worst-case scenario involving all potential hazards. Veteran riders accomplish this forward scan almost unconsciously in about one second, cataloging anything that could get them when they turn their heads.

In busy areas it is normal for sizable helpings of time to pass while the rider is unable to steal a single safe look-back. The artful rider recognizes these spells and respects them. If the road ahead becomes clear enough that its potential hazards are outweighed by the need to look behind, swivel the head smoothly to the left. If you just need a little semi-look to check on a passing car, a quarter turn of the head should be enough to pick up the car's general location and attitude in the peripheral vision. It's usually not necessary to turn the head all the way around. Keep both hands steady on the bars, just in case you missed a pothole or other trap with your initial forward scan. A half-second glance should be enough to determine whether vehicles or other cyclists are approaching, their position in the lane, and even their speed. The ability to make these determinations quickly will come only with experience. Sometimes a more thorough and time-consuming look-back is needed.

The physical act of looking back while riding a bike is not as simple as it sounds. It requires some skill to keep the bike tracking straight while moving the head around. Figuratively speaking, your head weighs a freakin' ton. Seemingly minor movements of the head have a profound effect on balance. Every time you wave it around in some direction, your bike will try to follow it. Practice in a safe location, such as an empty parking lot, glancing back quickly and smoothly without swerving even a little. Beginners should refrain from serious city riding until they can manage this skill.

The look-back, when practiced correctly, is actually quite a production. In tight traffic cyclists must check behind often enough that the process of scanning forward in order to scan backward consumes a great deal of attention and concentration. This information-gathering process becomes meditative, as it cleanses the mind of nonessential thoughts.

SEEING WITHOUT LOOKING

Given that diverting one's eyes from the road ahead is asking-for-it danger-ous, cyclists help themselves a great deal by developing a sense for what is coming up behind without relying on frequent look-backs.

The most solid, nonvisual clues about the netherworld behind the cyclist's back are gathered through the ears. Let your scraggly, rather bizarre looking human ears become your rearview mirrors.

The first audible indication of approaching vehicles is usually not engine noise, but the sound of tires on pavement. Most modern passenger cars are extremely quiet. Some are near silent at low RPMs. They can sidle right up on you at low speeds, completely undetected. At normal city speeds, however, their tires give them away. Tire noise can be a hiss or a sort of ripping sound. The sound will vary with different vehicles, tires, street surfaces, and speeds. Tires that are rolling quickly make noise at a higher pitch than tires that are rotating slowly. The noise from an accelerating vehicle rises in pitch. With practice a cyclist should be able to hear what type of car or truck is coming, how fast it is moving, whether it is speeding up or slowing down, and how far to the right it is.

Cars that are turning, stopping, and accelerating make noises that reveal a great deal about the habits of whoever is behind the wheel—the chirp of a tire accelerating hard out of a turn, for instance. Bicyclists should listen for the rip of tires that are struggling to hold the road, versus the dull nonnoise of a normal Sunday turn. Engine revs can also be very informative. Anger, impa-tience, conservatism, timidity—the attitude of the driver is revealed before the vehicle can be seen.

In recognition of the basic importance of ears for cycling safety, some cities—Philadelphia, for one—have banned the use of headphones by cyclists. They don't want folks out there weaving around, rocking out to Doug E. Fresh while unable to hear vehicles, horns, sirens, and screaming pedestrians. Coming from noncyclists, these laws are somewhat paternalis-tic and hypocritical. After all, the passenger compartments of modern cars are designed to keep out as much street noise as possible. Half the drivers seem to have the stereo cranked, and the rest are talking on the phone. They can't hear jack.

Like the typical passive motorist, the headphone-wearing cyclist willfully disregards a symphony of useful information. Rearview mirrors do much of the same work as ears, and therefore are absolutely recommended for riders who crank music through headphones or are hard of hearing.

A mirror won't provide a complete enough picture to eliminate the need to turn the head, but the helpful snapshots it provides will allow the rider to cut out a substantial percentage of necessary look-backs. Experienced riders prefer the eyeglass- or helmet-mounted style of mirror, because long-stemmed handlebar-mounted mirrors are doomed to be broken in any kind of sustained city cycling. Riding behind a friend who is using a good eyeglass mirror, and examining his or her little migrations on the road, will give an appreciation for the device. The mirrored rider, without turning the head, sees potential trouble early and starts dealing with it well before the nonmirrored rider becomes aware of it. Mirrors are very helpful on narrow, busy roads and in bustling downtown areas that have high levels of background noise.

Precisely because it negates some of the need to look back, however, reliance on a mirror can cause problems. The cyclist who looks back in traffic is actually sending helpful signals to drivers. Because riders with mirrors don't have to look back as often, they end up alienating themselves, in a sense, from other road users, often to the point that they are viewed as unpredictable and dangerous. On the other hand, a rider who swivels the head around to look back is clearly aware of the following traffic, a revelation that clarifies the bicyclist's movements and gives confidence to drivers. A bicyclist who looks back seems to be up to something. Even the most dense of motorists will usually figure out that the rider who checks behind in a certain way is preparing for some kind of turn or move. Turning back can have almost the same effect as a turn signal.

In addition to ears and mirrors, bicyclists can employ plain old common sense to visualize the situation behind them. The cyclist who passes the exit of a busy grocery store parking lot, for instance, knows there is a good chance that a bogie will appear on the street before too long. Artful bicyclists subconsciously calculate the possibilities and odds of what might be happening behind them, even if they can't see or hear it. It helps that they usually have a long history of navigating that street or, somewhere, a street very similar to it.

The look-back will never be made obsolete by these other techniques. No matter how uncannily aware you fancy yourself to be—with your well-honed sense of hearing, your nifty little mirror, and your eerie supernatural powers—don't make any significant lateral move on the road without first turning your head and getting visual confirmation of a clear path.

INSTINCT UNVEILED

An expert tracker might look at an elk track and know immediately how large the animal was, how fast it was moving, and, with startling accuracy, when the track was made. He notices a few blades of grass out of place in a field and can tell what moved through there and when. Some trackers have honed their craft to such a degree that they have actually learned to track ants over rock.

To the general public these skills can only be explained by a crazy sort of magic called "instinct." The tracker must be "tuned in" to the rhythms of the forest in some preternatural way.

But this talk of instinct cheats the tracker out of the credit he or she deserves. One does not enter the world with a mysterious talent for tracking already built in. One learns the craft by spending every waking hour in the forest, face in the dirt, watching. Trackers spend weeks at a time observing what fresh tracks of all kinds look like and how they degrade over time. It's not magic that gives them such a masterful knowledge of their surroundings, but painstakingly methodical work and intelligence.

Cyclists should take a page out of the tracker's book. Ride constantly, and consciously try to learn from the thousands of little interactions you will have on each ride. The city moves according to laws that are more powerful and more interesting than the traffic ordinances. These laws are mysterious, but not unfathomable. The cyclist can crank up the powers of observation and collect knowledge on a level so advanced that most folks won't be able to understand how it might have been obtained. They will call it instinct, but it's just active learning.

Some riders experience the tumult of heavy traffic as an incomprehensible chaos, an overload on the senses that could not possibly be sorted out. So when they go out into it, they attempt to put up a barrier between the city and their senses. They try to shut everything out. They may feel they are protecting themselves, but they are hindering progress.

In fact we are faced with a finite and manageable amount of useful information at any given time. There is only so much that can happen out there. There are only so many vehicles and pedestrians to be concerned with, and these are ultimately limited in their potential movements by the physical laws of the universe, if by nothing else.

Separate what is known from what is not known, and respect the unknown. Blind corners and alley entrances, the penumbra of hulking buses and trucks—what's back there? The world of traffic is teeming with hidden life, things that are moving and happening just out of view that could well be on a collision course with your personal well-being even if you can't yet see them. And it is full of vehicles and pedestrians in full view. We can see their current vectors, and might get some idea about where they're headed, but we remain uncertain of their next moves. What exists in the shadow of knowledge? The known, and the unknown. So much of what is called instinct could simply be a recognition of what is not seen and what is not known, and respecting the worst-case scenario.

Open your eyes and take it all in. See the whole playing field. Listen. Process the vectors, the sounds, and the possibilities. Identify that which is immediately relevant. Sort out the known from the unknown.

You will make many mistakes at first, and in your inexperience you will be subject to the mistakes of drivers, pedestrians, and other bicyclists. Don't waste these opportunities. Learn from your mistakes and the mistakes of others. At some point you will know the drivers better than they know themselves. In the end you are some pedal strokes ahead and laughing all the way when traffic reaches out to bludgeon you with one of its tentacles of disorder. It's not instinct that makes this possible but ordinary human faculties put to good use.

When tuning in Zen-like to one's environment, route repetition is massively helpful. Find a number of good routes and ride them consistently to become intimately acquainted with all of their idiosyncrasies. Like a tracker who has been watching the same track for a week, when some detail is out of place on your route, you will know how and why.

TURN SIGNALS

They leave the signal on for no reason, use the left signal when they want to turn right, or just forget their minivan was ever equipped with this startling new technology. Drivers are so unreliable about signaling their turns that bicyclists should approach the whole enterprise with an underlying skepticism. In fact it may be better if cyclists completely forget about trying to look for turn signals on cars and trucks in traffic. The act of looking for a turn signal reveals some degree of faith that drivers will actually use their turn signals properly, and no such faith should be forthcoming. Such faith is actually dangerous.

Now if you should happen to notice, through no fault of your own, some sort of light flashing on a nearby vehicle, by all means take it into account. But don't go searching for turn signals to answer any questions you might have about a particular driver's intentions. Instead, simply assume poor performance from all other road users and note any potential paths their vehicles might take. This is the cyclist's version of keeping an open mind.

A cyclist who is perturbed by a driver's failure to use a turn signal reveals a still-lingering reliance on the proper habits of others that holds disturbing implications for the rider's future. Expect nothing, and you will never be disappointed. Demand nothing, except from yourself. The proper response to a driver's failure to signal is calm indifference. Perhaps the cyclist's head is filled with things of real consequence and the turn signal is not even noticed, one way or the other. Turn signals matter little to the experienced rider.

HAND SIGNALS

Many states and cities require cyclists to signal every turn. The big problem with this law is that removing hands from the bars while riding is generally bad policy, especially in traffic. The cyclist needs both hands on the bars, to hold the rig steady over potholes and to keep in close contact with the brake levers. Signaling is a bit like looking behind. The road ahead must be verified as smooth and clear before the hands come off the bars. For this reason alone it is not recommended that cyclists signal each and every turn. Hand signals should be used only when they will really do some good.

Problems aside, there will be situations when the hand signal is very useful. At relatively high speeds, with a vehicle coming up from behind, the rider does well to pop a quick hand signal before slowing down for a turn. Moving from lane to lane might require looks back as well as hand signals. Group cycling is much safer when riders signal their turns and stops to surrounding riders.

The best way to signal a turn is simply to stick the arm out briefly in the direction you plan to turn or move—right arm for a right turn, left arm for a left. The ol' left-arm-bent-up-at-a-90-degree-angle-to-signal-a-right-turn method is quickly going out of style—if it isn't there already—and will be unrecognizable to many new drivers. Some riders put an arm straight down, palm open, to signal an impending stop. This last one is more useful as a signal to other cyclists in your group that you're slowing down, so they don't come up on you quickly and can prepare to brake.

IN DEFENSE OF GUTTERS

It is often declared, for many reasons, that cyclists should never ride in the gutter. *Never* is a scary word. It applies to many aspects of riding, but not to gutters.

Rarely is riding a gutter the best option, but we shouldn't be dogmatically opposed to it. Gutters can't be lumped together into a single category, any more than streets can. There is tremendous variety in gutters. Some gutters are quite wonderful places to ride, spotless runways of fresh white concrete. They provide a more hospitable riding surface than the road itself. But some are horribly dangerous debris-filled little canyons that fall away into gator-mouth drainage portals every ten meters. Most are somewhere in the middle.

Gutter riding is occasionally useful on busy, multilane roads with narrow curb lanes and no on-street parking; streets where the right lane is as well used as the left and cars are moving fast. In these situations, traveling in a smooth gutter for a short while may be safer and stir up less general hassle than riding in the lane.

Yes, there are good reasons to consider gutter cruising that have little to do with safety. Some folks get vigorously agitated when they hear any hint of a suggestion that cyclists might want to move over for the sole purpose of facilitating motor traffic. But the fact remains that riding the gutter can occasionally help keep traffic flowing and stress levels subdued, and this is a good thing. Using the gutter can also be a way for you to keep moving while motor traffic struggles to a halt around you.

The most often cited safety problem associated with riding in the gutter, which is that it presents a near-open lane to drivers and causes them to pass dangerously close to the rider on very narrow roads, is certainly a consideration, but not a deal breaker.

The most important traffic-related danger of gutter riding has to do with turning and crossing vehicles rather than passing vehicles. Gutter riders, tucked away in the peripheral vision, will often evade detection by drivers on cross streets looking left into the traffic lane (potential right turners). The gutter rider will also be less visible to oncoming drivers (potential left turners). Gutter riding and intersections don't mix well. Consider the gutter for a temporary option, but don't spend too much time there. Move there from a normal, established default position in special situations, and then move back into the street once conditions allow.

Safely leaving the gutter to climb onto a raised layer of asphalt may require lifting the front wheel, or both wheels, or subtle steering tricks to add angle to the exit. When exiting a gutter, don't veer weakly into a lip of asphalt, and don't start the turn before checking thoroughly for traffic.

There are other inherent physical difficulties in riding gutters, the most obvious of which involve proximity to the curb (although the presence of a gutter does not automatically imply the existence of a curb). It's possible to catch a pedal on the curb, for instance. Curbs also cause steering troubles. Due to the physics of countersteering, it can be very difficult to steer away from the curb, because pointing the handlebars to the left begins to turn the bike to the right (see Turning and Cornering, page 139). With the bike very close to a curb, steering in either direction is a challenge because you can't move the wheel. Curbs tend to have a troubling sort of gravitational pull.

Many cyclists believe quite passionately that riding in the gutter is necessarily demeaning, and that it sets a bad precedent that erodes the ability of all cyclists to navigate the streets in a proper "vehicular" fashion. People who buy into the emotionalist rejection of gutters cheat themselves by dangerously narrowing their range of acceptable options. A cyclist should be prepared to use every inch of available space on the road, including the gutters. Rather than banishing gutters to purgatory, cyclists should understand their inherent dangers and learn how to solve them.

You will need the gutters someday, so don't let them freak you out. The best way to learn the gutters is to ride them. Try it first at subdued speeds on streets with sparse traffic. Notice what kind of debris and obstacles are there and build a tolerance for these—a tolerance through mastery rather than passivity. Especially on skinny tires, there will be some types of street drainage grates that you shouldn't go anywhere near unless you're looking to enter the sewer in several pieces. Learn the grates. Get the feel of hugging the curb and moving between the gutter and the street (looking back prior to each move). Note how the curb is better approached with the right pedal positioned high. Pedestrians won't expect you to be in the gutter, and neither will motorists. The best way to avoid having to choose between the gutter and some other bad option is clever route finding.

THE DOOR ZONE

Some of the worst streets for cycling are narrow, busy streets (narrow, busy— you should see a pattern developing here) lined with parked cars, where the cyclist is faced with the choice of getting out in front of much faster motor traffic, or riding in the Door Zone (DZ). The DZ is the area within about four feet of the parked cars, where doors pop open seemingly at random into or in front of cyclists, with disastrous results. On bad cycling routes with oppressive traffic and lots of on-street parking, taking the lane can be a nasty prospect but is usually more palatable than venturing into the DZ.

The Door Zone is a brutal, sadistic taskmaster. The Door Zone is a total beeyotch.

Getting "doored," as it is universally known in the language of cycling, is a violent, completely unpleasant experience. Unfortunately it's also a rite of passage for urban bicyclists, who remain difficult to convince about the

THE SIZE OF THE DOOR ZONE VARIES WITH THE SIZE OF THE DOOR.

treacherous nature of the DZ until they experience it for themselves. Then they never want to go near a door again.

Smacking a door almost always results in the cyclist being launched headfirst. With luck the rider might hit the door square and fly cleanly over it to roll in the street beyond. That's a best-case scenario. More often a door disaster will result in violent secondary collisions with various things, like the bicycle, the door, the window, and the pavement.

THE DOOR ZONE

EVEN THOUGH THIS IS A NARROW STREET, THE RIDER DOES NOT NEED TO RIDE IN THE DZ TO ALLOW THE DOCK TRUCK (A) TO MAKE AN EASY PASS. IF THIS STREET WERE MUCH BUSIER, HOWEVER, WITH TRAFFIC IN BOTH DIRECTIONS, IT WOULD BE MORE THAN A LITTLE FRIGHTENING TO RIDE. THIS RELATIVELY QUIET INNER-CITY STREET HOLDS PLENTY OF DANGER AS IS, COMPOUNDED BY THE LINES OF PARKED CARS. THE RIDER HAS SPOTTED THE OPEN DOOR AHEAD (B) AND WILL BE POSITIONED NICELY TO AVOID IT—IF HE MAKES IT THAT FAR. HE WILL NARROWLY MISS HITTING THE DOG (C) THAT IS RUNNING OUT INTO THE STREET, AND WILL PROBABLY SMASH INTO THE CAR (D) THAT IS IN THE PROCESS OF ROCKETING BACKWARD OUT OF THE DRIVEWAY. THE RIDER'S VIEW OF THE MOVING CAR WILL BE BLOCKED BY THE PLUMBER'S VAN (E) AT A CRUCIAL MOMENT. THE DRIVER WILL GET THE TICKET, BUT THE RIDER WILL GET THE INJURIES. TO AVOID SUCH TYPICAL RIGHT-SIDE HAZARDS, THIS CYCLIST SHOULD CHECK BEHIND AND MOVE SEVERAL MORE FEET TOWARD THE CENTER OF THE STREET AFTER THE DOCK TRUCK HAS PASSED SAFELY.

Passenger-side doors also pop open, which means there are DZs on both sides of a car. This is of crucial importance for riders who like to "filter" between lanes when traffic is jammed.

Cyclists should realize the futility of trying to scan the passenger compartments of parked vehicles for potential door openers. We can never spot them all. Since there are no consistently reliable ways to tell if a door will open until it opens, cyclists should adopt a strict zero-tolerance policy about riding fast in the DZ. There are times when a little foray into the DZ can be helpful, but the DZ-cruising cyclist needs to slow enough that a collision with a door would be noncatastrophic. Luckily most streets are sufficiently wide that a cyclist can ride between the DZ and the path of passing traffic at a constant, comfortable pace. It is only on the really bad streets that the cyclist is confronted with the necessity of commandeering a busy traffic lane to avoid the Door Zone, and these uncomfortable streets can usually be deselected from the route.

Traditional placement of on-street bike lanes on many streets—sandwiched between traffic and parallel parking spaces—endangers inexperienced cyclists by encouraging them to cruise the DZ. Add this to the other criticisms applied to bike lanes (see Bicycle Lanes and Paths: Good or Evil?, page 144). Since almost all painted bike lanes are four feet wide or more, cyclists can usually cruise on the far left of the bike lane to stay out of reach of any evil doors. Some new bike lanes in Denver and Seattle have been placed out of the Door Zone in their entirety, proving it can be done.

Doors are far from the only hazards lurking in the DZ, unfortunately. A mob of potential dangers floats around any line of parked cars, like fish around a coral reef. There are strange creatures that live behind parked vehicles and then pop out at inopportune moments. These include adult jaywalkers, toddler ball chasers, drunken transients, dogs and assorted other locomoting balls of fur, and others. As if that weren't enough, parked vehicles outdo themselves by pulling out into traffic at exactly the wrong time and place.

READING PARKED VEHICLES

Several years ago a bike messenger named Ray was riding through the downtown of a midsize American city during the afternoon rush. Traffic was very heavy, four lanes, solid. There was a little silver Subaru parked against the curb in front of him, nothing out of the ordinary. Ray started to move around the Subaru. Suddenly, a guy came crashing out of the bank on the right and jumped into the Subaru's passenger seat headfirst. Bank robbery! Just as the guy threw himself and a gym bag full of loot and exploding dye packs half-way into the car, the getaway driver gunned the engine, popped the clutch, and fishtailed into Ray's lane, missing him by just a few feet. The guy didn't look once before he stomped the pedal, and Ray was almost toast.

The driver then put on a display of getaway bravado that was absolutely jaw-dropping and uncharacteristic of drivers in beat-up Subarus: He careened all over the road on the edge of control, jammed the car into tiny gaps in the choked rush-hour traffic, missed dozens of other cars by inches, and finally disappeared out of sight. It was like a television cop show condensed into twenty seconds. Ray tried to chase after, just to watch the driving, but the Subaru bandits escaped. His amazement turned to anger as reality seeped in: Those bastards almost took me out!

Ray then did something that was totally out of character. He went back to the bank where the cops were starting to gather and gave them a description of the vehicle.

Ray's near miss with the getaway Subaru is an extreme example of a common problem: parked vehicles pulling out suddenly in front of, or into, passing cyclists. In this case Ray should have been able to see trouble coming. When a passenger runs and jumps in a waiting parked car—especially when the passenger is running out of a bank with a bag of neatly stacked twenties—that car is probably about to burn rubber away from the curb.

There are other meaningful signs besides bags of loot, but cyclists shouldn't be overly obsessed with scanning lines of parked cars for clues. Instead of trying to pick up warnings of impending pullouts and door openings, just leave a minimum four-foot buffer between yourself and any parked cars, much more space if practical, and keep tabs on the little buggers out of the corner of your eye. But if the parked cars are talking, you might as well listen. Predict the future by taking note of the following details in parked vehicles:

- HUMANS—is anybody in there? If you happen to notice movement through the car's windows, or in the side mirrors, don't blow it off. The appearance of a driver is usually the first and most obvious clue that a parked vehicle could become a problem. Over time an observant commuter may begin to notice subtle patterns in the behavior of drivers and passengers—the slight shoulder hunch of someone in the first stages of opening a door, for instance. Where is the driver looking? A driver who is looking back over her shoulder or intently into the rearview mirror may as well be holding up a warning sign that she is about to thrust her car into the next gap in traffic—are you in the gap? Beware the Gap Effect. As always, be prepared for the worst, whether or not you see a driver. Darkly tinted windows, oversize headrests, tiny shrunken heads, and other problems keep the head-watching method from being consistently reliable.

- Is the ENGINE running? You may or may not be able to tell. A vehicle with its engine running is a vehicle that could move at any moment. During daylight hours, in the noise of the city, it can be nearly impossible to tell which engines are firing and which aren't. The only policy is to assume they all are. When the city tosses you a solid clue, such as TAILLIGHTS or visible EXHAUST, which is a common sight in cold weather, be thankful and put the sudden windfall of information to use as best you can. Always remain vigilant, even in the absence of such signs. NOISE from the vehicle is generally not a useful indicator when passing parked vehicles. By the time you can hear the modern engine idling, or distinguish it from others, it's too late. Sometimes there will be an audible clue or two—the clunk of a transmission, the change in rpms as a clutch releases—that can serve as a helpful warning for cyclists in close quarters.

- The TIRES tell a story too. Tires that are in the process of turning one way or the other are a definite symptom of vehicle movement. Either the driver is parking or getting ready to bolt. A sharp eye for the disposition of nonmoving tires is also helpful: Which way are the front tires pointed? Give special attention to cars parked against the curb on your right with wheels cranked to the left. Such a car could launch directly into the street, without the typical reverse adjustment needed to exit a curbside space. Urban cyclists are vulnerable to being smacked by harmless-looking parked cars that suddenly jump into the road with one vicious stomp on the gas pedal, not unlike the getaway car that nearly got Ray. At five o'clock they all become getaway drivers. On tires that are pointed into the curb, there can be no instant getaway.

- In a line of parallel-parked vehicles, REVERSE LIGHTS are a beautiful sight. Shining reverse lights represent at least two or three seconds of advance warning before a pullout, because drivers simply don't leave parallel parking spaces by backing out. Doesn't happen. As long as those soothing beacons shine from its butt end, a vehicle remains a known quantity, accounted for and predictable. Contrast this to streets with diagonally parked vehicles, and parking lots, where reverse lights are the opposite of soothing.
- Another comforting sight, among the innumerable frightening omens that the cyclist must recognize in traffic, is that of a DRIVER'S ARM poking out of an open window. Arms that are resting like that don't open car doors.

CLOSE COMBAT: POSITIONING IN HEAVY TRAFFIC

In many ways, very congested streets are easier to navigate than less-congested streets, because traffic tends to move at a reasonable cycling speed or lower when the streets are clogged. This speed matching allows the cyclist to claim an entire lane without difficulty, change lanes, and generally flow with ease. Proximity to vehicles is also a by-product of congestion, but proximity to vehicles that are moving in the same direction, at close to the same speed, is not necessarily dangerous and should not, by itself, cause a cyclist to freak out. Proximity combined with speed discrepancies and proximity to turning and crossing vehicles—these are more legit reasons to freak out.

When patiently cruising behind a car—a common situation in congested traffic—try not to stare grimly at the car's rear end. Instead, from a safe distance off the bumper, try to look through or around the vehicle to see what's going on ahead. The best riders notice red lights or obstacles ahead before the driver does, and have already decided how they will deal with the driver's likely reaction to them. Keep the fingers poised on the brake levers. As long as the rider has awareness of a vehicle and accounts for all its potential movements, it doesn't matter much if its driver sees the cyclist.

This point is hard to get across to bicyclists who figure that being seen is the most important thing.

One of the key points for riding in heavy traffic is to avoid passing or just squeezing into the space on the right of slower vehicles in the same lane. Those who succumb to this temptation put themselves in a position to be cut off or run over by a vehicle from the line on their left. Expect the vehicle to turn onto any side street, alley, or driveway, or to pull into any open parking space, even without a turn signal—especially without a turn signal, some veteran riders might say. Rather than pass on the right, stay behind slowish vehicles and observe. If you feel the need, pass these vehicles by switching lanes to the left, vehicular style. This lane switching opens the cyclist to a new set of dangers, however—like frantic drivers who have the same idea—and should (also) be treated with much caution.

Bicyclists in congested traffic could easily find themselves in a position to pass slower vehicles, especially as the right lane begins to back up. At these times the line of stop-and-go traffic in the right lane is possessed of a troubling sort of potential energy. It's likely that there will be some drivers stuck in that line who don't want to be there. Consider that these drivers are even less likely than others to see you, because they must use their mirrors or crane their necks around to do so. An insidious version of the Gap Effect is in full effect in these situations. To counter it, give all potential gap shooters— the overeager, the unaware, the nonnoticers, or the just plain nonlookers— a healthy buffer while passing, and maintain your awareness of a potential intrusion. Expect it and stay one step ahead.

The rider who exhibits much patience in regard to vehicles in front may remain vulnerable to vehicles behind. Any assumption that the drivers around are aware of anything beyond their own eyelids should be avoided. Cluelessness is a constant threat that causes, among other things, the common rear-end collision, *collisionus americanus.* As drivers and passengers in motor vehicles, most of us have at some point experienced a rear-end collision caused by drivers who momentarily fail to notice what is going on in front of them. They reach down to fiddle with the radio, or brush some McMuffin chunks off their Dockers, and wham! Rear-end collision. These wrecks are typically inconsequential for motorists, a matter for the insurance companies to sort out, but for cyclists the prospect of the rear-end collision is much more frightening. Can you imagine being smashed between two cars? Thanks for comin' out!

Cyclists should maintain rearward awareness of approaching vehicles when slowing for a stop. Use the ears for this purpose. A slowing vehicle makes a distinctive sound as the engine and tire noise both decrease in pitch. The rider who follows a car relatively closely should not execute a full look-back, but can turn the head about forty-five degrees to the left. This allows the cyclist to keep tabs on the lead vehicle as well as the trailing one. Some of the more jaded urban riders prefer to slide to the right, out of the way of potential rear-enders, as traffic slows.

Cars and trucks are kind of like bulls at a rodeo. As long as we can avoid the business ends of the beasts, we can contend with them quite easily. We can mess with them and use them as our toys. But if we get careless—horn up the yang.

RIDING A STRAIGHT LINE

Riding straight is a crucial skill for navigating many types of situations. If gutter riding feels sketchy, or you squirrel out in tight traffic, get busy with some straight-line exercises before you go too much farther. Don't try to jam your poorly skilled self into situations that demand good skills.

Urban riders have at their disposal an easy and effective teacher of straight-line skills built right into the transportation infrastructure. The traditional way for a cyclist to practice riding straight is by attempting to ride on top of one of the many solid white lines painted on the street. Use one of the standard four-inch-wide lines, not one of the honkin' eight inchers that are so popular these days. Look ahead instead of down, and let your eyes pull you along. The eyes are powerful. Relaxation is key. The bike is steered, veered, and jerked around with the legs as well as the hands and arms—relax them all. Do this straight-line exercise while pedaling. The pedaling motion should not cause the bike to weave.

When it becomes easy to roll right on top of the line for long stretches, get used to glancing back quickly while holding the line. Resist the natural inclination to veer left when swinging your head back to the left. Turning the head can start a chain reaction that causes the bike to go haywire. Break the chain by turning only the neck and keeping the shoulders relaxed and square. Don't lean the bike over, and don't turn the bars. It is not recommended that city cyclists succumb to their temptation to look back by pulling one hand off the bars and sitting up.

After you learn to ride easily on a four-inch line and learn how to hold a straight line while looking back, the next step is to learn how to ride a straight line at very slow speeds. Using the same four-inch line, slow to a walking pace, and then slow down even more, and see what happens. Ideally you should be able to hold the line at any speed, all the way down to zero miles per hour, while swiveling the head all over the place. This drill will expose any basic shortcomings in balance and control. The ability to balance and control the bicycle at low speed is another very important skill that should be viewed as part of the minimum requirement for safe cycling in crowded areas.

The rider's straight-line skills will be tested at some point on every ride in the city—suddenly narrowed gaps between side mirrors, grates to be traversed, long cracks and lips in the pavement to be avoided, not to mention most lane-sharing situations. When faced with such challenges, concentrate on the line you want to ride, and not on the obstacles you need to avoid. Any skier or mountain biker knows that if you fixate on a tree or rock, you'll run right into it. Instead of looking at where you don't want to go, look where you want to go and go there. Relaxation, confidence, and visualization are the key building blocks of bike-handling skill.

The ability to ride straight will generally decrease the space required to operate your bicycle and will thus open up much more of the road surface for your use. This can only be a good thing. It will instill confidence not only within the rider but also in other road users who observe and appreciate the rider's command of the machine. This keeps everything moving smoothly. Erratic weaving and floundering, of course, has the opposite effect—it causes following drivers to get frisky with the brake pedal and ruins the traffic flow.

This is not to say you need to ride straight all the time, but it is guaranteed that you will need this skill. Riding straight also saves energy and lets you go faster.

TRACK STANDS

One of the most exciting and strategically interesting events in all of bicycle racing is the one-on-one track contest called the match sprint. Although the match sprint is only three laps around the velodrome, the racers usually hold off until the final lap to unleash their full fury. The first two laps are usually spent playing mind games, jockeying for position, and keeping an eagle eye on the opponent.

During the first lap one of the racers is designated to lead at a walking pace or better. After the first lap the walking-pace requirement is scrapped, and the lead rider often slows to a complete stop, balancing on the bike in an attempt to force the other rider into the lead. Thus the term "track stand." Track stands are an important part of sprint strategy because, for most track sprinters, the trailing position is the coveted position. From the back a racer can launch a surprise attack or take advantage of the draft when the other racer attacks in full view. When both riders have it in their heads that they will steadfastly refuse to lead the final lap, a track-standing duel results—a race to see who can go nowhere the longest.

Track standoffs in match sprints rarely last longer than a few minutes and rarely test the human limits of track standability. Track-standing contests at messenger competitions are usually won by a rider who is able to balance in one spot for forty-five minutes or longer. These riders are such masters of low-speed and no-speed balance that maintaining balance is no longer an issue. Instead the track-standing contest becomes a bizarre test of physical endurance, as the muscles start to shake and seize, usually after about fifteen or twenty minutes. Some among today's messengers are such accomplished tricksters that their contests usually require riders to keep both hands off the bars and then balance with one foot on the pedal and the other hanging in the air, just to keep things interesting.

Probably the most useful application for the track stand, outside the velodrome, is that learning the technique helps riders achieve the low-speed balance that is very helpful and important for city riding. If you can ride zero miles per hour, you can also ride relaxed and under control at two miles per hour.

Solid points in favor of track standing at intersections are few, frankly. A true artist can employ track stands to smooth out and quicken a ride, just a little. Because the track-standing rider is able to keep both feet in/on the pedals throughout a stay at a stop sign or traffic light, starting from the intersection is slightly easier and the rider gets up to speed faster. But is it worth it?

Unless the rider is quite skilled, the attempt at a static balance will consume much more energy than it saves as the rider flounders around, strains, and struggles to hold position. A good track stand is silent and near motionless. Before the rider is even able to fake one of these graceful moves, he or she will have to suffer through dozens of sorry, energy-sapping performances. Even if the track stand is perfected, after years of practice, it is hard to imagine how the rider would actually conserve much energy by using it.

Also, the track stander's effect on nearby motorists and random passersby should be considered. This conspicuous activity has two effects on citizens of the outside world: (1) It confuses them and (2) annoys them. Imagine the nifty track stander at a four-way stop. The cyclist has come to a complete stop and is waiting lawfully. But the driver with the right-of-way has been hypnotized into submission by the track stander, who appears on the verge of powering into the intersection. The rider finally puts a foot down, everybody breathes a sigh of relief, and the normal sequence resumes. In areas with lots of pedestrian traffic, sloppy, substandard track standing often results in the rider's migrating up into the crosswalk and blocking it. Not smooth.

It is also worth considering, at least for a moment, how a noncycling citizen who has no appreciation for the limited practical benefits of a track stand might experience it entirely as an alienating force. To the untrained eye, a track stand looks to be little more than showing off, a cry for attention. And those in the metal boxes are left to wonder, even if they are not directly affected by the track stand, what kind of world is this where grown men and women have learned to stand still on their bicycles? Could this be one of the seven signs of the Apocalypse? These are fair questions.

That many drivers will feel an urge to exit their vehicles and knock track-standers over is undeniable and unfortunate. How much we should care about this, if at all, is unclear. The bottom line with track standing is that it's fun. Even if it won't save energy or put the rider on the short list for a Nobel

Prize, balancing and rocking back and forth on a stationary bicycle (the real meaning of the term "stationary bicycle") can add a little challenge and spice to a mundane commute or ride to the store.

Whatever the initial motivation, it is a natural progression for city riders to try to learn a passable track stand, just like basketball players eventually learn to spin the ball on their fingers. Start by looking at the street. Notice how it slopes downward to the curb. Some streets might have pronounced bumps at intersections around the recessed wheel tracks. This is all the incline you need to get a good track stand started. Because streets generally slope down from left to right where cyclists ride, most track standing is accomplished with the front wheel pointed to the left, up the incline. Don't use the brakes; just let gravity stop the bike, then hold it with a slight pressure on the crank. The back end of the bike can be pointed down the slope or up, as long as the front wheel is pointed up. Most riders find it easier to stand on the pedals, with the cranks near level, or with the forward pedal slightly above level. Track stands can be performed with either foot forward, but most riders find it easier to put the left foot forward when the wheel is pointed to the left. If nothing else, this position keeps the shoe from hitting the tire. Really smooth riders can balance with the feet in any position, and in any gear.

Micro-adjust the track stand using the cranks, the handlebars, and body position. It's easy, but you might want to go through the initial stages of learning in a semiprivate place. The track-stand learning process is not pretty, especially if the rider has not yet mastered a set of clipless pedals. Nothing looks uglier than a wobbling, meandering track stand followed by the toppling over of the rider, who then thrashes helplessly like an overturned turtle.

Master a regular track stand, then move on to sitting down, one hand, no hands, one foot. The ultimate is to learn to ride the bike backward while facing forward. That's when you know you're really going slow. You'll never lead out a sprint again.

TURNING AND CORNERING

It sometimes becomes necessary for cyclists to remind themselves of the freakish steering behavior of their bicycles. To do this, perform a little demonstration. Ride down the street with a very light touch on the bars, so light that you may as well be riding with no hands. Let the bike steer itself. Then, very gingerly, pull the right side of the handlebar toward you slightly, forcing the front wheel to point to the right. As most will probably expect, the bike begins to track to the right. But, almost immediately, the bike tips over to the left and the right turn becomes a solid left turn. This is a demonstration of countersteer in action: Turning the handlebars to the right turns the bicycle to the left, and vice versa. It sounds crazy, and it is.

Bicycle steering is a bizarre phenomenon that eludes complete understanding. Even highly skilled veteran cyclists may be quite surprised to learn of the fundamental madness ingrained in their bicycles. All this time they thought they were using their handlebars to steer their bikes. Turns out they've been using a mysterious combination of body English and handlebar adjustments to get the job done. Turning is achieved by leaning the bicycle, and the lean is controlled by adjusting the handlebars. Widespread ignorance of this strange phenomenon of countersteer isn't too surprising. When we're out riding we don't analyze how we steer the bike, we just do it. Our bodies have known how since we were kids, but our brains never bothered to figure it out.

The cyclist in a turn should not be thinking in terms of countersteer, or hitting the apex, maintaining speed, or anything sexy like that. The cyclist should really only be worried about tracking a safe line through any debris or road damage, and what large game—cars, pedestrians, other cyclists—they may encounter in the turn or when coming out of it. Save the fast cornering for races on closed courses. Overzealous cornering causes trouble in two important ways: (1) It increases the likelihood that the rider will wipe out, usually with sand or gravel on the road as a contributing factor, and (2) it often causes the rider to veer wide into oncoming traffic lanes upon exiting the turn.

The more the bike is leaned over, the more likely it is to slide out while turning. Straighten the bike up to vertical as you ride over sand, ice, wet metal, or wet brick pavers. This straightening of the bike makes the turning radius wider, so the cornering speed needs to come down in order to keep the bike in the proper lane. Scan for road damage and micro-adjust your line accordingly. Notice the variable slope of the street when cornering. A few degrees on the surface might make the difference between cruisin' and bruisin'.

One of the best cornering tips is to stay loose on the bike and unweight the saddle and handlebars enough that the arms and legs can act as the perfect shock absorbers they are. Don't push the bike away stiffly in the turn. Instead, let it come to you. Use your eyes to pull you through the turn. Don't look down, but instead look where you want to go. The bicycle has a tendency to track right where the eyes are looking.

PANIC STOPS

The formula for calculating g-force in braking looks something like this: g = (velocity)2 x .0333 / stopping distance, where velocity is miles per hour and stopping distance is measured in feet. Notice that there is no mention of weight or mass in this formula. G-force is a simple matter of speed and distance. A three-thousand-pound car executing a 0.6-g stop will have the same stopping distance as two hundred pounds' worth of cyclist and bicycle executing a 0.6-g stop, assuming identical reaction times and initial velocities for both. The car's brakes will have to do a great deal of work transferring kinetic energy into heat energy to achieve such a stop, but with power-assisted brakes on all four wheels and a low center of gravity, the typical car is actually able to stop in a shorter distance than the typical cyclist traveling the same speed.

For a very long time now, cyclists who think of themselves as quite knowledgeable have repeated among themselves the statement that the maximum g-force a cyclist can generate while braking is about 0.6 g. Conventional wisdom held that anything much more than 0.6 g would flip the bicycle and send the rider over the front wheel. This calculation was based primarily on the relatively high center of gravity of the cyclist and the coefficient of friction between rubber and road.

Few of these cycling illuminati have ever bothered to check their formulae in an actual physical experiment with skilled riders. If they did, they would find that skill level has a huge effect on stopping distance. In fact the really skilled cyclists among them, those having achieved a certain intimacy with their machines, would be surprised to learn they could generate 0.85 g or more under heavy braking and stay on their bikes. The rear wheel would stay on the ground the whole time. In real-world terms this means that a very good cyclist traveling at twenty miles per hour (thirty feet per second of initial velocity) can achieve a complete stop in about fifteen feet. Many cars can achieve this as well, but many can't.

How do great riders achieve such stops? First of all, they have practiced the maneuver, sometimes by necessity, and have learned to use and control their own body weight under forceful deceleration. At just the right moment, they throw themselves back to cancel some of the force sending them forward. Just enough of this forward momentum is canceled that the bike stays on the ground and under control. They have also developed a remarkable feel for the brakes on their bikes. Rather than simply squeezing the brake levers as hard and quickly as possible, they are able to apply a smooth gradient of force over a very short period of time. They understand that the front brake will do almost all the work in an effective stop.

Hard braking on a bicycle has much more to do with the rider than the bike. The rider who sits on the seat passively and jams on the front brake is going over the bars. While the old calculation assumed a static and seated rider, a successful and safe panic stop requires an exaggerated, well-timed body movement. It is an athletic move, like sliding into second base or dunking a basketball. The body's mass is hurled backward as far as it will go, with the arms outstretched. If you don't look too closely, the proper finishing position for a maximum stop looks a bit like that of a sprinter at the finish line, throwing the bike forward.

Unlike cars, bicycles are somewhat maneuverable under heavy braking, which allows for even shorter stops. Even under substantial g-force deceleration, a cyclist can turn the bicycle sharply. Such a turn may not be an available option in a tight space in traffic, but the cyclist in crisis should think immediately of turning as well as braking to avoid trouble. It may also be possible to enhance a maximum stop by pushing the rear wheel to one side, a smaller, quicker version of the "power slide" most of us performed as preteens. The rider may as well utilize the inevitable rear-wheel skid that occurs under hard braking.

Theoretically, the most effective stopping force that can be applied to a wheel comes at the moment just before the wheel locks up. This leads many to believe that the shortest stops will involve no skidding. On a bicycle, it doesn't work that way. Trying not to skid the rear wheel during a hard stop is like trying to keep the eyes open during a sneeze. The rear-wheel skid is almost automatic when the front brake is applied correctly. Maximum stops can only be achieved with a very forceful application of the front brake, and heavy application of the front brake tries to bring the rear of the bike off the ground. Even though a good cyclist can keep the rear tire on, or almost on, the pavement during all but the most intense stops, the rear end always lightens up enough that friction between the tire and the road is reduced, and a skid occurs. The front tire should not skid at all, but the rear pretty much has to, if it's not off the ground entirely.

Bicyclists should definitely practice this sort of hard stop. The damage that will occur to the rear tire—from the inevitable skid—will be worth it. Strap on a helmet and gloves and find a fairly deserted strip of blacktop. Start with slow speeds and work your way up, stopping as quickly as possible. Stay light on the bike and learn how to turn sharply to either side under heavy braking. Get a feel for what kind of force brings the rear wheel off the ground. Try some stops using only the front brake. This drill will quickly, perhaps ruthlessly, educate you about front-brake modulation and how the body must move under heavy braking.

The term "panic stop" is a bit of a misleading way to describe the braking maneuvers described here. There are still faster and more brutal ways for panic-stricken cyclists to stop, which involve increased levitation of the rear wheel. In the most extreme of these, the front brake is squeezed so hard that the front wheel sticks right where it is. This is occasionally necessary to avoid a collision, unfortunately. At decent speeds, no body movement could possibly counterbalance the forward momentum of the bike and rider involved in this last-ditch evasive maneuver. The bike flips over, and the cyclist is forced to eject. This is the real panic stop. Stopping the bike this way does not have to end in ugliness as some may assume. The cyclist can still retain some control. Rather than surrendering completely to head-first momentum and dropping like a rag doll onto the street, a rider might be able to clip out and hurdle the handlebars when the bike goes vertical, landing on the feet or on all fours as the bike crashes behind.

Short reaction times are even more important to the safety of the cyclist than panic stops. Reaction time is the time between the point when the need to stop arises and the point when the rider actually starts the process of stopping. You could be the best panic stopper in the world, but if your reaction times stink, you're still going to find trouble and pain on the streets. Reaction time can be reduced by such physical preparations as keeping the head up, the eyes forward, and the fingers on the brake levers, but the best way to cut reaction time is through disciplined vigilance.

It is good to master all versions of the panic stop, but it is better to anticipate problems well ahead of time and avoid situations where problems elude anticipation. Panic stops are a symptom of cyclists' mistakes. Riders who have mastered the art of anticipation rarely have to flash their most serious stopping skills. The riders who know best how to execute panic stops are the riders who least often need to.

Youth is wasted on the young, and experience is often wasted on the experienced.

BICYCLE LANES AND PATHS: GOOD OR EVIL?

What's food to one may be fierce poison to others.

—LUCRETIUS

Not long after the invention of the bicycle in the nineteenth century, bicyclists started angling for the construction of special paths on which to ride their precious machines. It's difficult to imagine now, but early bicyclists seem to have been even less excited about sharing the roads with noncyclists than we are today. The roads were often muddy and rutted; competition for available space was bitter, and their counterparts in road rage, the wagon drivers, were often armed. When the bicycle craze intensified in the 1890s, so did bike-path fever. Many of us have heard a bit about the wheelmen's historic fight for smooth roads, but their campaigning for separate paths has been difficult to square with our mythical visions of the past (and present) and sits in the dustbin of history.

Bike paths multiplied until the dawn of the automobile age, when everybody abruptly forgot all about them. Across the nation ostentatious projects for extensive path networks were left half finished and the existing paths faded back into the landscape, leaving few reminders of this remarkable episode in the history of American transportation.

During the Bike Boom of the early 1970s, Americans started taking bicycles out onto car-clogged roads in significant numbers, and the results weren't all that pretty. The cyclists didn't know how to ride in traffic, and the drivers didn't know how to deal with cyclists. Wouldn't it be great, folks started to wonder (again), if we could build separate facilities for all these bicycles, keep them off the roads and out of the way, and simultaneously make things safer and more pleasant for cyclists? Cyclists as well as drivers were asking this question. At about the same time, as the country experienced a fuel crisis and generally stank like a tailpipe, Congress allocated funds for alternative transportation projects, including bicycle facilities. Cities and states started to build bike paths (again) and paint bike lanes on their streets. These were popular projects all around.

The new "bikeways" came with unintended consequences. They were packaged and sold to the public as safer facilities for cyclists, but that didn't always seem to be the case. Bad news about the danger of bike paths did not fit well with the primary bicycle-related goal of urban-transportation engineers—to get bikes out of the way of motor traffic—so they ignored the negatives as best they could and kept building.

Many of the off-street bike paths of the 1970s were really just glorified sidewalks known as "sidepaths." Sidepaths are on the same plane as the street grid, so they tend to repeatedly send cyclists into intersections. Cyclists on sidepaths are less noticeable to drivers than are cyclists in the street, and they tend to be seduced by a false sense of security. They carry this false sense of security into the intersections and get crunched. Invisible and blind—it's an unfortunate combination. This issue with intersections negatively affects any sidepath-like facility.

Less important, the asphalt paths of the 1970s Bike Boom were structurally crude. They were often as narrow as suburban sidewalks (about six feet across) and didn't endure well. They often looked great right after construction, but before long they cracked obscenely and gave cyclists a very rough ride.

The first generation of painted bike lanes also had some unsafe design features. At intersections, the lanes often guided riders into slots to the right of right-turning vehicles, which led to conflicts and collisions.

Meanwhile, the cycling advocates who criticize bike paths, a type of human that does not seem to have existed during the original path build-out of the nineteenth century, did not help matters with the style of their delivery. John Forester and his likeminded antifacilities activists apparently never bought into the notion that a little bit of honey helps the medicine go down. For decades they have been delivering their lessons with a heavy dose of condescension and belittling ad hominem attacks, making it easy for observers to dismiss those lessons regardless of merit. The more they point out problems with the facilities, the sillier those objections seem to a general audience. Theirs is a peculiar form of advocacy.

As the decades passed, the engineers corrected some of their obvious mistakes, but not all of them. Bike lanes were repainted to the left of right-turn lanes, and the standard width grew, but some still lured inexperienced cyclists into the Door Zone. Off-street paths, for the most part, evolved into smooth cement surfaces. The paths are much wider now—the typical modern bike path is a ten- to fifteen-foot-wide behemoth. But sidepaths still exist and still send cyclists awkwardly into the street and cause confusion at intersections, although these days they are more likely to be known as "cycle tracks," a name that conjures comforting visions of northern European bike infrastructure. And all the paths are still crowded with inattentive joggers and walkers, novice riders who can barely stay upright, and those distributors of four-legged chaos commonly known as dogs.

Some of today's urban riders enjoy a new generation of bicycle paths that flow right under or over streets, just like urban highways. Such a path is known as a "fully separated facility," and it's a beautiful thing. These separate facilities were like science fiction during the 1970s Bike Boom but are now installed in several North American cities, doing double duty as parkland and transportation routes. One is tempted to call these paths "bicycle highways," but since almost all of them are shared with pedestrians, joggers, and in-line skaters, and pedestrians in fact hold the all-time right-of-way on them, these paths still have much more in common with sidewalks than highways. They are multiuse paths—MUPs. Still, if such a path cuts across town and takes you

THE "FULLY SEPARATED FACILITY." A BEAUTIFUL THING.

reasonably close to where you need to go, consider yourself very lucky and use the thing. Use it because there will be no interactions with motors, and no stop signs or red lights, along its entire length. Judicious use of a fully separated bike path could reduce travel time and stress—even if you have to go a bit out of your way to access it. Experienced riders understand that they may be more likely to hit something on the bike path than the street. But they still appreciate bicycle facilities, seek them out, and happily put them to good use.

Bike lanes are popular too, although the riders who enjoy them may find it difficult to explain the attraction. The advantages of bike lanes are primarily psychological. Most of these lanes are painted on streets that are

THE PERILS OF SUBURBAN SIDEPATHS

THIS ILLUSTRATION DEPICTS THREE CYCLISTS TRYING TO NEGOTIATE A TRICKY INTERSECTION AT THE ENTRANCE TO A POPULAR MALL. AS SHOWN, THE CYCLISTS ALL OWN THE RIGHT-OF-WAY THROUGH THE INTERSECTION. EACH IS IN A POSITION TO FIND OUT EXACTLY HOW LITTLE THAT MEANS.

CYCLIST ONE IS RIDING AGAINST TRAFFIC ON THE SIDEPATH AND MUST CONTEND FIRST WITH RIGHT-TURNING MOTORISTS IN THE NEAR LANE (A). THESE MOTORISTS LOOK ALMOST EXCLUSIVELY TO THE LEFT AND ARE PATENTLY UNAWARE OF ANY CYCLISTS APPROACHING FROM THEIR RIGHT. FOR THIS REASON THE RIDER IS SMART TO PASS BEHIND THIS VEHICLE. NEXT, CYCLIST ONE WILL HAVE PERFECT VISION OF THOSE TURNING RIGHT INTO THE MALL (B, F), WHICH IS GOOD, BUT WILL ALSO HAVE THE CRITICAL TASK OF KEEPING TABS ON FRANTIC LEFT TURNERS (C) OVER THE RIGHT SHOULDER. IF CYCLIST ONE MAKES IT ACROSS, HAZARDS ON THE OTHER SIDE INCLUDE THE AWKWARDLY PLACED SIGNAL BOX (D) ON A RAISED CONCRETE PEDESTAL, AND THE EVER-POPULAR MAN BEING DRAGGED BY A DOG ON LONG LEASH (E).

CYCLIST TWO ENTERS THE INTERSECTION FROM THE OTHER SIDE, LULLED INTO COMPLACENCY BY THE SIGHT OF THE LITTLE GREEN MAN ON THE WALK SIGNAL. DISPLAYING A TROUBLING LACK OF AWARENESS, CYCLIST TWO IS SOMEHOW SURPRISED BY THE RIGHT-TURNING YUKON (B) AND MUST SWERVE TO AVOID CONTACT. PASSING BEHIND THE RIGHT-TURNER (A), THIS RIDER WILL BE IN A PRIME POSITION TO COLLIDE WITH CYCLIST ONE.

CYCLIST THREE IS ABLE TO AVOID SOME OF THESE PROBLEMS BY RIDING IN THE STREET, BUT WILL NOT BE IMMUNE TO THE NORMAL HAZARDS OF BUSY CROSSINGS. THE SOCCER MOM IN THE HONDA PASSPORT (C), FOR EXAMPLE, MIGHT BE OVERWHELMED BY SHEER EXCITEMENT AT THE THOUGHT OF SHOPPING AND MIGHT TRY TO SNEAK ACROSS PREMATURELY. CYCLIST THREE WILL ALSO BE OBLIGATED TO CROSS UNCOMFORTABLY IN FRONT OF THE RIGHT TURNER (A). IN ADDITION, CYCLIST THREE MIGHT DRAW THE IRE OF IMPATIENT MOTORISTS BEHIND, LIKE THE LANE CHANGER (F), WHILE HAVING TO DEPEND ON THE AWARENESS AND GOODWILL OF THESE SAME MOTORISTS—LESS THAN IDEAL.

SIDEPATHS AND ROADS EACH BRING THEIR OWN SETS OF PROBLEMS. CHOOSING ONE OVER THE OTHER OFTEN BOILS DOWN TO A MATTER OF PERSONAL STYLE. THE SIDEPATH MIGHT BE THE BEST OPTION FOR A PATIENT RIDER WHO IS PREPARED TO STOP OFTEN—FOR DOGS, PEDESTRIANS, LEFT- AND RIGHT-TURNING VEHICLES, OTHER BICYCLISTS. IF TIME IS AN ISSUE, AND THE RIDER HOPES TO KEEP MOVING, THE ROAD IS PROBABLY THE WAY TO GO. UNFORTUNATELY, IN TYPICAL FASHION, THE LOCAL LAW BANS CYCLISTS FROM THIS PARTICULAR BOULEVARD. EVEN THOUGH THE MAN WITH THE DOG (E) YELLS, "GET OFF THE SIDEWALK!" AT EVERY CYCLIST HE SEES, THE SIDEPATH IS ACTUALLY THE ONLY LEGAL OPTION. CYCLIST THREE IS RIDING ILLEGALLY.

wide enough for cycling anyway, but the presence of the painted lanes gives cyclists an unmistakable territory of their own. This can be helpful around drivers who don't understand the law or don't respect cyclists as legitimate road users. Bike lanes might also serve as some legal protection for careful cyclists in case of a wreck—who can argue with a cyclist in the bike lane? There is an unfortunate corollary to this, that cyclists, conversely, might be legally compromised on streets with no bike lanes, or when they have to move out of the bike lane on a street that has one (for instance, when maneuvering for a left turn).

Whatever psychological protection they might provide, basic bike lanes of course provide little in the way of actual physical protection. Remember that bike-car wrecks usually involve vehicles that are turning or crossing, and a street rider will have to deal with these dangers, bike lane or no bike lane. Motorists smash into cyclists in bike lanes all day long.[13] It's logical to assume that confining oneself to a strip of real estate on the right side of the street could very well lead to a decrease in safety in some situations, as a far-right position is bad for both vision and visibility. Bike lanes are especially counterproductive on high-speed downhills with side parking or driveway entrances. In these situations the bicyclist should move left, away from typical right-side potentialities, if the space is available.

Some bike lanes are painted in their entirety, most often with green paint, with the hope of making the lanes and the bicyclists who use them more conspicuous to drivers. It seems likely that this scheme would enhance any of the bike lane's protective benefits. It also seems likely that the paint could enhance some of the negatives already mentioned.

The "protected bike lane" is still another step beyond the simple bike lane, with bollards or curbs placed between the bike lane and car traffic. Occasionally a line of parked cars separates the bike lane from the road. This type of souped-up bike lane tends to provide less physical protection from motor vehicles than its hopeful name implies. While they may improve the outlook with respect to same-direction traffic, "protected lanes" can cause additional problems for bicyclists with respect to crossing traffic and pedestrians. Riding into an intersection from one of these separated lanes is practically the same as riding into an intersection from a sidewalk. It's a design that tends to increase the chance of collisions with turning vehicles. If you've been paying

IS THE "SHARROW" A MORE EFFECTIVE AND HELPFUL FORM OF ACCOMMODATION THAN THE BIKE LANE STRIPE?

attention, you'll notice that these are the same problems that were associated with the sidepaths of the 1970s. Sometimes it seems like today's planners and cycling advocates are ignorant about the mistakes of the past.

Although John Forester and the dogmatic vehicular cyclists can cite all these practical safety concerns chapter and verse, they seem to be virulently opposed to separate facilities on principle alone. They argue to this day that bike lanes and paths represent the "ghetto-ization" of cyclists. The most strident among them feel that riding on a bike path is a shameful act, and that riders who use separate facilities are unwitting dupes in a long-term plan to push cyclists off the public roadways for good. Their view could not be more distant from that of the Euro-gazing advocates of today.

Unfortunately, the vehicular cyclists' warnings about the insidiousness of bike facilities cannot be wholly dismissed. A disturbing process seems to be at work that can be linked to the psychological implications of cycling infrastructure construction. There is always going to be a new generation of ignoramii out there, asking themselves, *What are those cyclists doing on the road anyway? Didn't we, the taxpayers, spend X-million dollars last year building the [insert name of path here] multiuse rail trail? Didn't the bicycle people themselves beg to get this path built? So why are they still on the roads?* Tantrums like this flare up from time to time among folks who have no understanding of the history of cycling in America or the needs of utility cyclists. In the future—as there does not appear to be any impending superabundance of people who can think their way out of a paper bag—we can expect more of these scattered antibike spasms. And certainly we can expect future builders of major roadways to exclude the simplest on-street provision for cyclists—the wide curb lane—in favor of pushing cyclists onto off-street paths, even the long-discredited sidepaths. As a result, the very idea of riding in the street among car traffic could be made to seem even more extreme and unwise than it already does. In this way the construction of separate facilities can lead to a deterioration of cyclists' safety and options. It's something to watch out for. So far, however, the fears of the bike path haters have not been realized. There is no widespread organized movement to remove cyclists from the nation's existing roadways, and on the whole, the use of separate facilities is still voluntary.

It's possible that cyclists are near the historical peak for access in urban areas, with nowhere else to go but down. Bicyclists currently enjoy a unique, some might even say privileged, status in the transportation realm. With a few exceptions here and there, we are allowed to ride on pretty much any street that would be worthwhile to ride. When barred from a new boulevard (that we would likely try to avoid anyway), there is almost always a sidewalk, sidepath, or some other sneaky way to two-wheel it. We can ride streets with painted bike lanes if we wish, but we are not required to. We can also ride on the separate paths, if we wish, but are (usually) not required to. With a legitimate place in both the vehicular and pedestrian realms, cyclists are having their cake and eating it too. Bicyclists have more freedom than any other class of road user. Rather than embracing, enjoying and cultivating this fortunate situation, many of us seem locked into perma-victim mentality.

Instead of getting bogged down in dead-end, personality-driven arguments about cycling facilities, think of all streets, bike lanes, bike paths—even sidepaths—as tools for you to use as you see fit. The more tools, the better. Just because a tool may be somewhat dangerous, like a busy street or bike path, does not mean it won't be a useful tool. If you went through the garage and threw out all the tools that could cause injury when misused, you wouldn't have much left over, except for maybe some tape. Would you let your precocious three-year-old use the radial saw? Probably shouldn't let anyone who is clumsy or careless around sharp objects, no matter how old, fire up the saw. But the radial saw remains one of the handiest tools in the entire garage. Its danger and usefulness cannot be separated. You don't trash it just because using it requires some caution. You reach for it every time you need to build a shed.

ON THE BIKE PATH

The appearance of large numbers of novice cyclists on the paths is a good sign. It means that new cyclists are entering the ranks. It also seems to indicate that bike-path proponents are right when they assert that separate facilities will attract more citizens to the bicycle option in transportation. Beginning riders often express their hatred for the idea of bicycling in traffic, but they seem to love the bike paths.

Beginners are their own worst enemy, of course, wherever they ride. Their assumption of safety on the paths is undermined by their own presence there. Because beginners flock to the paths, the narrow paths become much more dangerous than they have any right to be. This isn't just a bit of smack talk. Inexperienced riders are dangerous to themselves and others, just like teenage drivers after they've first gotten their licenses. They tend to weave around, misjudge distances and speed, and at times lose their balance on the paths. They often don't look where they're going and sometimes don't know where they're going in the first place. When new bicyclists have to cross an intersection, they are often unappreciative of the level of danger that intersections pose. They are wide-eyed, hopeful, and innocent, and the accident numbers reflect that.

Let us not forget our own humble beginnings, and while we're at it, let us bring some humility into our present. Give these novices a break. Give them encouragement, if not the benefit of the doubt. When navigating an off-street path, cyclists should treat these riders the same way they treat questionable drivers, with polite mistrust and the proverbial "open mind." That is, don't rule out any possible movement they might make until the movement becomes physically impossible to make. Eventually road users will think of every possible movement, no matter how ill-advised, and execute it right in front of you. That's what people do. That's what traffic is.

The best way to avoid the missteps and bad decisions of others—drivers, cyclists, and pedestrians—is to leave plenty of physical space between you and them. In this regard bike paths are problematic, because there is not much available space to escape into. Adjust for the lack of space by slowing way down around pedestrians and other path traffic. Commitment to slow riding around others requires patience. Patience is easy to come by on the path if riders can remind themselves of all the red lights they're not stopping at. There will still be sections of path where discreet cyclists can stretch out and crank it up a bit.

When passing slower cyclists on a bike path, wait until there is plenty of space, and no one coming the opposite direction, then pass on the left as you would a car on the highway. Say, "On your left," without a hint of alarm, as you begin the pass. This lets slower riders know you're coming, so presumably they won't swerve left into you. It is also polite and traditional among cyclists.

It may be useful and considerate, at times, to verbally warn pedestrians, but sometimes it is best for everyone if the bicyclist can pass a ped quietly, leaving a reasonable amount of space at a reasonable speed. Smarter cyclists use bells to good effect on the bike path; they warn pedestrians well ahead of time and don't have to slow down as much. "On your left" is a bike thing. Saying "on your left" to pedestrians is impractical, first of all, because they are moving too slowly and the cyclist is past them before they can process the words, and also because it causes about half of them to freak out and walk to their left, exactly the opposite of what you want.

One of the great features of the new generation of fully separated paths is the "on-ramp" that connects the streets and sidewalks with the path below. If the path is really top-notch, these ramps will be numerous. Unfortunately, while the ramps are a critical component of any facility's usefulness, they also encourage momentum-loving bicyclists to enter bike paths without proper

A RAMP CONNECTS THE PATH TO THE STREETS AND SIDEWALKS ABOVE.

care, at dangerous speeds. These things aren't supposed to function like freeway ramps, but that's exactly what happens. If you're lucky enough to have such bicycle freeways in your neck of the woods, notice the little stop signs at the bottom of the ramps—the most ignored stop signs in all the land. Obviously, don't assume anybody will stop at the bottom of the ramp (including yourself). Respect the blind corners. These ramps are also exit ramps, which creates another pernicious hazard: A rider making a surprise exit from the path suddenly grabs the brakes or turns across the line of someone following too closely. Use hand signals to warn other riders of your intention to exit. Don't assume they got the message.

Perhaps the scariest hazard on the bike path is the rider coming at you from the opposite direction. He's got his head down, he's pumping those pedals. He's drifting just a bit across the path. Bike paths are relatively skinny (eleven feet wide for a full-size path, six feet wide for a thin one), so a little drift goes a long way. Prevent extremely violent, dangerous head-on collisions with other cyclists—literal head-on collisions—by hauling enough awareness for yourself and everybody else. And try not to ride on a bike path at night without a light, even though the surface, if it is the typical white concrete, will be easy to follow in the dark. The light isn't there for you to see where you're going, but so others can see you coming.

Like streets, the bike paths themselves can sometimes be dangerous, even when they're empty. Ice can be a wicked problem on the paths during colder months. Even if the responsible agency deigns to plow the path after a snowstorm, large patches of ice will remain unless crews go out on foot and attack them with shovels and picks, which rarely happens. To safely cross patches of ice, ride your bike like a ghost. Don't put any extra pressure on the bars or into the bike through the feet, hips, spleen, or hair follicles. Breathe, relax, and float across.

Many paths are lined with soft grass on both sides, which is a nice inadvertent safety feature. Denver's Cherry Creek bike path, on the other hand, a fully separated concrete ribbon cutting into the heart of downtown, was bordered in places by fields of large, sharp rocks. Riders who wandered off the Cherry Creek path were sanctioned with serious injuries and broken bicycles, until the city rectified the situation by removing the boulder fields. (Today the Cherry Creek path has been widened, smoothed, rerouted, and improved in many ways, cementing its status as the most useful and advanced bike path in the nation.)

Hoarding responsibility never ends, even on an empty path. The obvious way to prevent these and other bike-path disasters is to keep your head up and eyes forward. *Watch where you're going.* Sounds simple, right? If it were really that simple, everybody would do it, and there would be almost no crashing at all.

On the fully separated path, the increased danger of minor collisions could very well be offset by the elimination of car-bike interactions. Removing cars from the picture decreases stress along with the likelihood of deadly accidents. No cars . . . We really must stand back and admire these words for a moment.

While somewhat dangerous for inexperienced users, the fully separated path is the newest, coolest tool in the cyclist's toolbox. No cars, no stops. Seekers after the Holy Grail of Momentum need seek no further.

SIDEWALKS AND THE LAW

Observe any downtown area in any major city in America, and you will see bicyclists riding on the sidewalk. Most of these riders will be riding illegally, and not out of ignorance of the law. Most have some vague idea of the illegality of their actions. The pedestrians there will be occasionally perturbed, and occasionally terrorized, by the sidewalk riders, but they are generally accepting of the situation. Sidewalk cycling has gained some measure of legitimacy in American society that does not match the letter of the law.

The typical sidewalk law of a large American city bans bicycles outright from sidewalks in the central business district (CBD). Many municipal codes allow only children younger than age twelve or thirteen to ride on sidewalks outside the CBD, but many cities also allow adults to ride sidewalks outside the CBD—where the sidewalks are usually only five or six feet wide. The rider is always required to yield right-of-way to pedestrians.

That's the typical law, but there are some noticeable exceptions around the nation. Seattle has a very bike-friendly code:

> Every person operating a bicycle upon any sidewalk or
> public path shall operate the same in a careful and prudent
> manner and at a rate of speed no greater than is reasonable
> and proper under the conditions existing at the point of
> operation, taking into account the amount and character
> of pedestrian traffic, grade and width of sidewalk or public
> path, and conditions of surface, and shall obey all traffic
> control devices.[14]

Sidewalk surfers are required to yield right-of-way to pedestrians, and to give an audible signal when passing, but otherwise, if you want to ride your bike carefully on the sidewalks of Seattle, go for it.

The cities of Portland, Oregon, and Madison, Wisconsin—great bike cities that they are—have some of the most enlightened and reasonable sidewalk laws in the nation. In Portland, the rider may hop onto a sidewalk in the business district if he or she is "avoiding a traffic hazard in the immediate area." We can live with that. In Madison, "bicycle riding on sidewalks is permitted," except "where a building abuts the sidewalk."[15] These laws are the product of some careful, logical thought, rather than arbitrary antibike sentiment or the conventional dogma that classifies bikes as vehicles and leaves it at that.

Regardless of what the law in your city dictates, you will likely find yourself rolling on the sidewalk at some point. Realistically, unless you are a strict vehicular cyclist who shudders at the thought of riding anywhere but a street, any trip into the downtown area will put you on the sidewalk, perhaps just for a short while as you negotiate one-way streets or make your way to a destination at midblock.

It's conceivable that limited, selective sidewalk riding could be accomplished in a safe and courteous manner, but it always requires a good deal of special care. It must be accepted, first of all, that sidewalks always belong to the walkers. You are just visiting in their realm. While riding on a sidewalk, slow to a near-walking pace. This is not enough, but it's a start. It's also easier said than done. Riding a bicycle under control at three miles per hour or less is beyond the abilities of many bike riders. They can't come close to riding a straight line unless they are rolling quickly. Wild weaving, overcorrecting, on the verge of toppling over—please do not inflict your drunken clown circus act on the good citizens of your city. It is strongly recommended that those in the balance-challenged set spend a good deal of time practicing and honing skills in a neutral location before dicing it up in traffic or inviting disaster on the sidewalks. These riders will simply need to step off their bikes and walk 'em if they have to use a sidewalk.

It's not good enough to simply avoid peds while riding on a sidewalk; ride in such a way that you do not alter or disturb their intended path. Allow them to walk the same direction, at the same speed, and in the same way they would if you weren't around. This is achieved by passing behind pedestrians whenever possible, and otherwise leaving a somewhat melodramatically wide berth in front of any walkers, large enough that their inner alarms stay silent and they don't even consider slowing down or changing course. This is an example of zero-impact cycling. If everybody rode sidewalks like this, there would be no bans on riding sidewalks. Not only is this a very courteous way to move, it also greatly reduces the chances of collision. Obviously, this tactic could be ruined by a moderately busy sidewalk or pedestrians executing sudden flip turns, which they all do at some point—*I think I'll go to that open-air drug market on Fifteenth Street before I go to the meeting on Eigh-teenth Street.*

Municipal codes quite often require the cyclist to let loose an audible signal when passing pedestrians on a sidewalk or path. Some experienced riders harbor cynical feelings about the whole audible-signal thing. Voicing a warning or ringing a bell is sometimes quite useful, especially when riding in the street or on bike paths where the rider is allowed to hold a bit of speed. On sidewalks an audible warning will often just gum up the works, especially when the rider is practicing a zero-impact style and can slip by a reasonable distance away from the walker, and at a speed only slightly faster than the walker. An audible signal may just confuse the ped, which defeats the purpose of this riding style. Audible signals have a way of startling small groups into stopping, turning, and roaming in random directions across the sidewalk. Best to just roll past gently, if possible. Do not disturb. If you're riding on a sidewalk, and a spread-out group blocks your passage, refrain from whistling, clicking your brake levers, or even saying "'scuse me." You will just have to wait. It's their world.

There is one way to continue practicing reasonable zero-impact cycling even on a fairly crowded sidewalk, and that is to ride the strip between the curb's edge and the parking meters and newspaper boxes. People rarely walk there. In fact peds strolling down the sidewalk pretty much forget about this space entirely, although they infiltrate it when jaywalking, when entering and exiting vehicles parked on the curb, or when staring in a daze at the parking meter. This strip is usually between one and a half and three feet wide. It can be negotiated only at small speeds, and even this will require a somewhat advanced command of low-speed balance and straight-line riding. Riding here is much more difficult, technically speaking, than riding on the sidewalk itself. There is often a nasty longitudinal crack between the sidewalk slabs and the curb proper, and there are always hardened obstacles brushing the cyclist's shoulder and occasional car doors opening from the street side. Riding the strip remains useful, polite, and, like sidewalk riding in general, quite illegal in most situations.

Cyclists run into more trouble when riding on the other side of the sidewalk, next to the buildings. When a building directly abuts a sidewalk, people will be stepping directly out of the building onto the sidewalk. It also means, quite often, that the corners of the building will obscure the view of alleys or sidewalks lining intersecting streets. With respect to alleys, sidewalk riding necessarily reduces the buffer zone between the cyclist and alley intersections. Expect cars and trucks to roll out of the alleys, and expect pedestrians (and other cyclists) to come bolting out from the hidden sidewalks. Always expect the worst from an alley or a blind corner. Roll slowly at the far side of the sidewalk, away from the building, to avoid these hazards.

One of the strongest among many good reasons not to ride a bicycle on city sidewalks is the problematic interface between sidewalk riders and street traffic. Motorists who cross sidewalks or crosswalks will often swivel their heads in only one direction to check for traffic: the direction from which they expect traffic to come. So if you're on the sidewalk and rolling against traffic, don't expect these drivers to look your way, or to see you even if they do. Definitely don't roll in front of their vehicles. Roll behind them, or, if the sidewalk is completely blocked, put a foot down and wait.

Many cyclists are run down, perhaps deservedly so, as they roll off the sidewalk and into the street at the end of the block. This is pure kid stuff: failure to look, failure to appreciate common dangers or to stay minimally alert, general failure to pull the head from the arse. These are the types of riders for whom the vehicular-cycling principle would do a lot of good. They aren't ready to handle the available freedoms of cycling, especially sidewalk riding.

It should be noted that, in addition to legions of resentful pedestrians, a large contingent of serious cyclists are staunchly in favor of sidewalk bans. Some of these are strict legalists with good intentions; others are vehicular cyclists who claim they would like to see every last off-street bike path rolled up and crushed into gravel, but they are turned into hypocrites every time they have to go downtown. Lots of idealists in this group.

RIDING IN SUBURBIA

Most Americans now live in areas that could be described as "suburban," and it is clear that much, if not most, of American bicycling occurs in these areas. It is a mistake to think of suburbia as the monolithic, homogeneous entity that many do—endless rows of similar split-levels on curvy streets on the outskirts of town, the lawns, the mowers and blowers, the angst. These days the suburbs contain lots of apartment complexes for inhabitants of all incomes, parking lots, open space, retail conglomerations, parking lots, office parks and industrial complexes, parking lots, and some of the most cutthroat traffic anywhere. Did I mention angst? And parking lots. The structure of the 'burbs is all about travel by car. Unfortunately a car cannot be cinched up into a tiny stuff sack when not in use, like a good windbreaker.

Probably the toughest, most ridiculous form of traffic exists on the big multilane arterial boulevards of suburbia. Invariably these are the roads that are lined with the 'Marts and the malls and the chain restaurants, and the associated vast seas of parking. Vehicles zip in and out of these lots with furious abandon, the drivers dazed and drunk on entitlement. The sheer traffic volume can be immense. The drivers themselves may be somewhat more prone to fits of abject stupidity than drivers downtown, where there are a lot of professional drivers. And the ubiquitous messengers and commuters constantly pedaling through relatively cramped downtown spaces foster familiarity and effective, if not cordial, relations among road users, but no such familiarity is apparent out by the Old Navy parking lot.

The city centers were constructed for foot travel, horse-drawn carts, and streetcars. Automobiles have never been completely at home there. The suburban shopping centers and their access roads, on the other hand, were constructed just for individuals in their cars. The sight of a bicycle invading the dragon's lair of the car-centric universe is often surprising and unwelcome. In some communities it must seem downright outrageous. Developers and civic leaders have further thrown us under the bus by constructing most new suburban arteries without much thought for bicyclists—the right lanes of these roads are often too narrow to share and bicyclists are expected to stay on the sidewalk. Sometimes the cyclist is outright banned from using the roadway. But, due to the speed discrepancies, traffic volume, frequency of turning and crossing, and bad attitudes that are usually associated with these roads, many cyclists would just as soon find another route anyway.

Ah, yes, route finding in the suburbs. It's not all it's cracked up to be. You'd rather not ride the hellish arterial boulevard that would take you directly to your destination, so you make a foray into the land of quiet side streets. But soon you find this street you're on does not seem to want to take you where you assumed it would take you. You used to be going north, now you're going west. All the other streets seem to do the same thing. It's a very curvy neighborhood. Soon you are looping back to a point very near where you started. What's this—back to the same arterial boulevard you were trying to escape! A half hour's riding has produced about a quarter mile of actual progress toward your destination. This is a typical suburban cycling adventure, at least for those who are unfamiliar with the territory and all its little tricks and shortcuts.

A good map is much more useful for navigating the suburbs than city centers, where streets tend to be laid out in predictable, orthogonal grids. These days that map will probably be on your smart phone/tracking device, and that might even be attached to your handlebars giving you turn-by-turn instructions.

Once a good route is located, perhaps using sections of multiuse path along with quiet, hospitable streets, the suburbs can provide much more relaxed and carefree riding than dense city centers. It is true that the width and curviness of suburban streets can tempt some people into aggressive driving, and the speed matching that comes easily while bicycling downtown is a rare commodity on suburban side streets. Here, you're getting passed, but the road is generally wide enough to facilitate easy coexistence with drivers, and there aren't that many drivers to worry about anyway. On suburban side streets, where citizens loll about in ultra-low-density housing, there are fewer cars parked on the street, and there are far fewer pedestrians to account for. With all those flat green lawns, sight lines are longer and clearer, and there are fewer places where you have to look. The lowest intensity of traffic in any municipality is generally to be found on its suburban side streets, while the highest is likely to be found on the suburban shopping-frenzy arterials—downtown streets would fall somewhere in the middle, in my opinion.

While riding in quiet sections of suburbia can safely be said to allow for a less acute level of concentration than riding elsewhere, successful suburban cyclists nonetheless have the same basic untrusting mind-set of their downtown counterparts.

RIDING AT NIGHT

Night riding is an important component of the cycling experience. This is especially true in North America, where the winter months bring early darkness for commuters.

Discussion of night-riding techniques can often be quite interesting, as it can reveal the underpinnings of one's whole cycling philosophy, and perhaps other personality traits as well. Some will say, for instance, that a cyclist need only gear up with the proper lights and reflectors and stick to classic traffic-law principles to be able to ride safely on the busiest streets on the darkest nights. Others will insist that no amount of lights and reflectors can make night riding safe. As usual, the truth is somewhere between these two extremes.

Night cycling looks very dangerous on paper. About half of cyclist traffic fatalities occur between six o'clock in the evening and six o'clock in the morning.[16] This amazing stat is even more impressive when you consider that relatively few cyclists ride at night. Many of these night victims are run down from behind by drunks or sleepers on high-speed roads and never stood a chance. Some of these victims, however, as with their daylight counterparts, are riding irresponsibly and erratically, without proper equipment, and have only themselves to blame. At night the garden-variety bonehead mistakes of cyclists are massively compounded.

It stands to reason that some of these cyclists-turned-statistics would not have been hit at all if they had been using proper lights and blinkers. Ideally a night rider has a helmet light as well as a handlebar-mounted light, and at least one bright red flashing reflector to clip on the back somewhere. In most jurisdictions this equipment is legally required for night cycling (although the law may not always be enforced). But are the lights and blinkies enough? Echoing the helmet debate, it must be said that attitude, style, and experience are more useful and important for cyclists than safety equipment. Undoubtedly some of these victims could have saved themselves by drastically altering their routes and techniques to make up for their lack of lighting.

Although one hopes that cyclists will keep their lights charged and blazing, they should also take a lesson from those who have learned to ride in the dark without any lights at all. Is it possible to go lightless safely, and if so, how? Riding at night without a light is not only possible, it can also be a very instructive drill. That's not to say we should make a habit of it! But even those who are religious light users—the true believers worshipping at the altar of Visibility—would probably benefit from at least considering the implications of this alternative, just to gain a partial understanding of it. (And realistically, a dedicated cyclist will be forced into this less-than-optimal situation from time to time anyway.)

The style that is required to safely pull this off is a version of what has been called the "invisible style." It is, by necessity, extreme antisocial cycling. The rider starts by choosing the quietest route within reason, to minimize interactions with cars. Then, whenever cars are encountered, the rider proceeds as if he or she is totally invisible—which is probably the case, frankly, if the rider is out at night with no light. This means slipping behind cars at intersections, adjusting speed to avoid situations where the rider is dependent on being seen by a driver, and so on. It is an extremely defensive, conservative, and patient style. It is a style that requires constant engagement, constant thinking ahead. There is an element of sneaking and creeping to this style that is very unpalatable to many of us.

Now, before lashing out, consider some of the interesting advantages of using the invisible style at night. From one point of view, the night rider's lightless paranoid-invisible style is extremely liberating. There is no pretense of being seen, and no dependence on it. It is all up to the cyclist to avoid the moving "obstacles," rather than up to the drivers to see and avoid the cyclist. The rider thus seizes control of his or her own destiny, in theory. Some riders who are devoted to this style claim that visibility to motorists is occasionally a complicating factor—a disadvantage—in car-bike interactions. Some veteran night riders have been known to switch their lights off from time to time, for precisely this reason.

A rider utilizing a reasonable vehicular style, on the other hand, well lit and dedicated to riding in a predictable manner, will enter situation after situation that should rightly be characterized by a gnawing uncertainty: *Does that driver really see me?* Guesswork. The invisible cyclist is not plagued by this question. The invisible cyclist has gotten inside this question, and has beaten it from within.

The problems associated with this invisible style are well known and probably outweigh the advantages. It is a style that could be criticized as selfish, and even unfair to other road users—because even if the rider is shrouded in darkness, there will still be a few drivers here and there who will notice and might be confused or startled by the rider's presence. It is true that some drivers will not notice a cyclist on the street, but it is also true that many drivers will notice and be pissed. As cyclists we must somehow respect and reconcile these two opposing facts of life, whether it be day or night. For this reason the invisible style is not practical for use on busy streets, or with other riders in close proximity.

Riders who practice the no-lights method will likely have some serious trouble with the city surface. Lights don't reveal surface anomalies with flawless precision, but they are far superior to flying blind. The new generation of bike lights with LEDs are remarkably powerful and provide a good field of view.

There are important elements of the invisible style that we should master and adopt for everyday riding. The same could be said of the vehicular-cycling principle. Enlightened cyclists achieve an artful blend of these two styles, the end result of which could be called a modified invisible style, or a modified vehicular style, depending on one's point of view. Their method in fact shifts fluidly along this continuum between the vehicular style and the invisible style as they adapt to a multitude of variables. It is no different for night riding.

Due to the presence of potholes, and the practical unavoidability of at least occasional encounters with motor vehicles—not to mention other cyclists—night-riding bicyclists should use proper lighting whenever possible. This means using at least one headlight (ideally one that not only makes the cyclist more visible to other road users but also illuminates the road ahead) and at least one flashing red blinker for the rear. But don't stop there, put lights on your wheels as well.

Lights are effective, necessary equipment. But they are not enough. The night rider must adopt the cynical mind-set, vigilance, and flexibility of the invisible cyclist, even while flashing like a UFO.

RIDING WITH OTHERS

Cyclists in traffic are shadowed by a tricky dualism: the need to take precautions against drivers who may not see them and, at the same time, ride predictably for those who do. Unfortunately, these demands are not one and the same. In fact they often pull and tug against each other, and cyclists must decide how the balance should be tipped.

Every move that the cyclist makes in traffic is subject to the perceptions of other road users nearby. There is usually an audience, although that audience doesn't always pay much attention. Whether we like it or not, this adds another degree of complexity to our decisions. Will they be able to react to what we're doing, and if so, how will they react? Will they freak out? Will they back off? Will they be calmed and assured? Or maybe they won't even notice.

Accounting for the perceptions and reactions of others is one of the cyclist's primary tasks. This is true concerning motorists and pedestrians, but especially so for other cyclists riding in close proximity.

The "organic" method of riding described on the previous pages is a method for the singular rider, alone in a flow of cars and trucks. It is a somewhat selfish style. It is not always suitable when two or more cyclists are riding together through town. For instance, this book advises individual riders in traffic to affect subtle but near-constant lateral moves, in the interest of safety and efficiency. These same moves, however, could surprise the hell out of an unsuspecting riding partner. When in the company of other riders, it may be necessary to abandon most of the free-form movement in favor of a more structured style, falling back to something akin to a strict vehicular style, with accompanying hand signals no less.

In traffic it becomes glaringly obvious when two riders are practicing different styles. But even two riders who are totally in agreement on style and are seeing and anticipating the same things can still come into conflict with each other. If both riders are very experienced in traffic, they will both feel compelled to occupy the same space on the road, and they will have to share the safe zones. The position of one rider determines the available maneuvering space of the other, and mobility is necessarily limited for both. By riding more robotically than one otherwise might, it is possible to find relative safety in city traffic in the company of other cyclists, but there is always some degree of compromise involved. That is why some highly experienced riders will express a preference for riding alone.

Bike-bike wrecks are not uncommon and are of two basic types. The first type is that which results from the sort of conflicts already described: Two or more experienced cyclists are out for a ride, together, and run into each other. Pace-line mishaps and misunderstandings at intersections are common in this genre.

In the other major type of bike-on-bike accident, one or both cyclists are beginners who are practicing the most primitive and dangerous form of cycling, "absentminded anarchy," and they randomly come together, often at a blind corner. They are hauling ass on the sidewalk, or cruising in the cycling space on the wrong side of the street, things like that. They are tumbling through your city like meteors looking for a planet to hit. They will eventually find the trouble that they appear to seek. In the meantime there is not much that we can do or say that will keep these people from their appointment with destiny. The best we can do is know they're out there and watch out for 'em. Be prepared to swerve when the time comes. Let's not become part of some other rider's learning process.

CHAPTER 4

BICYCLE ACCIDENTS AND INJURIES

THE STATISTICAL QUAGMIRE

You would probably like to see solid statistical evidence to back up the claims made here about accidents and injuries, and the author would like to oblige. Just one problem: It doesn't exactly work that way. Using statistics to quantify the danger of cycling is like trying to trap a mouse under a taco shell.

Statistics fail to paint an accurate picture of the overall risk of cycling. The biggest reason for this failure is simple: The vast majority of bicycle accidents never get reported, written down, or noticed in any official way. Researchers can't count the numbers if the numbers aren't there. You see, when a cyclist gets smashed by a car, there is usually a police report saying so; when a cyclist visits an emergency room, there may be some record of the visit with a general description of the accident. But when a cyclist wipes out in a dime-a-dozen solo wreck—the most frequent sort of bike wreck by far—even though that cyclist may be hurt, she or he will usually not seek medical attention or file any kind of report, and therefore leaves no paper trail. Bicyclists do the bulk of their suffering in silence. They tend to limp home, tough it out, and chalk it up to experience—all without notifying the Department of Transportation.

Paper chasers have estimated that about half a million bicycling-related injuries are treated in American emergency rooms each year, with an additional half a million seeking treatment in doctors' offices.[1] That's a substantial bloody mess of significant injuries. But this number (which, remember, is still only an estimate) is just a drop in the bucket.

If one million or so cycling wrecks require emergency or outpatient treatment each year, then how many injuries go untreated? Three million? Ten million? More? We can only guess.

At the same time, a large portion of people who do show up at emergency rooms are there for very minor injuries, boo-boos if you will. How should we define *injury* anyway? Do these boo-boos count? Should we care? When we expand our concept of danger to include not just the ER-worthy mishaps but also the more common injuries—the sore ribs, sprained shoulders, pavement burns, and bruises—then cycling suddenly looks like a very dangerous activity.

Piling confusion onto confusion, the cycling accidents of young children are combined with those of adults in most studies, creating a meaningless statistical mush. As most of us can remember, kids do particularly silly things on bikes, like riding out of driveways into the street without looking or jumping ditches on Kmart specials. They stack it up with far greater frequency than adult cyclists, which is part of what makes a kid a kid. (Kids under age sixteen still account for an astonishingly large portion of reported cycling injuries—about half of those aforementioned ER visits and a third of hospital admissions, according to a recent glance at the government's numbers. In the 1970s and 1980s, when kids were a lot more excited about bicycling, their share of the carnage was even larger.) Out on the street, kids' pattern of collisions with cars, the type of wrecks kids are likely to have and their likelihood of being at fault, is nearly the opposite, or the mirror image, of the pattern shown by adults. Still, their learning experiences are embedded in the statistics and become distracting, misleading clutter when we try to quantify the danger of cycling for adults.

Because kids' crash rates are so high relative to the crash rates of experienced adults, a huge drop in the popularity of bicycling among kids over the past several decades has profoundly distorted the picture in yet another way: As kids became less likely to ride, it looked like cycling was becoming safer for everyone. Suffice it to say that any cycling study that fails to separate kids from adults is hopelessly compromised from the start. Unfortunately that includes the most influential papers in the cycling universe.

The rise of mountain biking has thoroughly jacked up the stats as well. Most of the recent studies of injury data fail to differentiate between off-road and road bicycling accidents. Some of these studies have a designation for "nonroadway" wrecks, but this category can include parking lots, playgrounds, driveways, and other nonpublic thoroughfares, in addition to the local BMX tracks and homemade vacant-lot jumps.

Even if we could somehow account for every single cycling mishap, sort out all the kids' wrecks and the off-road wrecks, and obtain perfectly detailed information about injuries, the numbers we would end up with would be averages over cycling populations and, therefore, close to useless for you as an individual. The so-called "average cyclist" . . . does not exist. Why are we so concerned about the accident rate of a fictional character if the rates of the vast majority of living, breathing cyclists are not even close to that?

The true nature of the urban bike wreck will always elude statistical analysis. You can't qualify or quantify a bicycle accident. Every wreck is a mystery wrapped in an enigma, born of multiple factors not completely recognized or understood even by those who experience the incident firsthand. Every accident is as unique as a snowflake.

The key to escaping statistical tyranny is to not strain your brain too much about it. One must realize and accept that there will be more art than science to this enterprise. Beware of engineers, cycling advocates, spokes models, and authors who come at you spewing official-sounding statistics about cycling accidents. Numbers are not the ultimate authority here.

Rather than searching for answers in piles of paper, let us seek knowledge from the cyclists themselves, those with literally hundreds of thousands of miles' worth of experience and decades of truck dodging behind them. These men and women have plenty of stories to tell. We are wise to listen to them well, and to read their scars with a careful eye, while taking the stats with a grain of salt.

THE STATS AT A GLANCE

After bad-mouthing accident statistics, it should be noted that the statistically evident phenomena described in this section are confirmed by cold, hard experience. Without getting too specific or excited about criticizing the various studies, it is possible to pick out some undeniable patterns in the accident statistics. Some of these patterns may be quite surprising to beginning riders.

The first lesson to be learned here might be a bitter pill to swallow: There is no greater danger to the cyclist than the cyclist's own incompetence. As a whole it turns out that cyclists are not an entirely smooth and skillful lot. The majority of cycling accidents are embarrassing solo incidents, with the cyclist sliding out on turns; stacking it up after ramming potholes, curbs, and other obstacles; or just generally losing control.

Collisions with motor vehicles are potentially more damaging but account for no more than about 15 percent of all cycling accidents. Admitting it is the first step toward moving beyond it. That surly looking character in your bathroom mirror is often your worst enemy out on the street.

Now, let's talk about collisions. The vast majority of all car-bike accidents in urban areas involve turning or crossing. The possibility of parallel-path collisions (in which a car sideswipes or hits a bike from behind) causes heaps of worry in bicyclists, but these are relatively rare in city traffic. Hits from behind are more common in rural areas and on rural-style roads within cities, where they are disproportionately deadly.[2]

Almost half of all car-bike accidents are caused by cyclists who ride out into traffic without looking, ride on the wrong side of the street and pass in front of drivers who aren't looking in their direction, or otherwise mess up in some really obvious way. This means that about half of car-bike collisions could be eliminated lickety-split with a simple change in behavior.

Assuming you're an adult with a reasonable sense of self-preservation, you've already eliminated most of those boneheaded mistakes. Now, what about the rest of the car-bike collisions? Most *adult* cyclists who are involved in collisions with motor vehicles are riding lawfully when their wrecks occur. As far as you're concerned, the typical car-bike collision involves a looked-but-failed-to-see error by a driver who pulls out or turns in front of a bicyclist. In this reality, simply riding lawfully and predictably proves to be a woefully inadequate safety strategy.

Dissecting the subset of car-bike wrecks that can be legally blamed on motorists, we find that the most frequent of these involve drivers turning left into cyclists, pulling out from stop signs into or in front of cyclists, and turning right into cyclists. Anticipating and avoiding these motorist mistakes is really what this book is all about, and what traffic cycling is all about.

If you're like most people, you'll be surprised to learn—maybe even angry to learn—that the intentional stop sign–running and light-running for which cyclists are famous, so annoying to the general population, causes relatively little carnage in the stats. Despite the constant warnings from law-and-order cycling advocates and noncyclists, despite the burning desire for scofflaw riders to pay in blood for their deliberate transgressions, they rarely do.

Consider fourteen years of crash data from North Carolina. From 1997 through 2010, about twice as many of the state's adult cyclists were hit from behind by motorists—a crash type that is considered to be rare, remember—than were hit when riding, deliberately or otherwise, through stop signs or red lights. Across the country, in Boulder, Colorado, a little city teeming with law-ignoring college students on bikes, only about 4 percent of car-bike crashes are caused by cyclists running lights or stop signs, according to a recent study. That includes little kids on bikes.[3] This is not what one would

SHOULD CYCLISTS BE ALLOWED TO TREAT STOP SIGNS LIKE YIELD SIGNS AND RED LIGHTS LIKE STOP SIGNS? STATISTICS SUGGEST YES.

call ambiguous evidence. Bicycle safety education these days, which focuses primarily on encouraging bicyclists to obey traffic signals while wearing a helmet, is a complete miss. It doesn't begin to address the most important safety issues facing adult cyclists.

Obviously, breaking the law deliberately, with awareness, is going to be less dangerous than breaking the law inadvertently, without awareness. The stats take us another step beyond, suggesting that breaking the law with awareness is probably less dangerous than following the law without (see Running Green Lights, page 88). It should go without saying, but unfortunately does not: This is not an endorsement of law breaking, just an observation of statistics that are confirmed by experience. But understanding the reasons behind these numbers will make you a much better, safer rider.

CYCLING FATALITIES

Researchers concerned with bicycle accidents have focused much of their attention on fatalities rather than injuries, probably because the fatality numbers seem to be so much easier to deal with. Unlike the murky injury stats, crunching the fatality numbers involves relatively little guesswork. A fatality, after all, is a fatality, while nobody seems exactly sure what an injury is.

Just because these fatality stats are easy to obtain does not mean drawing conclusions from them is a straightforward matter. For instance, because fatal cycling accidents are rare, focusing on them alone gives an overly rosy impression of the risks of cycling. While it is a sketchy enterprise to estimate the total amount of bicycling that occurs for a given unit of time, and thus to conjure an estimate for the danger of bicycling in terms of fatalities per hour or fatalities per mile, let's just say that your next bike ride is relatively unlikely to end in death.

By any estimation, the chance that any of your bike rides will kill you is infinitesimal—somewhere around one death per million hours of riding.[4] These happy, reassuring numbers do no justice to the overall danger of cycling, as its rate of serious injury is about thirty times the fatality rate, and the rate for ER visits is roughly fifty times the rate of serious injury, or six hundred times the fatality rate.[5]

The stress on fatalities leads naturally to a narrowing of focus, with the spotlight placed on a specific type of injury at the expense of all others. Cycling fatalities are most often the result of head injuries resulting from car-bike collisions, but head injuries actually represent a relatively small portion of all injuries from car-bike crack-ups, and car-bike collisions are a relatively small slice of the pie when considering all painful bicycle accidents. Overall, head injuries probably account for less than 5 percent of all bicycle accident-related injuries.[6]

There is another more specific way that the attraction to cycling fatality statistics has fostered misconceptions. Studies show that a substantial percentage of cycling fatalities (about 25 percent) result from cyclists getting hit from behind by a vehicle. This type of accident, however, is not among the more common urban car-bike accidents. The hit-from-behind scenario is typically a rural or suburban phenomenon. It usually occurs on high-speed roads, with drunk driving as a common factor. Still, the fear of hit-from-behind collisions continues to be used as justification for controversial traffic engineering decisions in city centers.[7]

The annual tally of bicycle accident–related deaths has declined noticeably since 1975. In 1975, the year of the American Bike Boom, there were about one thousand fatalities, and in 2013, if the general trend holds, there will be around seven hundred.* The number of cyclist fatalities has bounced along between six hundred and eight hundred for the past fifteen years.

To what should we attribute the welcome decline since the 1970s? Nobody knows for sure, but that doesn't stop us from theorizing with wild abandon. Could it be traffic calming that did it? Better brakes on cars? People driving slower, with more awareness of cyclists? How about the growing popularity of bike helmets? These are some hopeful shots in the dark. Each of these things has had some effect.

Sadly, the decline has probably had more to do with kids' dwindling bike usage. According to the US Department of Transportation, the portion of total cyclist fatalities involving children under sixteen years of age dropped like a rock over the past forty years (from roughly two in three in 1975, to one in three in 1998, to one in five in 2004, to one in ten in 2011). Meanwhile, as the number of child victims has dropped off the charts, the number of adult victims has been creeping steadily upward for the past twenty years or more. Obviously, the most powerful force in the fatality count has been the drop in child cycling. What appears to be good news on fatalities, well, it's something else entirely.

---

*The number of bicycle-related traffic fatalities is very close to 2 percent of the total yearly number of traffic fatalities, reported at 32,367 for 2011. (National Highway Traffic Safety Administration)

THE PARADOX OF EXPERIENCE

Another thing the stats confirm quite clearly is the value of experience. The numbers are inexact at best, but when we put together all the studies of different cycling populations over the decades, we see that the more experience a cyclist has, the fewer wrecks he or she has per mile or per hour of riding. This effect is dramatic. A decade of experience seems to reduce the mythical average cyclist's accident rate by about 80 percent.[8]

It's important to understand that this does not necessarily mean experienced cyclists have fewer total wrecks—they have far fewer wrecks per mile or per hour of riding than beginning riders, but they tend to ride far more. In the end, beginners and vets tend to have about the same number of serious accidents per year.

Could it be, as John Forester and others have argued, that more experienced bicyclists are simply more likely to follow the rules of the road, and that adherence to vehicular-cycling principles is what gives them their low accident rates? Well, consider a study of Boston bicycle messengers performed by a Harvard professor. His study suggested that the messengers were carrying a collective per-mile accident rate hovering around the lowest ever recorded for any group of cyclists.[9] The older, more experienced of the couriers must have achieved a far better rate than that to make up for the rookies, who combine their unlawful riding with lack of experience.

Bike messengers are among the safest riders in the world per mile? Ack! This makes zero sense if following rules is the ultimate key to safety. But if experience is more important than following rules, the Boston study makes perfect sense—the only cyclist who can match the in-traffic experience of an old bike messenger is another old bike messenger.

As any cyclist accumulates hours and miles on the bike, the clumsy floundering is weeded out of the repertoire. The city has to cook up increasingly bizarre and complex scenarios to get the better of a quick-learning cyclist. The total number of wrecks per mile will decrease, while the percentage of the total wrecks that involve collisions with a car or truck will increase. The accidents become much less frequent but more serious over time.

THE ACCIDENT IMMUNE SYSTEM

Please forgive all the drama about crashes and injuries in this book. I'm just trying to save you a spot of trouble, using the power of the written word. I'm not confident it will work, but it's worth a shot.

There is a painful catch-22 involved in cycling—the best way to avoid wrecks is to wreck. By God I wish it weren't true, but pain is the best teacher. You never forget what Professor Pain tells you.

After you've been on the bike for many years, it becomes difficult to escape the notion that you're collecting one of each type of wreck. There will be one wipeout on diagonal railroad tracks, one loss of control after unseen pothole, one slide out on gravel, one door, and on and on. Once you get clipped by a stop sign–busting delivery truck, you will forever onward think of stop signs, and delivery trucks, in a different light. All it takes is one time. Call it the Accident Immune System.

Unfortunately there is no shortage of different accident types to collect. Like viruses, they seem to mutate in response to our defense mechanisms. They become less frequent as time goes on, but the wrecks keep on coming, surprising you with their endless variety.

The badge of experience is the scar. Experience hurts. Are you sure you want it? Some don't. They suffer one good fall and stuff the bike into the back of the garage behind the snowblower. Can't really blame them too much, but this book is for the rest of you.

ROAD RASH

Road rash is the cyclists' term for the most common bicycle-related injury, the abrasions that result from falling onto pavement and sliding across it. A little bit of road rash is just the cost of doing business.

Road rash is a precious gift. Road rash is your friend. Bask in it, appreciate it, love it. Above all, learn from it.

The time-release pain of road rash, a constant companion for a week or so after any decent tumble, serves to remind the victim of What Not To Do.

Don't fight it. Listen to what the road rash is telling you: "You're not that great of a cyclist. Maybe you should try a Segway. You're dangerous to yourself and others. You need practice . . ." Allow the humility of road rash to enter your consciousness, where it will displace malignant pride* and help keep you out of the ER through your cycling career.

Abrasions result from almost every type of bicycle wreck, even car-bike collisions, because almost every type of bike wreck involves hitting the tarmac at speed. Road rash leaves its mark anywhere the body meets pavement. After a really action-packed wreck, the victim is often surprised to find pavement burns on both sides of the body—hips, knees, ankles, elbows, wrists, shoulders, back, and elsewhere. There may not be any memory of rolling like that, but the road-rash record proves that it happened.

Road rash laughs heartily at Lycra clothing. A short slide on the road surface can rip a pair of Lycra cycling shorts halfway off, leaving the haunches bloody and raw, a fairly common sight at the local amateur races. This type of injury can show up beneath layers of heavy clothing as well, quite insidiously, even on skin that was "protected" by jeans and jackets. This is a sobering indicator of the destructive power of sliding on the street.

Treatment for all but the worst road rash is fairly simple and do-it-yourself. The least enjoyable part of treating these abrasion-type injuries is cleaning them. It's important to remove the debris from the wound, and this is usually a bit painful. Use antibacterial soap and water, treat the wound with a topical antibiotic ointment, and then cover it with a sterile dressing. A nonstick bandage is best. Pro racers have been using a special type of dressing that is water based, designed to keep the wound moist so it will heal faster.[10] Uncovered road rash can be repeatedly irritated by layers of clothing, which impedes healing and hurts like hell.

The only ways to prevent road rash are to ride with humility and intelligence and perhaps cover your skin with leather the way motorcyclists do. In any case, wear gloves on every ride, along with your helmet. When you fall properly, the hands make first contact with the street.

---

*Cyclists are no more susceptible to this disease than any other group but are more vulnerable to its side effects, especially the false sense of security that leads to a decrease in vigilance.

COLLARBONES

"I didn't hear it," says Christie, "but other people did."

What Christie didn't hear, and what ruined the appetite for lunch in the pedestrians around her, was the sound of a collarbone breaking as her body hit the pavement. She had wrecked hard after riding over some severe waves in the asphalt that she hadn't noticed (see Waves, page 50). The unseen waves twisted her bike out from under her and threw her down so quickly and violently that she had no chance to duck, roll, or otherwise prepare for the impact.

Although Christie didn't hear the actual snap, she understood immediately what had happened, because her arm had been rendered suddenly and completely useless. There was no moving it. That, and the tremendous pain that flooded the area about ten seconds later, made for an obvious diagnosis. When a collarbone goes, it's not subtle.

Faced with the knowledge that one of the biggest bones in her body had broken clean in half and was trying to poke out through the skin, Christie quickly began to go into psychogenic shock.* She laid down and put her feet up on a snowbank. Cell phones were put into action, and the paramedics were on the way.

The collarbone, or clavicle—sometimes known as "nature's shock absorber"—is the bone at the top of the chest that runs from the shoulder to the sternum, or breastplate. There is one collarbone on each side. These are the prominent bones that you can see in the mirror and grab with your hand. Clavicles are broken with some regularity in bicycle accidents, usually due to a serious impact with the street, when the cyclist is thrown down directly onto the shoulder (like Christie) or hits the ground with an arm held out stiffly.

---

*Psychogenic shock is a fear reaction that rapidly dilates the blood vessels and causes decreased blood flow to the brain. Fainting is the extreme form of this most mild version of shock, which is usually "self-correcting." The general public tends to confuse psychogenic shock with other forms of shock that are far more serious. Severe bleeding is the major cause of "real" shock (hypoperfusion), during which the body's cells and organs are starved of blood. In response to a hemorrhage, the body sends signals to the heart to pump more juice. The heart rate is increased, causing additional blood loss. If this downward spiral is not interrupted, it will end in cardiac arrest and death. The first outward signs of this deadly form of shock—restlessness, anxiety, pale skin, rapid heart rate—mimic the symptoms of psychogenic shock and, sometimes, life itself. Paramedics are taught to watch carefully for and treat signs of shock if there is the slightest possibility of internal hemorrhage. (J. David Bergeron and Gloria Bizjak, *First Responder* [Upper Saddle River, NJ: Prentice Hall, 2001], pp. 322–24.)

"All I got was four pain pills and a sling," Christie says of her hospital experience, which she insists was decidedly unpleasant, especially when the doctors had to cut her favorite sweatshirt off and then abandoned her to wait half naked and helpless on a gurney for hours while they attended to more critically injured patients. Nonchalance in the ER is a fairly typical reaction to this painful but relatively nonthreatening injury.

A fractured clavicle is usually pretty straightforward stuff, but it's not an injury that can be handled without professional treatment. If you snap a clavicle, head to the ER. (If nobody is around to drive you, you have earned a trip in an ambulance—don't attempt to ride with a broken collarbone.) The docs will want to look you over, take an X-ray or two, and make sure that none of the major blood vessels or nerves in the area of the fracture have been damaged. Beyond that, immediate medical treatment will involve little more than strapping you into a sling or specially designed "figure-eight" harness, giving you some pain pills and words of encouragement, and sending you out the door. Installation of metal plates or pins (surgery) probably won't be necessary. You will be asked to return in about six weeks for a follow-up.

Adults usually require about six to eight weeks, maddeningly slinged up, to heal their snapped collarbones. After the pain goes away, it's a good idea to start some physical therapy to regain strength and range of motion. Even with a good rehabilitation regimen, however, the arm and shoulder on the side of the break may never function quite as well as they did before the accident. Unless you opt for surgery, there could be a permanent funky lump or other minor deformation in the area of the break—total badge of honor and usually quite inconsequential.

Six weeks is probably not enough time for a clavicle to heal to the point that it could withstand another hard blow, so when you get back in the saddle, be patient and ride conservatively. Christie understands this all too well: About six months after her accident, she was surfing the city streets on her bicycle again, and yes, she hit pavement again. This time her chain slipped off the big ring and caused a minor tumble. Her clavicle snapped at the exact same spot of the original injury. Back to the hospital, another sling, a few more pain pills, and the whole deal all over again.

Even after her two collarbone incidents, Christie continues to ride through the city every day. She says the experience has made her a more vigilant cyclist and left her with a physical reminder in the form of a minor deformity known as a "winged scapula" (one of her shoulder blades sticks out).[11]

The fractured collarbone, painful and frightening though it may be, is really just the extreme version of road rash. Call it a warning from the streets. The crash victim left with a broken collarbone as the most severe injury is actually a lucky individual who has been granted a reprieve of sorts, because any crash violent enough to cause a fractured clavicle is a crash that could quite easily have caused, with just a bit more speed or an inch here or there, serious head trauma. And while collarbones magically stitch themselves back together over time, a damaged brain may stay that way forever.

Some have suggested that cyclists might be able to prevent collarbone fractures, and other fractures, by eating foods rich in calcium and vitamin D. Total nonsense, others say. The best way to avoid such injuries, of course, is to avoid falling—or to fall correctly.

HOW TO FALL

"The ship was turning gradually on her nose—just like a duck that goes for a dive. . . . The band was still playing. I guess they all went down."[12]

—HAROLD BRIDE, SURVIVOR OF THE *TITANIC*

Many painful and debilitating injuries, especially the collarbone fractures and severe road-rash incidents previously detailed, could be avoided if cyclists would apply more finesse to their crashes. There is a right way and a wrong way to fall off a bicycle.

Crashing is an important skill for cycling. Some do it well, and some cyclists are hopeless crashers. Unfortunately it's a skill that seems to require innate athletic talent, or perhaps needs to be learned early in life—in rough-housing, peewee football games, and such—and not one that can be easily acquired as an adult. It may be possible to practice this skill, by heading to the local park or soccer pitch and taking some dives off the bike. Everyone around will think you've completely lost it, which is always a nice bonus. In our current litigious environment, however, guys can't go around recommending that people fall off their bikes on purpose.

The key to a good crash is to roll with it, and thus distribute the force of the impact. This is not always possible, even for a skilled crasher, because some crashes are just too violent and sudden. This is precisely the difference between a "good" crash and a "bad" crash.

The process of crashing begins with a frightening flash of realization: *I'm going down.* This is a moment that really pumps the adrenaline, a moment of complete raw fear and life, without distractions. It is pure action combat with the street at that point.

The talented crasher recognizes this point of no return—which will be different for each rider in any given situation—at the earliest possible moment and abandons fruitless attempts to avoid the inevitable, leaving more precious time to set up for the fall. The first thought is for the hands—get them off the bars and out. Separate from the machine. Some really poor crashers maintain a death grip on the bike and ride it right down into the pavement. Not good.

So you're falling away from the bicycle with your arms out, checking out the landing zone. That's not to say you should try to absorb the whole impact with the hands—far from it. But the hands should make the first contact with the street. For this reason gloves are among the most important bits of safety equipment, along with attitude and helmets. Much better to lead with the hands than with the shoulder or head. If the crashing cyclist is able to get the arms out, half the battle is won.

The idea is to minimize the force of the impact, and to keep your head from smacking pavement, while, if possible, initiating the roll. Don't hold the arms out stiff—you'll break your wrist or collarbone that way. It might seem silly to suggest, but deliberately try to relax your body while falling, and as the blacktop rises quickly to meet you, think consciously about how you can soften the encounter. *Hello, street. It's me again.*

Upon touchdown, the outside arm collapses, absorbing as much of the fall's energy as possible. First with the hand—the bottom of a fist—then the forearm, rolling onto the back of the shoulder and over. A perfect roll is harmless to a gloved hand. Lucky for us most falls naturally send the rider off to the right or left, which begins the rolling process nicely. Complete the crash by getting the heck out of the street. When executed correctly, the worst you'll end up with is some minor road rash on the forearm and shoulder and a wicked adrenaline rush followed by an overwhelming sense of relief.

The sequence outlined above is a rather optimistic scenario. It assumes that the crash has been "telegraphed"—that you can feel it happening in time to execute the roll. This is simply not the case with many types of bicycle accidents. Even the most talented and cat-quick bike handlers get slapped down awkwardly and hard more than a few times in their lives. Their shoulders get torn up, their helmets crack open like raw eggs, before they even realize what happened. For these violent falls, by definition, there is no magic technique that can help. The only answer is prevention, in the form of a conservative, defensive, and very focused attitude in the rider.

Falls are not pleasant, but if we ride well enough to make them infrequent occurrences, and know how to fall correctly, a few crashes are a small price to pay for the great privilege of riding a bike through the city. The injuries to the head and face described in the next section, however, make the transaction far less favorable.

FACIAL INJURIES

Due to cyclists' face-forward position and high center of gravity (recumbent riders being an exception here), we are vulnerable to having our faces smashed in sudden, violent wrecks. Bicycle helmets are great for protecting the top of the head and perhaps the brain but offer scant protection for the lower face. The average cyclist rarely considers this particular vulnerability, which is why it is being given so much attention here. Allow me to enrich your paranoia.

Serious facial injuries, as with brain injuries, often result from impact with motor vehicles, either moving or stationary. These are wrecks where the bike is suddenly stopped cold in its tracks, while the rider continues forward. With the front wheel blocked, the rider flies forward and tends to catch his or her legs on the handlebars, which forces the head and upper body to pivot downward and slap against whatever immovable object is there. Facial injuries also occur from particularly nasty versions of solo crashes, especially slide outs from high-speed cornering and wrecks caused by sudden displacement of the front wheel. Slide outs and slap downs.

In the mountain of bicycle accident statistics on the desk here, the term "head injury" usually refers to any injury above the neck. Got a bloody nose? Head injury. Knock some teeth out? Head injury. In this way the numerical incidence of head injuries, as we traditionally think of them, is overstated, while the incidence of facial injuries is forgotten. Circumstantial evidence suggests that bicyclists are more likely to suffer an injury to the face than a concussion or other brain injury, but facial injuries are lost in the statistical purgatory.

Many dedicated cyclists can confirm having had teeth knocked out at some point, or fracturing one or more of the fourteen irregularly shaped bones of the face. These events provide some of the least-beloved memories of their entire lives.

Unfortunately, traditional road-cycling helmets provide no protection against these common injuries.[13] Full-face mountain-bike helmets, like those used in downhill racing, should be considered for use by riders who like to take a lot of risks in heavy traffic but want to stay pretty.

HEAD INJURIES

Head trauma is the grizzly bear of all cycling disasters—rare but deadly. Although head injuries account for a very small percentage of all cycling-related injuries, they are implicated in about 85 percent of cyclist fatalities.[14] Across the board, severe head injuries result in death for about half the people who suffer them.[15]

A cyclist who smacks his or her head in an accident will, if lucky, escape with only a concussion. Concussions cause confusion, headaches, sleepiness, and short-term memory loss. Recovery is usually quick, but the individual may be left with a particular vulnerability to repeated concussions, a "syndrome" that is a bit of a mystery to the medical community.[16]

A more serious accident may bruise the brain below the site of impact, or bruise both sides of the brain if it "rattles" in its hard case (a coup-contrecoup injury). A violent blow may fracture the skull. In these cases it is not the contusions on the brain or even the skull fracture that pose the greatest danger. Such injuries may involve broken blood vessels that bleed into the space around the brain, and the swelling caused by this bleeding is the most dangerous and deadly complication of head trauma. In extreme cases a hematoma (collection of blood) around the brain can compress and destroy brain tissue, or it can push the brain through the opening at the base of the skull. Such severe swelling is immediately life threatening.

Because intracranial hematomas can grow slowly, anybody who has been in a crash involving the head needs to be watched closely afterward. Symptoms of brain swelling may mimic intoxication. "Raccoon eyes" are an ominous sign of intracranial bleeding. An even more ominous sign is bleeding from the ears.[17] Any person who has suffered significant head trauma should be immobilized due to the danger of spinal injury, and of course, professional medical help should be summoned immediately. For severely injured patients, every minute is critical. For the walking wounded, an MRI will reveal any hidden hematomas and damage to the brain.

To prevent head injuries, the cyclist should strap on a certified crash helmet for every ride. Bicycle helmets seem to provide some protection against such injuries but are no magic bullet. The most effective safety device is not the helmet but that hunk of rock it is supposed to protect.

OTHER INJURIES

Road rash, busted collarbone, smashed face, and cracked skull are, unfortunately, not the only injuries common to cyclists. Falls from the bike cause all manner of damage to the upper extremities. Broken or dislocated fingers; broken or sprained wrists; cracked elbows; and sprained, strained, or dislocated shoulders are all familiar. (Muscles get strained, and ligaments get sprained.)

Damage to the rib cage is a typical result of various types of sudden drivetrain failures, in which the rider is thrown violently into the stem and handlebars (see Drivetrain Maintenance, page 245). Catastrophic mechanicals are also known to cause painful contusions around the knee.

Cyclists who get hit by cars often end up with broken legs from the initial impact with a low bumper. The cornering slide outs so popular among beginners often cause a broken or badly twisted ankle on the inside leg. Occasionally these same wrecks can fracture a hip.

"Soft" injuries, such as saddle sores and knee pain, are extremely common, but they result from poor bike fit and other issues, not from accidents. For more on these problems see Bike Fit on page 232.

HELMET DISCLAIMER

First of all, let's get one thing straight. Cyclists should wear a certified bicycle helmet whenever they ride. There.

This needs to be stated first, because without it, the information contained in the following sections could get me thrown from a high place. This helmet stuff tends to get folks all riled up.

If you are like most cyclists, the following information will probably make you feel uneasy and will challenge most of what you think you know about helmets and their effectiveness. Please read the entire section with an open mind before freaking out. Remember: Knowledge is power. The information is important and, in the end, learning it will probably provide more protection than the helmet itself.

THE HELMET CONTROVERSY

. . . no falsehood is so fatal as that which is made an article of faith.[18]

—THOMAS PAINE

The first hard-shelled bicycle helmets for mass consumption appeared in the late 1970s. Thirty years ago only a small percentage of cyclists wore them.

Today, however, the use of helmets is thoroughly entrenched in cycling culture.[19]

From the racers to the commuters, it is almost taken for granted that cyclists should wear helmets on every ride. You buy a bike, you buy a helmet to go with it. Cyclists who choose not to wear them suffer pangs of guilt and are widely considered to be nuts. In Australia, New Zealand, and parts of Canada, adult cyclists are required to wear helmets. In the United States, many state and municipal codes require children to wear helmets, and their parents are held responsible if they don't. These laws are becoming more popular. While helmet use is still voluntary for almost all adults in this country,* American cyclists purchase millions of bicycle helmets each year and wear them religiously.

So, what's the controversy? Isn't the push for helmets supported by solid and incontrovertible evidence? Well, it depends on whom you ask. Those untiring preachers of helmet usage—like the US Consumer Products Safety Commission, the National Center for Injury Prevention and Control, the Snell Memorial Foundation, the Insurance Institute for Highway Safety, and dozens of other private and government agencies—rely on just a handful of research studies to make their case. These groups seem quite happy with the available research. But the studies they cite are not immune to the pitfalls that have plagued other studies of bicycle accidents and injuries, and so the studies have attracted critics like thrashing, injured fish attract sharks.

If you spend any time at all looking at this issue, you'll quickly and repeatedly come across the claim that "helmets reduce the incidence of serious head injuries by 85 percent," or something similar. This figure is derived from a series of studies that gathered data from Seattle-area emergency rooms in the late 1980s and early 1990s. The researchers simply looked at the injuries of cyclists who wore helmets versus the injuries of those who did not, and they found that the helmeted riders treated in the ER suffered fewer and less-severe head injuries.[20]

Critics of these Seattle studies are quick to point out that severity of injuries could not be pinned on helmets alone. As the studies' authors themselves

---

*Those in Dallas and large portions of Washington State, including the otherwise great city of Seattle, being notable exceptions.

acknowledge, riders using helmets tend to be more experienced and safety conscious than riders who don't, and therefore may suffer less-severe accidents and injuries. Helmeted riders—being more affluent, in general, with much better access to health care[21]—might be more likely to seek treatment for less-serious injuries, which would skew the results in favor of helmets. Likewise, helmet-wearing children tend to have more-concerned parents who might rush their kids to the hospital even after minor falls—just to be sure. All of this would result in helmets looking more effective than they actually are. By what amount, it's impossible to say. The Seattle studies, though enticing, assumed an authority in the helmet debate that is not justified by their methodology.

If helmets are the lifesavers they are advertised to be, then we should expect to see a significant drop in cyclist fatalities as helmet use rises. On the face of it, the correlation seems to be there: Helmet use has gone up drastically in the United States and fatalities have dropped (by about 25 percent) since the late 1970s. When we use pedestrians as a control group, however, helmets don't look so good. The number of fatalities among pedestrians has dropped right along with cyclist fatalities, both in the United States and Canada.[22] Since helmets have never been very popular with pedestrians in either country, it could be argued that the decrease in deaths is due to other factors.

In a possible preview of legislation coming to the United States sometime in the future, the Australian states of Victoria and Western Australia enacted mandatory bicycle helmet laws for adults in the early 1990s. Years after the laws were implemented, there was little or no indication of any statistically significant reduction in the rates of head injuries or fatalities due to vastly increased helmet usage.[23] Even before a similar law was passed in New Zealand in 1993, there was a great increase in the number of cyclists there who voluntarily donned helmets, and yet no corresponding decrease in the rate of serious head injuries could be found.[24] The primary trend associated with these mandatory helmet laws is a general decrease in cycling. The population statistics have not been helpful, at all, for the arguments of those favoring mandatory helmet laws for adults.

The obsession with bicycle helmets seems particularly irrational when the danger of cycling is considered alongside the danger of driving and walking. Compared to the danger faced by other road users, there is nothing all that special about bicycling that is particularly likely to cause a head injury. Statistically, an hour of driving seems to be in the same range of risk for serious head injury. Driving and walking helmets—hypothetically speaking— would prevent many times more deaths and brain injuries than would bicycle helmets, simply because there are so many more drivers and walkers. But if someone were to seriously suggest that a law should be passed forcing all drivers, passengers, and pedestrians to wear helmets, that poor someone might be burned at the stake. Many of the same people who think unhelmeted cyclists are completely insane would consider any helmet-wearing drivers and pedestrians to be, well, completely insane.

When a bareheaded cyclist suffers a head injury, people shake their heads and sigh: "Shoulda been wearin' a helmet." But when a helmeted rider suffers a head injury, nobody seems to doubt the effectiveness of the helmet. Instead, there is an automatic assumption that the injury would have been worse without the helmet. In fact, there is rarely any evidence to prove that an unhelmeted rider's brain injury could be blamed on the lack of headgear, or that a helmet would have made any difference at all. We just assume. There is a great deal of hopeful superstition behind our faith in bicycle helmets.

WHAT ARE BICYCLE HELMETS BUILT FOR?

Some emergency room doctors have seen firsthand the limitations of bicycle helmets. What these doctors know, the rest of us should try to understand: Bicycle helmets are built to soften relatively minor blows to the head, like those that can result from falls, but are explicitly not designed to save the bacon of a cyclist in a high-speed collision with the road or a car.

If you look on the inside of a new helmet these days, you should find a sticker stating that the helmet meets the standards set by the Consumer Products Safety Commission (CPSC).* If you have yet to buy a helmet, make sure the sticker is on any helmet you purchase. But don't get too excited about it.

---

*The CPSC has certified all models of bicycle helmets sold in the United States since 1999. Prior to that, helmets were certified by the American National Standards Institute (ANSI), the American Society for Testing and Materials (ASTM), or the Snell Memorial Foundation. Snell's remain the most rigorous among all the standards, including the current CPSC rating.

DON'T GET TOO EXCITED ABOUT THE STICKER.

Helmet models are tested by strapping them onto fake heads and dropping them straight down onto anvils of various shapes. If the so-called head form slows down gradually enough, as measured by a device called an accelerometer, the model passes. The CPSC sticker means that the helmet is certified to protect your head in an eleven-miles-per-hour impact with a jagged surface like a rock or curb, or a fourteen-miles-per-hour impact with a flat surface.[25]

Fourteen miles per hour? Obviously the CPSC's testing conditions are exceeded regularly by any decent cyclist on the way to the grocery store, and absolutely blown away during other common cycling scenarios—fast descents, for instance, or some car-bike collisions when the speed of the rider is compounded by the speed of a vehicle. That CPSC certification is not going to keep your skull together in a really bad crash. It's no surprise that many of the most vocal helmet boosters are pediatricians, as bike helmets are designed to provide effective protection in the kind of low-speed accidents suffered so often by kids.

Adult cycling consumers don't want anything on their heads that might slow them down. They want helmets that are slick looking, lightweight, and well ventilated. These demands create a conflict with safety concerns. If manufacturers wanted to produce a much more protective and safe helmet for adult cycling, they could do that.

In fact such models already exist. Consider using a more protective style of helmet designed for mountain bike enduro racing. These have fewer vents and legitimately hard shells, but are still reasonably light.

With the tension between safety concerns and consumer demands to guide them, helmet makers have designed bike helmets to gradually slow the rate of the head's deceleration in a wreck, not so much to protect from the blunt force of the impact. The term "hard-shell," when applied to today's road-cycling helmets, is a complete misnomer, an anachronism left over from the 1980s. Supposedly built to collapse, the modern bike helmet consists of a layer of expanded polystyrene (EPS) foam covered with a literally paper-thin sheet of plastic. Its apparent solidity is an illusion.

When a bike helmet is compromised by a hard fall or an accident, it needs to be replaced. Helmets can sustain fractures in the foam that are invisible yet seriously reduce the helmet's ability to dissipate energy. Likewise, when a helmet gets much over five years old, the foam becomes so brittle that it's time for retirement.

Bicycle helmet manufacturers have done a remarkable job within the confines of the market. Which is to say, they really know how to make money selling bicycle helmets.

ITS APPARENT SOLIDITY IS AN ILLUSION.

TORSION INJURIES

At 8:15 a.m., on July 28, 1998, Robert R. strapped on his helmet and started riding his bike to work. At 8:30 a.m. he rode head-on into a Mercedes SUV and was knocked out cold in the middle of one of the busiest streets in the city. A few homeless guys dragged him onto the sidewalk so he wouldn't get run over. About an hour later he woke up in the hospital, surrounded by doctors, technicians, and beeping medical equipment. He was lucky to be alive.[26]

On a monitor by his bed, a strange scene was unfolding. He couldn't quite figure out what he was looking at. "That's the inside of your carotid artery," someone explained helpfully. A tiny camera had been inserted into the large artery in his groin and was threaded all the way up to his neck, allowing the medical team to observe a life-threatening blood clot in the artery feeding his brain. "Cool," Robert said, and fell back to sleep. The pharmaceuticals were really kicking in at that point.

Later on the doctor came to Robert's room and explained how he might have received such a dangerous neck injury. The helmet may have saved your life, the doctor told him, but it almost killed you at the same time. He had seen this type of injury before in cyclists. Due to the wide, oblong shape of most bicycle helmets, an off-center impact on the helmet's surface can translate into a violent twisting of the head and neck. Furthermore, the "sexy, high-performance vents"[27] of the typical high-end helmet can catch in a wreck and twist the victim with disastrous results. This is particularly scary news for loyal helmet wearers, because torsion-type head injuries, in which the brain stem and the blood vessels in the neck can be torn, are among the most deadly of all injuries.

It is certainly very disturbing to think that a bike helmet, due to design features based on aerodynamics, ventilation, and style, might actually cause more harm than good in some crash situations. Keeping this frightening complication in mind may cancel the false sense of security that some cyclists feel when wearing a helmet, and that can only be a good thing. In recent years some helmet makers have been making helmets that are specially designed to absorb the energy of oblique impacts, using a new technology called MIPS (Multi-directional Impact Protection System). The aforementioned enduro helmets use this technology.

Robert, for what it's worth, has weighed the consequences and continues to wear a regular bike helmet on every ride.

THE HELMET VERDICT

As humans we are attracted quite naturally to easy answers. Quick fixes. To cyclists the bicycle helmet can seem like the easiest answer of them all. It is not.

The purpose of the previous sections has not been to disparage use of helmets, or to suggest that they shouldn't be worn, but simply to inject a needed dose of sobriety into a microculture that has come to revere the bicycle helmet as some kind of magic force field against head injuries. In reality, bicycle helmets should be recognized as a compromise between safety, style, ventilation, and weight.

Considering the limitations, and the fact that some are so light and comfortable they are barely noticeable when worn, bicycle helmets do a nice job protecting heads in most falls and low-speed impacts. Violent collisions are another matter, but—you never know—a bike helmet's three-quarter-inch layer of expanded foam could be the difference between a nasty concussion and a lifelong handicap. Legions of cyclists have pieces of broken helmets stashed away somewhere, to remind them of what might have happened to their skulls. Experience, not some spotty research study, has made helmet believers out of them. Others without helmets will be launched head-first toward the street, and just before impact a single thought—perhaps the clearest thought they will have for some time—will flash into their minds: *I sure wish I had a helmet on right now.*

The brain is too important and vulnerable to forgo this easily applied preventive measure. Strapping on a helmet won't make us immune to accidents or injuries, even brain injuries. But while we dismantle some of the claims made by the pro-helmet groups, we must emphasize that bicycle helmets can provide a significant net gain in safety for cyclists who wear them.

Wear a helmet properly or don't bother. The worst thing you can do is put on an ill-fitted helmet and believe that it will work when needed. For a good fit, the helmet should be low on the forehead and sized so that your skin moves when the helmet is pushed around. The chinstrap must be snug and the Y-straps evenly adjusted and close to the bottom of your ear. If you're unsure how to properly adjust your helmet, any local bike store should be happy to help.

Cyclists should wear helmets and ride like they don't. Wear a helmet, but don't let it go to your head.

CHAPTER 5

AIR POLLUTION AND THE CYCLIST

A HISTORICAL REALITY CHECK

Climb into your time machine and go back to New York City, 1890. It's educational.

Of course you can expect, in addition to seeing plenty of ladies in funny hats, a notable absence of cars and trucks. A total lack of freeways and over-passes. No diesel-spewing buses, and not a single parking garage in sight. Sounds great, right? Before you get all romantic about the old-fashioned unmotorized city, realize that the first thing you're likely to notice about the old New York is its god-awful smell, a combo of rotting garbage, sewage, coal smoke, and of course, horse dung. To the intrepid time traveler visiting the most overcrowded city on Earth,* it becomes painfully apparent that exhaust comes in many forms and originates from sources other than motors. The nineteenth-century cities were so heinously dirty that living within them was considered a grave threat to human health.

Much of the blame for this pollution was placed on the popular trans-portation technology of the era—the horse. New Yorkers in 1890 had to con-tend with a frightening yield of horse exhaust. Deposited on the city's streets each year were tens of thousands of gallons of urine and two and half mil-lion pounds of manure, which created clouds of dried dust or, depending on the weather, green puddles. The buildings lining the streets were stained by splash from the pools of excrement. The draft horses themselves were so overworked that they would frequently drop dead in the streets, to the tune of some fifteen thousand per year in New York alone.[1] Cycling through the nineteenth-century city without fenders will put a nice greenish brown stripe up your backside and pretty much ruin your knickers.

It's no surprise that the automobile's arrival into this stinking, soupy envi-ronment was celebrated by affluent city dwellers. They figured it would bring a vast improvement in terms of cleanliness and health, in addition to a revolu-tion in mobility. The danger of motor-vehicle exhaust was the furthest thing from their minds. Newly motorized Americans enjoyed several decades of blissful ignorance until the insidiousness of the internal combustion engine wafted into the national consciousness from the Left Coast.

---

*New York's Lower East Side, near the turn of the twentieth century, housed more than three hundred thousand people per square mile. Today the most densely packed areas of Manhattan hold about one hundred thousand people per square mile.

Around 1950 the air over Los Angeles, the world leader in all things auto-motive, had achieved a shocking density and brown hue. A new word was born: *smog.* No matter how much folks wanted to, the strange new cloud could not be blamed entirely on industry. Angelinos weren't about to give up their cars at that point—nor could they, one could argue, as the city's rapid-transit system had just been torn out in its entirety—but they demanded that their elected officials pay attention to the region's air quality, or lack thereof. With a cloud like that, something had to give.

Decades of regulatory experiments in California set an example for the whole nation, culminating in the tough federal Clean Air Act of 1970. This legislation eventually forced a significant cleanup of industrial pollutants and emissions from new vehicles.

THE GOOD NEWS ABOUT AIR POLLUTION

Going through the long list of poisons that hang over our streets and pump in and out of the lungs of city cyclists is a scary exercise that tends to make horse crap sound pretty nice, so let's start with some good news.

Due to government regulations and advances in technology, a new car today produces about 10 percent of the pollutants produced by the typical 1970 model.[2] The use of the catalytic converter, a device attached to a vehicle's exhaust system that changes harmful pollutants into such benign substances as oxygen and carbon dioxide, is the primary reason for this massive improvement. Basic catalytic converters were introduced in 1975, and more sophisticated "three-way" converters (which reduced emissions of carbon monoxide, hydrocarbons, as well as nitrogen dioxide) were mandated by law in 1980 and today appear on all gasoline-powered cars sold in America.* The

*Catalytic converters force the exhaust stream through a tight honeycombed structure made of ceramic material. The ceramic honeycomb is coated with precious metals, such as platinum, rhodium, and palladium, that catalyze the pollutants into nonpollutants. Platinum, for example, strips the nitrogen atom away from the noxious nitrogen dioxide molecule (NO_2) and "holds" it, leaving oxygen (O_2); the leftover nitrogen atoms then bond to form harmless N_2. Voila!

The catalytic converter was the American auto industry's response to the stringent mandates of the 1970 Clean Air Act. It's worth mentioning that the American car companies did not go gently into this new era. In fact they put everything they had into fighting it, claiming that the new laws would cause a "business catastrophe." Their full-court press of lobbying swayed Washington for a few years, until foreign competitors such as Volvo, Honda, and Mercedes showed they could exceed the new US guidelines years before they went into effect, and the American companies were shamed into action. (For a decent account of the fight over the Clean Air Act, see Jack Doyle, *Taken for a Ride* [New York: Four Walls Eight Windows, 2000]).

1990 amendments to the Clean Air Act brought still more stringent emission controls, but there have been only minor modifications since then.[3]

The gasoline used today is not your father's gasoline. In the cities with the worst pollution, "reformulated" gas is used. This new fuel contains additives that boost its oxygen content to make it burn more completely, reducing harmful emissions.* Federal laws have also tamed diesel fuel by removing most of the sulfur content. In city buses and maintenance fleets, conventional diesel has largely been phased out in favor of cleaner-burning fuels, from propane to recycled cooking oil.[4] And lead has been gradually phased out of gasoline over the years, so this extremely toxic ingredient has been virtually eliminated from air in America (not so for many developing nations, where leaded gas is still in use).

Smokestack emissions from factories, refineries, and power plants have also been cleaned up significantly. Generally speaking, about half of our human-made air pollution comes from these "fixed sources," although this percentage has been rising steadily as auto pollution has been reduced.

Air quality in the United States actually improved throughout the 1990s and early 2000s, even as the number of vehicles on the road and total miles driven increased.[5] The early 1980s were probably the worst years for air pollution in this country, due to the combination of the total automobile population and the relatively high number of older, unregulated vehicles that remained in service. The attrition of older vehicles was one of the best things ever to happen to urban lungs.

There could be more good news on the horizon. It seems possible that the nation's vehicle fleet could, at some distant point in our future, run substantially on electricity instead of gasoline. That's what we keep hearing anyway. If all that hypothetical energy were generated from clean sources such as solar or wind power, as opposed to burning coal and natural gas, the nation's air pollution problem would cease to exist as we know it. Perhaps there will be a further revolution in air quality and some of us will live to enjoy it. Most

---

*The use of oxygenated fuels produced an unfortunate frying-pan-into-the-fire situation. Although it has been phased out, until 2005 or so almost 90 percent of oxygenated fuel contained MTBE (methyl tertiary butyl ether). While we know that MTBE is toxic to humans, and is a likely carcinogen, it is not yet known what level of contamination is safe, if any. MTBE has been detected in drinking water supplies throughout the country, especially in areas where reformulated gas was mandated, where it had a nasty habit of leaking from underground storage tanks. MTBE is particularly frightening because it doesn't break down easily under natural conditions and persists for years. (Blewett and Embree, *What's in the Air,* pp. 61–65; see also the EPA's MTBE homepage at www.epa.gov/mtbe.)

experts would say this is an overly optimistic and naive outlook, considering the nation's curiously persistent attachment to large gasoline-powered vehicles and the big picture of climate change.

WHAT AM I BREATHING AND WHAT DOES IT DO TO ME?

The fact remains that cyclists are still subjected to dangerously high doses of a multitude of poisons, despite the improvements in air quality. Here are the main pollutants we should be concerned about.

- CARBON MONOXIDE. Carbon Monoxide (CO) is a poisonous product of the imperfect, incomplete combustion of gasoline and other hydrocarbon fuels. (During complete combustion, the carbon in the fuel is fully oxidized into carbon dioxide [CO_2], a nontoxic gas.) Back in the day, CO was the most obviously toxic of all the tailpipe pollutants, and the first to catch the world's attention, because of its uncanny ability to knock folks out and put them to sleep—forever. Even with the improvements in engine technology and fuel composition, and the addition of catalytic converters, CO gas still reaches dangerous concentrations in American cities on a regular basis.

  Breathing CO reduces the flow of oxygen in the bloodstream. The national standard for CO dictates a maximum allowable concentration of nine parts per million over an eight-hour period ("not to be exceeded more than once per year," according to the US National Ambient Air Quality Standard), but readings have been taken among groups of idling cars at about one thousand parts per million![6] If you were to hang out for too long in that much CO, you would pass out and die. Luckily, such concentrations do not last for long, as cars eventually move, the air mixes up in the breeze, and so on.

  CO concentrations vary wildly and depend on many factors, so it's difficult to say for sure what kind of dose urban cyclists receive in their day-to-day travels. That said, an average of ten to twenty parts per million is probably a safe estimate of a cyclist's exposure during a spin through the typical large American city, with the occasional spike far in excess of those levels.[7] At these concentrations cyclists often notice the more subtle effects of CO, in the form of headaches, light-headedness, and general blah. Although CO is odorless and tasteless, it comes as a package deal with other ingredients of exhaust that you can detect, so if you're smelling that nearby traffic jam, you're also sucking down a good dose of CO.

- HYDROCARBONS. Hydrocarbons are molecules made of hydrogen and carbon atoms in various combinations. The volatile hydrocarbons in gasoline are what explode and make engines turn. Unfortunately, because there is no such thing as perfect combustion, a portion of these hydrocarbons remain unburned and come out in the exhaust. A large portion of the hydrocarbon molecules in fuel don't even make it that far, evaporating into the air from engine compartments and gas tanks. This is a very bad thing for cyclists and everyone else, because hydrocarbons cause cancer. Perhaps the most notorious of these hydrocarbon molecules is benzene, which has been found to increase cancer risk at very low levels of ingestion. Benzene constitutes about 2 percent of American gasoline.[8]

  Hydrocarbons cause additional problems by combining with nitrogen oxides (NOx) in sunlight to produce ozone (O_3), another harmful irritant.

- NITROGEN OXIDES. In the combustion chamber of an engine, extremely high temperatures cause oxygen and nitrogen atoms—the main ingredients of pure, lovely air—to form nitrogen oxides. The most notorious of the nitrogen oxides in exhaust is nitrogen dioxide (NO_2). The complete catalog of effects of NO_2 on individuals has not been pinned down, but scientists have shown that breathing lots of it can damage one's immune system and cause injury to the lungs. Normal exposure levels in urban areas could decrease lung function and exacerbate such existing problems as asthma and bronchitis.[9] Nitrogen dioxide is a key ingredient in acid rain and teams up with hydrocarbons in sunlight to form "photochemical oxidants" such as ozone.

- OZONE. Ozone (O_3) causes a lot of confusion. On the one hand, we're supposed to be worried about the destruction of the ozone layer, because it protects us from the harmful rays of the sun. On the other hand, we're told that ozone is a harmful pollutant and an indirect product of automobile exhaust. In fact both are true.

Ozone is the three-atom version of oxygen. It exists naturally in the environment and forms a thin layer high above our planet, where it intercepts ultraviolet radiation. Ozone molecules are also created by a photochemical reaction when nitrogen oxides and hydrocarbons from motor-vehicle exhaust and industrial emissions are cooked in the sunlight. Cyclists should be concerned about this human-made brew because ozone is an oxidant that attacks the body's cells and tissues, especially in the lungs.[10] Inflammation and damage to the immune system have been shown to result from ingestion of ozone. At low levels it makes you cough, wheeze, and ache. It constricts the airways and wrecks lung function. Damage from ozone may be cumulative, progressive, and irreversible, but this has not been proven.[11]

In short, ozone is bad news unless it stays in its place: about thirty miles up in the stratosphere. An expanded awareness of the health effects of O_3 led the EPA to recommend tightening the standard for this pollutant in 1997 to an eight-hour average of just 0.08 parts per million, down from 0.12 parts per million. The new standard survived a concerted challenge from industry and a long period in legal purgatory, and when it emerged as law most major American metro areas stood in violation of it. In 2008 the standard was changed to 0.075 parts per million—"Annual fourth-highest daily maximum 8-hr concentration, averaged over 3 years."[12] Sounds like a really complicated way to get away with some $#!*, doesn't it? Many cities still struggle to meet the pre-1997 standard.

- PARTICULATE MATTER. This broad category includes many different types of pollutants, including some of the hydrocarbons listed above, which emerge from tailpipes as solids that float in the air. Black hydrocarbon-filled clouds of diesel exhaust are the most obvious culprit in terms of suspended particulate matter (SPM). But suspended particulates come in many other forms and from many other sources.

Regulators have turned their attention to particulates in recent decades, primarily because a number of case control studies have shown a causal relationship between SPM and what scientists call "morbidity." Simply put, researchers found that people in areas with high levels of SPM die sooner than people in other areas; perhaps even more frightening, they found that more people die on specific high-SPM days. Particulate pollution has a way of pushing folks with existing conditions, such as heart disease, right over the edge. Not to mention the fact that many of the particles in question are known to be carcinogenic. So if it doesn't get you now, it might get you later.[13]

At some point you may have heard someone jabbering on about PM-10. PM-10 is the favored term for particulates 10 microns in width or smaller. A 10-micron particle is about one fifth the width of the typical human hair. Such particles float around all day and can be breathed deeply into the lungs, where they are likely to stay. The PM-10 scare gave birth to the PM-2.5 scare. The 2.5-micron-and-under specks appear to be even more sneaky and dangerous.

In addition to exhaust particles, SPM consists of a multitude of other ingredients. Some of the most common of these include pulverized sand and gravel, masonry dust and dirt from construction sites, and, my personal favorite, tire dust. A single vehicle tire, as it wears down, can lose several pounds of rubber each year; some of this rubber stays on the streets, but some of the particles are fine enough to become SPM. Allergists have identified tiny black specks of rubber in the mucus coughed up by their patients.[14]

BREATHING STRATEGIES FOR THE CYCLIST

As with crashes and traffic accidents, there is no way for the cyclist to completely eliminate the danger of air pollution—it's just part of the game. But we can employ a multitude of strategies that will help minimize the risk.

- BREATHE THROUGH THE NOSE. Breathing through the nose, rather than the mouth, is the easiest and one of the most effective ways to minimize ingestion of harmful pollution, especially particulates. The human nose has evolved over millions of years to function as a high-tech air filter. When you inhale through the mouth, there is a good chance that unwanted particles will end up buried deep in the lungs, but if a particle is to make it all the way through the nasal passages and into the lungs, it must somehow pass through a gauntlet of defenses to get there. The much smaller size of the nasal airways, first of all, makes it more likely that pollutants will get snagged against the side. The nasal passages are lined by mucus membranes that secrete, of course, mucus (also known as snot in some circles). Nasal mucus moistens inhaled air before it reaches the lungs and also traps unwanted particles in its slimy grip. The other defenses include the obvious and visible nose hairs, but also the equally hardworking ciliated cells that lie deeper in the nasal cavity. Each of these cells sprouts what is essentially a microscopic hair made of protoplasm. The trapped particles, caught in the pleasantly named "mucus blanket," are constantly swept out of the airways by the movements of the cilia and usually end up in the stomach, or back in the street, perhaps after a farmer blow.[15]

- EASE UP. During strenuous exercise we obviously consume more air, and we tend to breathe through our mouths in an effort to suck in more oxygen, so consequently our lungs can be exposed to much higher levels of pollution.[16] When the air gets nasty, slow down enough to keep your breathing steady and your mouth closed on the inhale. Slower riding is usually safer riding anyway.

- REJECT BAD AIR. Micromanage your breathing. No two puffs of air are created equal. If you are about to pass through a cloud of dust or diesel exhaust, hold your breath for a few seconds. When you catch the unmistakable whiff of hydrocarbons entering your nose, there is no law that says you have to inhale that junk deeply into your lungs. Blow it out! Reject it! With any luck, ten or twenty meters down the road you will find a relatively crisp, clean volume of air for your breathing pleasure.

- CHOOSE A CLEANER ROUTE. Studies using personal dosage-monitoring devices show that pollution concentrations vary quite a bit from place to place within any given area. The distribution, however, is not random, and can be predicted to some extent. The concentration of auto-sourced air pollution is governed largely by a few simple rules: (1) High-traffic areas tend to be about twice as polluted as quiet residential neighborhoods. (2) Downtown areas, with streets packed tight into concrete canyons between tall buildings, tend to hold higher concentrations of pollution than open areas with the same traffic patterns, because of restricted airflow. By the same token, air in tunnels and parking garages is the most polluted air in the city. (3) Stop-and-go driving produces more emissions than highway driving. Not only do cars on the highways spew less exhaust, their speed churns the air and thus disperses toxins. That's not to say you should be out riding on the highway—it's probably illegal anyway—but you might want to think about avoiding the lurchy, stop-and-go routes. (4) Finally, on a smaller scale, there is more pollution hanging around in the middle of the street than off to the sides; the farther away from the cars, the cleaner it gets. Air around an off-street bike path will be cleaner than air in the street.[17]

Looking at these factors—especially the first one—you can see that the cleanest routes in terms of air pollution might correspond nicely with the cleanest routes in terms of traffic. What luck! Once again, a little patience goes a long way. Charting a route through residential areas, away from busy arterial streets, can save you a lot of headaches (literally), although it might cost you some time.

- AVOID RUSH HOUR. Schedules often demand that the cyclist be right out there in the mix with the twice-daily flood of auto commuters. If you have the luxury of doing so, ride during off-peak hours and significantly reduce your exposure to air pollution, as well as bad drivers.

- AVOID RIDING ON HIGH-POLLUTION DAYS. Most major cities have programs that notify residents about high-pollution days, usually in the local paper or on the cheesy morning faux-news program. Forget about all that. Your nose and eyes are probably better detectors than the remote meters set up by your local health department (which may have placed their monitoring stations well outside the high-traffic areas to avoid violations of the federal clean-air standards, as such violations may cost your city precious millions of federal highway dollars under the Clean Air Act). If you walk outside in the morning and immediately smell the pollution, or see it hanging in the trees like fog, it may be a good day to use the public transportation system if it's available.

High-pollution days take on a whole new meaning in areas that are prone to temperature inversions, such as Los Angeles and Denver. A temperature inversion is a topsy-turvy meteorological phenomenon during which cold air becomes trapped beneath a layer of warm air. An inversion will trap pollution below the warm layer as surely as if a Plexiglas dome had been placed over the city. Avoid riding on such days, if possible.

- USE A MASK. Wearing a mask with a carbon filter will keep the particulates and ozone out of your body, although it does nothing to stop carbon monoxide, the density of which is very similar to air itself. Aside from the material benefits, some of these masks give a very eerie postapocalyptic look to the wearer, an effect that seems to shake a lot of people out of their comfort zone. Such masks make drivers, at least for a second or two, think about the poisons they're producing. Making a point through fashion—this fits in nicely with the passive-aggressive tendencies of many cyclists.

DOES AIR POLLUTION CANCEL THE HEALTH BENEFIT OF CYCLING?

Who knows? Opinions are divided. The truth is that nobody knows for sure. It's a rather complex issue when you try to sort through the science.

The concern is that cyclists—by virtue of their being out in the air and at times breathing more of it, more deeply, than other folks do—might be doing themselves undue harm. On the other hand, cyclists are able to escape many traffic jams and other high-pollution situations in which drivers have no choice but to sit and stew. And cyclists, thanks to the physiological effects of exercise, tend to be healthier than average people and their immune systems tend to be more robust. What pollution they do breathe in may be more effectively neutralized. (So, a better question might be: Do the health benefits of cycling cancel the negative effects of air pollution?)

You don't have to travel too far out on a limb to claim that cycling is plenty healthy, given the alternatives. Let's be realistic: If you're not going to ride your bike, what are you going to do? Never leave the house? Ride the bus? Walk? Or sit on your bum in a car, breathing slightly less of the same bad air while suffering at stoplights, in traffic jams, dying of frustration and stress? Come on! Any real cyclist already knows the answer to these questions.

Given the availability of the defensive strategies mentioned above, the choice is clear. Ride your bike and be happy.

CHAPTER 6

PUNCTURES AND FLATS

FLAT PREVENTION

Short of using solid rubber tires like the wheelmen of the 1880s (not recommended), there are several common methods of preventing punctures, each with varying degrees of effectiveness and slightly different side effects. Lots of riders like to use flat-resistant tires, which use harder and thicker rubber than regular tires and often have Kevlar strips embedded in them as well. Some folks use plastic strips that are installed between the tire and tube. Another strategy involves the use of a liquid sealant, commonly known as "Slime," inside the inner tube. (And tubes can be purchased pre-Slimed.)

The primary downside of using these things can be summed up in two words: rolling resistance. The use of thick, heavy tires, plastic strips inside the tires, and especially liquid in the tubes adds significant resistance and makes riding noticeably more difficult. Many experienced riders would also say that making the bike more sluggish subtracts a little enjoyment from the ride as well. But these are subjective valuations. Worth it or not, there's no free lunch when it comes to flat prevention.

Flat haters will also learn that none of these crude mechanical methods is completely effective. Despite spending extra money and time and enduring the pig-like feel of Kevlar-encased, goo-filled tires, you could very well find yourself with a puncture anyway. With this in mind, perhaps it is best to focus on different methods of prevention that are more about route choice and riding style, and to learn enough about patching inner tubes that the thought of doing it isn't nearly so intimidating.

FLAT REPAIR EQUIPMENT

Even with flat-resistant tires and tubes, flats happen. Flats are common enough that cyclists, to achieve any semblance of self-sufficiency, must be able to repair them anywhere they occur in a reasonable amount of time. This means that all the necessary tools—a pump, patch kit, and two tire levers—must be carried on every significant ride. Consider this equipment part of the bicycle and take it wherever the bike goes. Some experienced riders would consider an extra inner tube and cab fare to be included on the essentials list.

THE AIR INSIDE THE TUBE AND TIRE COULD BE THE MOST IMPORTANT COMPONENT OF THE MACHINE.

TIRE LEVERS, MINIPUMP, PATCH KIT, AND A SPARE TUBE

Having experienced a host of problems with self-adhesive, or "stick-on," patches, I recommend using the traditional-style patch kits with "glue."* These kits work wonders when the directions are followed. Some folks claim that the so-called "glueless" instant patches have been greatly improved over the decades, but even if they do the job as well (highly unlikely), the time saved by using them would be, at best, about five minutes. And not five minutes of work, mind you, but five minutes of relaxing and sitting around. On the other hand, they are less likely to dry out than that tube you've been carrying around for a couple of years. So the glueless patch may work when you need it most. It couldn't hurt to carry both.

Make sure your pump matches the style of the valve stems on your bicycle (Presta valve stems are the thin type with the locking pin, and Schrader valves are the old-school type, like those on car tires). Many pump heads can be set up to fit either type of valve stem. CO_2 cartridges are easy, fun, and useful—they're nice to have on board—but unfortunately they can't take the place of an actual pump.

THE "GLUE" IN TRADITIONAL PATCH KITS IS REALLY VULCANIZING FLUID.

PRESTA VALVE

---

*In reality, "glueless" patches are the kind of patches that use glue (the adhesive on the back of the patch), while traditional patch kits really are "glueless." The little tubes of "glue" in traditional patch kits actually contain vulcanizing fluid, which works in a completely different way.

FIXING A FLAT: A PRIMER

It may be glass or a thorn or some random piece of metal that does the deed. It may be a pinch flat, or the dreaded blowout. Chances are you will collect several of each type of flat as the miles accumulate. These occurrences should not send you into fits of frustration, nor should they send you into the bike shop for assistance. Flats should not even raise your eyebrow with the slightest hint of surprise. The inconvenience of dealing with them is easily overcome by a little knowledge and experience. Fixing flats is no big deal.

Readers with a good working knowledge of flat repair can skip this next section. For the rest of you, here is an opinionated how-to in fourteen steps. Yes, fourteen is a lot of steps for something that is supposedly "no big deal." Don't be alarmed; it's really five general steps broken down into more specific components.

1. Remove the wheel from the frame. The rear wheel can be tricky to remove and install. It will be a lot easier if you take note of which cog the chain is wrapped around and place it back onto that same cog when reinstalling. All of the fork dropouts on late-model bikes have "lawyer tabs," a ridiculous bump that undermines the concept of quick-release wheels.

2. Quickly check the outer surface of the tire to see if you can locate the puncture. There may be a visible thorn or shard of glass sticking out or an audible hiss of escaping air. If you can locate the puncture before actually removing the tube, this will make your job easier. If not, no worries.

3. If the tube is still holding some air, release the air by using the valve.

4. Use the tire levers to pry the tire off the rim. With the first lever, gingerly crowbar one side of the tire out of the rim, and hook the back end of the lever around a spoke to hold it in place. Then use the second lever, a few inches away from the first, to continue prying the tire off the rim, section by section. Be careful not to "pinch" the tube, which would create an additional hole.

5. Pull the tube out of the tire, but leave the valve poking through the rim to make things a little easier. There is no reason to completely remove

the tube unless the puncture happens to be right above the valve stem, or you can't locate the hole and need to submerge the tube.

6. Very carefully, run your fingers (or a wad of easily snagged material like pantyhose) all the way around the inside of the tire to find any objects poking through it. It will likely be very small, and very sharp. Remove the objects from the tire and note their locations, which will help you find the hole(s) in the tube. At this point, become an active learner. Observe the perpetrator. What is it? Where did it come from? How did you pick it up, and how can you avoid it in the future? Refrain from tossing the little beast, whatever it is, back into the street.

7. Pump about fifteen or twenty squirts of air into the tube, enough to reveal the puncture's exact location with a hiss. If pumping up the tube fails to give the tube any shape, the hole is quite large—probably caused by a blowout or a pinch flat–type event. If you can't find any puncture, remove the tube entirely, submerge it in water while inflated, and look for telltale bubbles. Obviously, this method might be problematic while out on a ride. Mystery punctures are a great reason to carry an extra tube.

8. Once the puncture is located, use the sandpaper in the patch kit to rough up an area about one and a half inches in diameter around the hole. This removes the shiny substance that coats the tube, which will prevent any patch from sticking well. Also take care to sand off any ridges around the puncture, or these could create tiny air passages under the patch.

9. Spread a thin layer of the "glue" in the patch kit around the puncture point, enough so the area covered is bigger than the area of the patch.

10. Let the vulcanizing fluid dry—long enough that it no longer feels tacky to the touch. This usually takes a few minutes at least.

11. Peel the patch away from the foil backing and press it over the hole. Press hard all over the patch. Using a tire lever or similar object might help. There should be no bubbles under the patch or loose edges. It is not necessary to remove the clear plastic on top.

12. Stuff the patched tube back into the tire—some folks like to add a few pumps of air to the tube to give it some shape prior to this—and work the tire onto the rim with your thumbs. Usually you can get the bead

most of the way on and then curl your fingers around the tire and roll the rest on with your hand. Some rim-tire combos are extremely problematic. Avoid using tire levers to install a tire. If the last bit of tire refuses to go on the rim, pump up the tube a bit, then let the air out completely and try again.

13. Pump the tire back up to the desired pressure. Make sure it's properly seated, with no sections of tube caught between the tire bead and the rim. Be careful pumping if you are using Presta valves, because vigorous, uncivilized motion will break the valve or tear it away from the tube, effectively ruining the tube. Don't seriously tighten the bolt that holds the Presta valve where it comes out of the rim until you're done pumping.

14. Does the tire feel like it's holding air? Put the wheel back on the bike.

Whatever you do, don't skip Step 6, 8, or 10. These steps are absolutely crucial to a successful flat repair, but few cyclists give them the respect they deserve.

It's a good strategy to carry a spare tube (or two) while cycling, especially in thorn-prone areas. That way you can just slap the new tube in and save a lot of time. Fix the bad tube later, and make that your spare tube. If you employ this strategy, don't forget Step 6!

A note on rim strips—the piece of rubber, plastic, or cloth that covers the inside of the rim. Its purpose is to protect the inflated tube from the sharp edges of eyelets and spoke nipples on the inside of the rim. The cloth strips are best because they stay in place and last. The rubber strips can move and expose the edges they're meant to cover, and plastic strips fall apart. Usually, a rim strip is a no-brainer and demands very little, if any, attention. But if you find yourself suffering multiple flats on the underside of tubes, suspect a disintegrating or improperly seated rim strip.

BROKEN GLASS

Nationwide, broken glass is the most time-honored and feared perpetrator of punctures for road cyclists. It's evil powers, however, are much overrated.

There are two general types of broken glass to be found in American cities: tempered glass and "bottle glass."

Tempered glass is hardened by forced cooling during the manufacturing process. The faster-than-normal cooling compresses the surface of the glass, leaving it much more resistant to breaking than nontempered glass. This kind of glass is used in the rear and side windows of motor vehicles (windshields are a shatter-resistant laminate). When fractured, a car window made of tempered glass collapses into a pile of soft-edged pebbles. The pieces usually aren't sharp and rarely puncture bicycle tires. Feel free to ignore it. Bottle glass (and the glass from automobile side mirrors) is another matter entirely. It shatters into jagged pieces, any one of which has the potential to cause a flat.

On the street it's possible to distinguish broken bottle glass from broken tempered glass, even while riding. Along with the obvious difference in appearance, location can provide additional clues. Tempered glass is generally confined to streets and parking lots and, due to car break-ins, is often found in piles in the gutter or just outside the parking lane on narrow streets. Bottle glass, on the other hand, is found everywhere. If there's glass on a bike path or anywhere else that is off-limits to motor traffic, it's almost always bottle glass. Bottle glass is occasionally green or dark brown, a dead giveaway, or has beer-related writing on it, also a dead giveaway.

Avoid bottle glass if you can. Steer around it if no other vehicles are present, but please keep your priorities straight—flats are the least of your worries as a cyclist. Pick a new route rather than ride over batches of bottle glass each day.

GLASSPHALT

Don't be afraid. It's only "glassphalt."

Glassphalt paving material can cause hopeless glassophobes to suffer flashbacks and convulsions. This special asphalt sparkles in a way that mimics very closely the appearance of a biblical amount of glass shards scattered on the road. If it looks like crushed glass, well, that's because it is crushed glass. Glassphalt incorporates a small percentage of recycled glass, called cullet, into the aggregate mix.

Decades ago the use of glassphalt was driven by economics. There were so many sources of cullet around that it was considered a useless waste product. It was being given away, and those responsible for paving and resurfacing streets had the bright idea that it could be used in the road mix as a way to cut expenses. Today, however, with the widespread use of plastic bottles and the general decrease in sources of glass, asphalt containing crushed glass costs more than regular asphalt. Even with the added expense, it is still used occasionally, because it significantly increases the durability of the road surface.[1]

Like some sort of cruel prank, the sparkly bits of embedded glass disappear as you ride toward them, while still more come into view beyond, flashing like mad. Even knowing that glassphalt won't cause flat tires, it's hard not to experience a tiny panic attack while gazing upon what appears to be a vast sea of broken glass.

GOAT HEADS

Puncture Vine, Goat Head, Sandbur, African Devil Weed . . . call it what you want, it doesn't matter. The thorny seeds produced by *Tribulus terrestris,* as it is known in the science books, are the number-one cause of punctures for urban cyclists in some cities in the western United States. Thorns in the west, rust in the east.

Tribulus terrestris forms a mat along the ground, with tough vines that sprout very small dark green leaves and nice-looking little yellow flowers, in addition to the spiked seeds that start out green and soft but mature into thorns as solid as hardwood. The mat formed by one tribulus plant, from a single taproot, can easily grow six feet across, and it can produce several thousand seeds. Tribulus seeds fall away from the plant, and some of the lucky ones go off to see the world.[2]

Strangely enough, hopeful weightlifting-type guys have been buying supplements said to contain extracts of the *Tribulus terrestris* weed, which is supposed to give them bigger muscles and more serious erections, you know, the usual. To just about anyone else, tribulus is considered to be a noxious weed, an invasive species, and a major source of frustration. Accidentally introduced with a load of Mediterranean livestock some time in the 1800s, low-maintenance tribulus is now fully living the American Dream. It thrives in so-called areas of disturbance, the sandy, infertile, chemical-soaked soils where other plants fail. That's why it loves cities so much—a city can be described as a vast area of disturbance, and cities are full of rolling rubber, which is tribulus's best friend.

In the early years of the automobile, tires were essentially the same on cars and bicycles, so goat head thorns frequently stranded motorists along with cyclists. In California, where the Mediterranean-like climate is particularly friendly to tribulus, the highway department used to douse the roadsides with diesel fuel hoping to vanquish the evil weed, to no avail. Making very thick tires was the only answer.[3] Ironically, tribulus was the mortal enemy of the rubber car tire, yet the rubber tire was the best thing ever to happen to tribulus. Having adapted over millions of years to stick in the fur and paws of passing beasts, the patient tribulus plant was gifted one of the greatest windfalls in all of evolutionary history with the near-simultaneous inventions of the rubber pneumatic tire, the safety bicycle, and the automobile. Together these technologies provided the perfect mechanism to transport tribulus's seeds across the continents.

Once confined only to the dry southwestern states, tribulus has now been found in all states except Massachusetts, New Hampshire, Vermont, and Maine. We can only assume that New England is next on its list. The various agencies responsible for controlling tribulus have failed, primarily because of the remarkable properties of the thorns. Not only do goat head seeds hitch rides cross-country and around the world, they can lie dormant in the ground for many years, perhaps decades, before sprouting—spiky little time bombs. Back in the 1960s, the government recognized, for a moment, the futility of dumping chemicals on Puncture Vine and imported tribulus-eating weevils into the States. The success of this plan has obviously been limited, although the weevils seem to be enjoying their new home.

Tribulus terrestris is the most well-known member of the Caltrop family (Zygophyllaceae). In medieval warfare, a caltrop was a small iron device composed of four spikes. It was designed in such a way that it could be tossed on the ground in front of advancing cavalry and, no matter how it landed, one of the spikes would always be sticking up.

Tribulus thorns work much the same way. With one impaler always pointed skyward, those little caltrops cut right into your rubber, effortlessly. Tubes advertised as "thorn-resistant" should be looked upon with a healthy degree of skepticism, as should tubes that are supposed to patch themselves with green goo. The thick knobs of mountain-bike tires, by simple virtue of their being thicker than the thorns themselves, can keep the thorns from making contact with the inner tube. But since the knobs cover only part of the mountain-bike tire, protection is incomplete. Some brands of touring tires are said to be thick enough to foil thorns, and some cyclists report good results from protective plastic strips, but these

SHARP!

exact a significant toll in increased weight and rolling resistance.

Technology probably won't save you from thorns, but a little bit of common sense might. The most effective strategy for avoiding thorn flats involves using the thorn's own frightening power against it—thorn jujitsu. Since the thorns are collected by any tire or soft-soled shoe that presses down on them, simply ride where other bicycles, cars, or pedestrians have gone before. Ride near the center of bike paths and away from debris fields that collect in the least-used areas of streets, when possible. If you find yourself cruising through a vacant lot or across some random dirt patch, find the most established path and don't stray from it. Riding this way will drastically reduce your chances of being stung.

It's time we started giving this plant the respect it deserves after giving us a century-long ass-kicking. Hail tribulus! We surrender! Those living and cycling in the thorn zone should get to know the plant that produces the thorns. Learn not only what *Tribulus terrestris* looks like but also where and when it likes to grow. Where it now lives, it's there to stay. Where it doesn't live, it's probably on its way.

A THORNY DILEMMA

Let's say you look down at a stoplight and notice a nice-looking goat head thorn stuck in your front tire. Despite your consistent practice of thorn jujitsu, you've been stung. This presents a dilemma—to pluck or not to pluck. Eyeing the disposition of the goat head, you ask yourself a tough question: *Has that damn thorn pierced the tube?* Probably, but maybe not. There is the small chance that the thorn is askew and somehow failed to penetrate the inner tube. There is also the nagging possibility that the thorn has yet to puncture but will do so if it is not removed. You reach down and press on the tire with your thumb. Seems full enough, but that still doesn't answer your question. If the thorn has already pierced the tube, the leak of air caused by the perforation could be quite slow or nonexistent—thorns, you see, have a way of nicely plugging their own holes. In such a case, pulling the thorn out would only open the hole and allow the tube to deflate rapidly.

Do you feel lucky? It takes a confident and experienced cyclist to roll the dice and pluck away, happily and fearlessly, knowing that deft tube-patching skills will handle whatever consequences await. Those more fearful of having to fix a flat on-site will want to leave the thorn in the tire for as long as possible, where it serves as the perfect custom-size plug for any hole it makes.

These painful dilemmas become more urgent when the cyclist's tire is stuck with multiple thorns, a demoralizing but fairly common occurrence in thorn country. Two extra tubes, one for each wheel, provide some peace of mind when nothing else will.

RANDOM SHARPIES

Goat heads and bottle glass can be blamed for the vast majority of cyclists' punctures, but certainly not all of them. A small percentage of flat tires will be caused by a rogue's gallery of random debris. Among this group, nails, screws, and tacks of various kinds form the most common family of objects: the construction-grade fasteners. There are also staples, pop-tops, pins, campaign buttons, busted CD covers and other shards of plastic, dress shoe taps, pieces of wire, broken pencils, lawless twigs, valve cores, and an endless variety of unidentifiable machine parts lurking on the streets, waiting for unlucky cyclists to roll over them at just the right angle. It is quite useless to prepare for random encounters with random objects, aside from learning well how to patch a tube.

The punctures caused by this wreckage are generally violent and obvious and result in a rapid loss of air from the tube. In the case of nails and other tough, elongated pieces, the foreign object tends to penetrate all the way to the rim, leaving two big holes in the tube. Punctures of this sort can usually be patched in the normal way, provided there are enough patches left in the kit. If the object punches a hole in the tire casing that is large enough that the tube balloons out of the hole when inflated, the tire itself will have to be patched.

An interesting aspect of random-object punctures is that these punctures almost always occur in the rear tire rather than the front. We can imagine why. Most of these objects are lying flat on the street and are harmless in their sleeping position. But when a tire rolls over an object

THE SLICE IN THIS TIRE WAS CAUSED BY A SHARD OF PLASTIC IN THE STREET. THE TIRE IS NOT SALVAGEABLE.

like a nail or shard of plastic, the object snaps to attention, popping up off the ground. With two tires rolling over the object in quick succession, the front tire causes the object to stand up straight, and the rear tire receives the brunt of the attack.

PINCH FLATS

In general, pinch flats occur when a tire is underinflated for the conditions at hand. This type of flat is often associated with mountain biking on rocky trails, but it can occur in the urban setting. The mountain bikers developed tubeless tire systems that eliminated pinch flats even at low tire pressures, but tubeless tires also entail a number of fiddly logistical issues and aren't yet in widespread use among utility cyclists. Skinny tires are especially vulnerable to pinch flats when striking curbs, railroad tracks, potholes, or rocks in the road. Because they are associated with underinflation, pinch flats are symptomatic of a prior undetected slow leak, or simple negligence on the part of the cyclist. The occurrence of pinch flats on well-inflated tires calls into question the handling skills of the cyclist—fast, furious, and clumsy.

An experienced rider can feel a pinch flat at the exact moment it occurs. The tire "bottoms out" as it strikes an obstacle, and the wheel's rim impacts solidly with a clunk. This impact causes the inner tube to be pinched harshly in the tire casing as it comes together. Pinches like this cause a small but significant slit to open in the tube, or two matching slits arrayed in the familiar double-fanged snakebite pattern—which is why pinch flats are often referred to as "snakebites." When patching a pinch flat, always search for a second hole, usually about one centimeter apart from and parallel to the first. But don't stop there. If the cause of the underinflation leading to the pinch flat is a mystery, then search for a third hole and carefully grope the inside of the tire for the cause of a possible slow leak.

Pinch flats can be prevented easily by maintaining proper tire pressure (very firm to the thumb test) and by riding in a less than reckless manner.

BLOWOUTS

The frightening term "blowout" can be used to describe a few different types of events. Most commonly when a cyclist claims to have had a blowout, it means that the tube has exploded due to improper installation of the tire. Sometimes when a tire is worked onto a rim, a section of the tube is stuck between the rim and the tire bead. The faulty installation may go undetected even after the tire is pumped up hard. The unsuspecting cyclist goes out to ride, the tube steadily works its way to freedom, then *blam!* With nothing holding it back, a section of the tube explodes (contrary to popular belief, a tube can't explode spontaneously inside the tire). If the blowout occurs while the cyclist is cornering fast, there could be painful consequences. Blowouts like this can also occur when the bike is just sitting there in your house, which can cause heart attacks. *Blam!*

To prevent this most-common form of blowout, simply exercise some care when installing a tire. Make sure the tire is seated properly, with no sections of tube visible. As a way of ensuring good tire positioning, some like to inflate, deflate, then reinflate the tube after they install a tire, but this is really not necessary.

Another form of blowout occurs at the local gas station, when the recreational cyclist attaches the air compressor built for automobile tires to the Schrader valve on his or her bicycle. Damn, that thing fills up fast, don't it? *Blam!* Remember that the gas station compressor is designed to fill tires with vastly more volume than bicycle tires hold. The same source that requires a minute or two to fill a car tire could blow out your bike tire in about fifteen seconds.

A third type of blowout event is associated with excessive tire wear. And I'm talkin' excessive. When a tire—a rear tire, more than likely—is so absolutely finished that its rubber is completely gone, and even the inner casing is totally worn away in spots, there is nothing left between the inner tube and the road. The tube pokes out of the opening, grinds onto the road surface, and *blam!* (Actually, this sort of blowout sounds more like a *pifft!* than a *blam!*) Obviously, flats of this sort can be forestalled by replacing the bad tire. If gross tire wear looks likely to cause a flat in the immediate future—say, while you're out on a ride—switch the front tire to the back and you will probably make it home, or to the nearest bike shop.

If a tube pops due to excessive tire wear—*pifft!*—you must boot the tire in addition to patching the tube, or the tube will flat repeatedly. Ideally, use a small piece of rubber or denim and fit it on the inside of the tire to cover the worn-out spot. Some cyclists claim success using folded-up dollar bills for this application, but paper products will not last long. A strip of electrical tape or the like on the inside of a bedraggled tire can prolong its life another few hundred miles.

CHAPTER 7

EQUIPMENT

CYCLING EQUIPMENT

It is not really the place of this book to dole out too much detailed advice about equipment, clothing, maintenance—these sorts of things. If there is one point that consistently gets lost in the shuffle and should be reasserted here, it's that very little special equipment is required for most trips by bike in the city. To any new cyclists out there: Don't think you have to acquire hundreds of dollars' worth of gadgets and flashy clothing items before you can live the dream.

It is recommended that the rider obtain a helmet (of which the cheap models protect about as well as the fancy ones[1]), gloves, pump, patch kit, and tire levers to start out. Maybe a water bottle. Basically just a bike and the tools to fix a flat. You can wear regular clothing, for the most part. Many a happy mile has been ridden in tennis shoes. Soon you might decide to try out special pedals and shoes, padded shorts, and so on, and the fat will get burned off your bank account right quick. Or you may just decide that the add-ons are not helpful for your needs, in which case you will save quite a bit of money. However, you will miss the reassuring feeling that comes from joining a cult, which, to many cyclists, is actually their favorite part of the whole bicycle experience.

Bicycle equipment choices are often based on personal superstitions and arbitrary preferences. People hold zealous views about bikes and bike parts they've never seen. Cyclists become quite testy about their equipment choices. Criticizing the equipment choices of another rider can be as personal as calling them out on religious or family issues.

In fact, many very different choices will work. A mind-boggling number of equipment choice combinations are possible. There are many different paths to paradise. But there are also some dead ends.

In general, the cyclist buying equipment gets what he or she pays for and should look with a cynical eye at ridiculously cheap equipment. Cheap parts generally don't work as well or last as long as the expensive stuff. As the saying goes, choose any two: light, strong, cheap. There's a lot of truth in that. However, just because something is ungodly expensive doesn't mean it's important or well made, or that it's a good idea to buy it.

LIGHT, STRONG, CHEAP: CHOOSE ANY TWO.

Faddish parts have been an annoying problem in the bike industry from the beginning. The latest thing that everybody must have is forgotten three years later. Many of us have had experiences with gimmicky parts that we're still trying to forget.

At this late date there's almost no fancy idea that hasn't been conceived, fooled around with, and discarded. There is very little uncharted territory in bicycle technology. The most significant improvements of the past one hundred years have been materials related. Carbon frames, for instance, offer good benefits in terms of weight and strength.

Especially in the past few years, new materials have helped bikes become lighter and stronger—nicer—than ever before. But bikes are still bikes. Most contemporary cyclists will never own a bike as nice as the sub-twenty-pound race bikes of the 1890s. No doubt if steel were discovered tomorrow, it would be touted as the "greatest thing since carbon," or some such BS.

There have been some improvements in bicycle components, but few radical ones. An example of a very nice and relatively recent improvement in componentry is the incorporation of the shifters into the brake levers on road bikes, sometimes called "brifters." The mechanism allows the rider to keep both hands on the bars—on the brake levers, no less—while shifting and to shift easily while standing out of the saddle. This innovation is an important safety enhancement for city riders on road bikes.

SHOES WITH RECESSED CLEATS ALLOW THE WEARER TO WALK EASILY, ON THE TRAIL OR AT THE GROCERY STORE.

Another improvement is the clipless pedal, an innovation from the mountain bike realm. Wearing recessed-cleat cycling shoes in the city allows the rider to enjoy the power transfer and control of clipless without having to click around and waddle like a duck when off the bike. Don't be afraid to throw some freedom-enhancing mountain bike pedals on your road bike.

When choosing equipment, watch out for components that are designed specifically for rac-ing, unless that is what you plan to do with them. If something is made as light as possible, it may not stand up to the rigors of everyday riding. Beware of titanium bolts, for instance, as they are known to snap. Remember that when a pro racer's bike fails, a fresh one appears as if dropped from the clouds by the hand of God. Sure would be nice if all cyclists could enjoy such fancy service.

When choosing bikes and equipment, know that what everybody else rides or what everybody else does will probably not be the best guideline for you personally. Beware the sales associate at the bike shop who informs you of things you "need." Just get out and ride, and you will find out soon enough what you need and what you don't.

BIKE CHOICE

Which type of bicycle you choose to ride depends on convenience, style, personal priorities, what routes you ride, and what you need to carry. Three speeds, cruisers, BMX bikes, track bikes, cyclocross bikes, mountain bikes, folding bikes, recumbents, cargo bikes, and straight road bikes have all seen extensive action in America's cities, and all work well for certain purposes. Each has its own advantages and disadvantages. (Riders should shy away from ultracheap department store bikes, some of which are known to spontaneously disassemble themselves at the most inopportune time.)

The popular appeal of the mountain bike has to do with fashion; the more upright position, which attracts many beginners; and the fact that they are just plain awesome machines. Some curmudgeons wouldn't dream of putting a mountain bike into regular service on the city streets, but these rigs bring some real advantages over their lighter, faster road cousins for this application.

A real mountain bike enjoys potholes, a real road bike does not. Some of the most brutal drainage grates, those that eat road wheels for breakfast, can be tamed by a mountain bike. Curbs are less threatening to a mountain bike. And, since mountain-bike tires put more rubber between the pavement and the inner tube than road tires do, they are much less prone to flatting from glass and thorns.

Light mountain bikes with rigid forks work especially well in the city. Knobby tires are unnecessary on pavement until it snows, but big tires can be helpful all year long.

Full-suspension downhill bikes, built to jump off cliffs, are overkill for street riding, but many cyclists enjoy them and put them to good use. Other riders like a mountain bike with slick tires pumped up hard. Whatever works.

In general, road bikes are faster and roll farther with less effort, but they are somewhat more vulnerable to the city's little obstacles. It is natural for riders to gravitate to the road-bike option as their skill level and confidence grows. Road bikes are for pavement, and the city is paved, no denying it. Most longtime riders who have tested many different types of bicycles in the urban setting prefer classic, lightweight road machines.

A MOUNTAIN BIKE WITH A RIGID FORK MAKES A FINE MACHINE FOR
GETTING AROUND THE CITY.

Bicycle manufacturers have created new categories that mix the trendy
look and plush ride of the mountain bike with design features specific to the
needs of commuters; sometimes these bikes are called "hybrids" and "city
bikes."

Cyclocross is a rapidly growing sport in the United States that has been
popular in Europe for decades, particularly in Belgium. It demands a beefy
style of modified road-racing bike with cantilever brakes and clearance for
wide tires. Invented long ago, these bikes are designed for a punishing form

of off-season racing called cyclocross, but they turned out to be quite suitable for everyday use in the urban setting. Some riders find a good "cross bike" to be the ultimate ride, especially in winter.

An advantage that touring-style bikes, city bikes, and some of the hybrid/comfort family of bikes have over their sleeker cousins is that they have eyelets brazed onto the frame near the dropouts. This feature greatly eases the installation of effective front and rear fenders and racks. Anywhere outside the desert, fenders are extremely important tools for everyday commuters, because they keep rainwater and oily road grime from splattering all over the rider's clothing. A rear rack, when combined with panniers or some other container, allows the rider to avoid hauling a backpack and thus avoid a sweaty back.

Long popular in Europe, cargo bikes are an emerging trend on this side of the pond. The station wagon of bicycles, these have modified frames with platforms to haul your groceries, beer, and toddlers, sometimes all at once. Bike trailers are another option for hauling the goods home, though they add another degree of complexity to the ride.

Whether one rides a mountain, road, city, "Dutch," or hybrid model is not all that important. What is most important is that the bike be reasonably well maintained so that the bike itself does not cause an accident, and it should fit the rider very well.

SUSPENSION ON THE ROAD

Unnecessary.

That is, for riding on the paved surfaces of the world, crumbling though they may be, any suspension added to the suspension already provided by your arms and legs, a decent set of twenty-five- to thirty-five-millimeter-wide tires, and the natural flex of a bicycle frame and saddle rails and such would be superfluous. More harm than good, probably. It took us a few years to figure this out.

For a normal civilian road cyclist, suspension forks add unnecessary weight, cost, and complexity to the machine. Quality suspension forks are expensive. One nice mountain-bike fork costs as much as two or three decent commuter bikes combined! So any fork spec'd on a modestly priced hybrid or commuter bike is going to be a bargain-basement rip-off of the real thing, and will function appropriately.

On the road, even a great shock will sap energy, turning some of your forward motion into up-and-down movement. A low-quality or poorly tuned suspension fork will significantly diminish out-of-saddle acceleration and climbing. That's a high price to pay for some moments of comfort over pot-holes or rough stretches of road.

You already possess four extremely high-tech and very effective shock absorbers: two arms and two legs. Human limbs (and the neck) function so well as suspension components while bicycling, it's almost as if they evolved for that specific purpose.

For any type of cycling, keep the arms and legs bent. Occasionally we find ourselves locking out the knees or elbows for a spell while coasting along, and that's fine, but otherwise keep the limbs relaxed, bent at least a little. This helps you to absorb bumps in the road and makes it much easier to control the bike, especially in turns.

Keeping the grip on the relaxed side helps you relax the wrist, elbow, and shoulder, which in turn allows the whole arm to function as the perfect natural spring that it is. To utilize the magical suspension powers of the legs, simply get over the saddle with the knees slightly bent. Now get both sets of shock absorbers working at the same time. The air cushion in the tires smooths the ride even more.

The bottom line: You already have more than enough suspension on the road. Just learn how to use it.

TRACK BIKES AND FIXED GEARS

These days an urban cyclist is about as likely to be on a fixed-gear bike as any other sort of bicycle. We're not entirely sure how we got to this point, although it's clear that fashion has been one of the forces fueling the fixed-gear fad.

According to one charming theory, fixed-gear fever came to the United States in the 1970s with immigrants from Caribbean islands like Jamaica, where the people had grown used to riding colonizers' leftover nineteenth-century machines. Bikes of that vintage had fixed gears, and most were essentially brakeless as well. The immigrants came to the United States and started working as messengers in New York City, using the style of machine they were comfortable riding. While this was no big deal to the immigrants themselves, it happened to cause a sensation that spread through the messenger community and then to citizen cyclists around the world. It's a nice story. I hope it's true.

It's possible to ride a fixed-gear track bike with no hand brakes in a crowded city. Thousands of American cyclists do it every day. A very different style is used—a much slower style—because the lack of brakes pretty much eliminates the possibility of the full panic stop.

A skilled rider can stop a fixed-gear bike pretty well, but not as quickly as he or she could on a freewheel bike with hand brakes. For this reason many fixed-gear riders slap a front brake on their bike to add significant stopping power, although this cancels some of the cool and doesn't solve the problem of stopping a fixed wheel. (Single-speed bikes with freewheels always have at least a front brake, and usually a rear brake as well.)

Interestingly, the limitations of the brakeless bike seem to cause its riders to compensate by riding more conservatively, and perhaps with more awareness, than they otherwise would. As with the "Idaho Stop," there is no epidemic of crashes we can point to that proves the extra danger of riding brakeless.

Track bikes and fixie-converted road bikes are not necessarily the most practical machines for getting around a crowded city and are limiting in many respects. Like the other bicycle types, however, the fixed-gear track bike has its own set of advantages. Fixed-gear riders have more precise control of the machine in one sense, because they can change the bike's speed instantly through a direct connection to the drivetrain. The simplicity of the bike is also a major plus: It's cheaper than a regular road bike and can be built in about twenty minutes by an experienced mechanic.

In winter the track bike has no gears or cables to freeze up, and the bike's "brakes" still work in wet conditions. (This was a big deal for messengers, who never got days off for bad weather.) A real track machine is also lighter and quicker than a road-racing bike. An added bonus of the fixed-gear bike is that not very many dime-store hooligans know how to ride one. This reduces the chance that a bike thief will successfully pedal away on it. If someone tries, it could provide the afternoon entertainment.

TRACK BIKES HAVE CHANGED VERY LITTLE IN THE PAST 120 YEARS.

Practitioners might try to tell you that riding a fixed-gear bike teaches proper pedaling technique. It's true that having one gear forces constant pedaling no matter the grade or speed, so riders might get used to high-revolutions-per-minute spinning, which could be a good thing. However, because the cranks turn automatically when the bike rolls, those who are accustomed to riding fixed naturally learn to rely on the gear to supply part of their pedaling motion. If the helpful mechanism is suddenly removed—the rider installs a freewheel—that dead spot on the backside of the stroke becomes obvious. The pedal stroke that was efficient and appropriate for the fixed gear is revealed to be halting, unsmooth without it. Fortunately, the faulty pedaling can be unlearned after a short time. The myths about the benefits of training on a fixed gear are a lot harder to kill.

Track bikes are very smooth, elegant machines. If you're riding it primarily as a fashion statement, however, you're several decades behind.

BIKE FIT

No matter what type of bike you use, the most important consideration will be the fit of the bike. Does it feel comfortable? Does it feel right? Do you like it?

If you purchase a new bicycle and have no idea how it should feel, be sure to shop at a local bike shop instead of a big-box national retailer. Scope out the most experienced and helpful employees, and have them set up the bike the way it generally should be before you roll it out the door. Some shops have a special system of fitting bicycles to customers in a meticulous way, but some will just eyeball it, and that will probably work out just fine.

Like many things in the bicycle world, there is no real consensus on the subject of bike fit. But there are lots of old cycling coaches, racers, and self-appointed gurus out there who would love to tell you what they think about it. This proselytizing would seem to be a dubious exercise, as bike fit and position eventually boil down to matters of personal preference. Attempts to make a science of bike fit are frustrated by the unique physical proportions of each cyclist.

Even with all the differing opinions and differing body types, there are still a few areas of common ground. For instance, when the pedal is in the six o'clock position and the ball of the foot is over the pedal axle, the leg should be slightly bent. The saddle should be set just below the point where the rider's hips rock back and forth during pedaling. That loosely covers seat height, which is arguably the most important aspect of bike fit, and perhaps the easiest.

From this baseline, tweak the remaining adjustables until the bike "disappears" beneath you. The level of the handlebars will probably be an inch or two below the level of the saddle, although some of the aforementioned gurus advocate higher handlebar positions. Some riders will want to feel more stretched out, others will prefer to be a little more upright. Saddle fore-aft position is another topic that inspires a lot of heated arguments. The idea is to get the most out of your pedal stroke, but the best position will vary depending on the type of seat and the type of pedaler. You may find that you like to have your saddle pointed ever so slightly downward, that you prefer a shorter top tube and a longer stem, or any number of personal eccentricities. Most important, the bike should feel very good to you.

There is one possible exception to this if-it-feels-good-do-it rule. A lot of rookies have the seat way too low and the bars way too high, and it somehow feels right to them. They don't like the classic road-cycling position, wishing that their bicycles were chairs instead of bicycles. These position-challenged riders—while they represent a huge chunk of the bicycle-buying public—have it all wrong. One shouldn't sit so heavily on the bike seat. While this is the position prescribed by the "comfort bike" setup, it will lead, ironically, straight to discomfort and bad attitude. This terminally faulty positioning is the reason for many novices' lack of love for bicycling. They will never love it until they learn to distribute the weight. On the other hand, if a comfort bike gets someone out the door instead of sitting on a sofa watching *Duck Dynasty,* it can't be all bad.

Comfortable, efficient cycling means that the feet, the hands, and the butt all share the load. Even while "sitting," one is really standing on the pedals, while using the hands and sitting bones to ease the burden. The saddle is something on which to prop yourself up. Bicycling is not a passive activity for heavy sitters. The rider should make very frequent adjustments over the saddle, easily sliding back or forward to keep the muscles fresh. Absorb road shock with the arms and legs rather than through the seat.

Poor bike fit typically leads to some common ailments. Setting the handlebars too low results in the rider's putting too much weight on the hands, and therefore pain and numbness in the hands. Improper seat height is more serious, causing various types of knee pain, and also some very annoying crotch-oriented problems. Riding with a too-low seat causes sharp pain in the front of the knee. Riding with the seat too high causes pain, sometimes severe, in the hips. Seats that are pointed up too much are known to cause numbness of the package in men and excessive chafing in women.

There is some evidence that cycling could cause fertility problems in men. Research in this issue is ongoing, and there is currently much uncertainty and hot air surrounding it, but men would be wise to take extra care of their nether regions. Try to sit and pedal in such a way that you're not crushing the plumbing in the perineum area. Circumstantial evidence suggests that most avid cyclists are doing just fine in the fertility department, but it's easy to imagine how a feller might damage himself. Any kind of serious pain and numbness in the genitals is not a normal, acceptable feature of bicycling.

Many, but not all, women prefer a saddle built for the wider spacing of their ischial tuberosities (aka sit bones). Some saddles are also designed to protect the woman's sensitive parts.

Micro-adjust seat height and angle until it feels perfect—half a centimeter up or down can make a huge difference—and carefully choose a seat that matches your particular, unique backside. Once you find a setup that is very comfortable for long rides, don't mess with it.

BIKE SECURITY

Once you've chosen a bike and set it up just right, you'll want to hold on to the thing. Don't leave it sitting around outside the coffee shop. Lock it up.

The familiar "U-lock" provides the most surefire security. (Avoid thin cable locks, as they can be snipped with bolt cutters, but a very thick cable will do the job well enough.) Unfortunately, U-locks and other worthy locks are pretty heavy, by necessity.

U-locks come in two sizes, generally speaking. The large U-lock allows you to lock the front wheel and frame to a pole. The smaller version doesn't, leaving room only for a frame tube and a thin post, but it is significantly lighter. Trade-offs.

Even though the smaller U-lock is the perfect size to stuff into the back pocket of a pair of jeans, I don't recommend traveling like that. That's a convenient way to carry a lock, but if you crash and land on the lock, it's going to do bonus damage to your hip.

Even the mighty U-lock can be defeated by a determined thief. A while back it became fairly common knowledge that U-locks could be picked using simple plastic pens. The locks were improved to fix that vulnerability but in fact there are still several different ways to bust them open. So don't lock your bike outside overnight or in places that are hidden from view, no matter how great your lock is. Even if the lock can't be beat, a thief might strip the bike of its best components.

TOOLS

To achieve complete self-sufficiency, a cyclist must have a set of tools that could rival a bike shop, in addition to a grip on mechanical reality that few of us will be able to attain. Many devoted riders opt out of total self-sufficiency and settle for a substantial, but ultimately incomplete, level of control. Lacking full sets of tools, they are happy to retreat to the bike shop for some of the more involved fixes, bleeding a set of hydraulic disc brakes, for instance. There is no shame in this. Even riders who learn to perform every possible mechanical operation on their bikes still go to the old-fashioned, barely surviving local shop to get frames tapped and straightened, and to get headset cups removed or installed, which requires even more special tools than the other special tools.

Tools can be dauntingly expensive. One way to ease the pain is to accumulate tools slowly year after year. For example, one might buy a tire on sale and get a pedal wrench with that extra ten bucks. Tools are the gift that keeps on giving. Tools are an investment. This sounds cute, but on a strictly financial level, it holds true. The avid rider who spends on tools and knows how to use them will save money in the end.

When accumulating tools, one should discriminate between tools that might be needed today or tomorrow and tools that will be needed down the line. Decide which are more likely to be needed early, and get those first. Beginning riders have some fairly urgent tool purchases to make. The proper order of tool accumulation might look something like this:

1. PUMP, PATCH KIT, AND TIRE LEVERS are tied for number one. These should go along on pretty much every ride. To achieve the minimum level of self-sufficiency, the cyclist must be prepared to fix a flat. Combined with a spare tube or two, these three tools will keep you pneumatically secure.

2. Number two is pretty close: a set of ALLEN WRENCHES. Allen wrenches are also known as "hex wrenches" or "hex keys" because of their hexagonal cross section. Perhaps all you need is a Y-shaped three-way wrench at first. Later on, accumulate all the little ones, some of which will eventually be needed. Allen wrenches with really long handles are

nice to work with but impractical on rides. And make sure you get the large Allen wrench that is needed to tighten or remove the cranks. (Most modern bikes also have headsets that can be adjusted with a standard-size Allen wrench. If you're riding an older bike with an older headset or bottom bracket, you'll need to acquire the assorted wrenches necessary to service those areas of the bike.)

3. GREASE AND CHAIN OIL. A controversial choice—is lube really a tool? Not necessarily something to take with you, but you'll need it early and often. (In an emergency out on a ride, you can get by using lip balm.)

4. SPOKE WRENCH. Wheels aren't what they used to be. Most of the wheels these days are built by drunken robots, and sometimes the spokes chronically get loose and just plain need to be tightened. Often it is just a single spoke that is the culprit. In these cases there usually isn't much fancy trueing involved, but you still need the wrench. Get a spoke wrench that matches the spoke nipples on your bike, or get one that fits lots of different sizes.

Wheel trueing is a bit of an art, but anyone can do it. Find where the rim is bent out of alignment. One way to do this easily is to turn the bike over and

MAKE SURE YOU HAVE A WRENCH THAT FITS YOUR CRANK BOLTS.

USE A LIGHT TOUCH WITH THE SPOKE WRENCH.

watch the rim spin past the brake pads. Look at the rim and not the tire. If the rim is bent to the left, find a few spokes around the bent area that connect to the right side of the hub and give 'em a small twist to tighten.

Just remember that to tighten, the spoke nipples are turned counterclockwise with respect to the visible surface of the rim. Just a quarter turn or so at a time. This will pull the rim slightly to the right. Then loosen a few of the spokes there that go to the left side of the hub. This has the same effect as tightening the right-side spokes, but the combination of loosening and tightening keeps the rim round, as well as straight. If you just tighten one side without loosening the other side, the rim will develop a flat spot.

It takes practice to learn which spokes to mess with, and how much to mess with them. Spin the wheel and check your work. Then readjust with more twists of the wrench if needed. It doesn't have to be perfect. Be careful not to overtighten. A classic rookie mistake is to tighten, tighten, and tighten the spokes over the course of a few months until the spokes begin to pull through the cracked rim.

5. CHAIN TOOL. If you're riding around in the middle of nowhere someday, you might suddenly find yourself in need of a chain tool, and the ability to use it. If you're like most riders, however, you won't have one or both of these things, which means you'll be scrambling for a hand-up from a fellow cyclist or making that dreaded Call of Shame.

KEEP YOUR HOOPS STRAIGHT AND ROUND.

THE MYSTERIOUS CHAIN TOOL

Even if you don't carry a chain tool on every ride, you'll like to have one around. Most new chains these days use a master link that lets you remove and install the chain by hand. Know how to use the master link, and carry an extra one if possible, but get the chain tool also to take care of the many situations where master linkage won't do the trick. For instance, you may have to remove some links from a new chain to make it fit properly. Also called a "chain breaker," the chain tool can also put chains back together or, in the wrong hands, mangle them.

6. You probably already have a small PHILLIPS HEAD SCREWDRIVER. Keep it with the bike tools. You will need it to adjust your derailleurs.

7. PEDAL WRENCH, although many pedals can be removed/installed with an eight-millimeter Allen wrench. Remember that the left pedal has reverse threading. Right is right, left is wrong.

8. CONE WRENCHES. The hubs depend on strangely shaped bolts known as cones. Adjusting the cones can be a somewhat delicate operation, and you may do well to consult a maintenance manual or experienced colleague. Or you might just learn to do it yourself. *Banzai!* A cone wrench can also be used to adjust some types of brakes.

9. BOTTOM BRACKET TOOLS. Now we're starting to get into territory beyond the everyday adjusting tools. These are tools that are used for building up bikes and cracking open their vital organs. To get a standard bottom bracket apart, you need an eight-millimeter Allen wrench, a crank puller (a little device that slowly yanks the crank arms off the bottom bracket spindle), and tools to remove the bottom bracket itself.

THE PEDAL WRENCH IS A THIN FIFTEEN-MILLIMETER WRENCH WITH A LONG HANDLE FOR LEVERAGE.

Different brands of newer bottom brackets require different splined tools for removal or installation. Older, classic-style bottom brackets require a two-sided wrench to remove the fixed cup (which is reverse threaded like the left pedal) and lock ring, and a separate tool to hold/move the adjusting cup.

10. CASSETTE TOOLS. As with most bottom brackets, a special splined tool is required to remove the cassette body. A chain whip is also indispensable for removing the cassette. Use the skewer to hold the splined tool in the cassette as you torque the wrench.

11. Going along with the bottom bracket tool and the cassette tool is the ten-inch CRESCENT WRENCH that is used to turn them. Problem is, bottom brackets and cassettes are supposed to be tightened to within a specific range of torque. A torque wrench is a nice addition to any home, but people get along without them easily enough.

12. True bicycle lovers own their own CABLE TOOLS. This includes cable cutters to cleanly cut the housing and little needle-nose pliers to pull the cable to the proper tension. It's also good to have plenty of extra cable and housing around, and ferrules to cover the cable and housing ends.

13. FLOOR PUMP. A good-quality floor pump makes your life much easier.

14. REPAIR STAND. A stand grips the bike and holds it steady so it can't get away. This saves you from the backache of constantly bending over and lets you easily turn the pedals and wheels.

A BOTTOM BRACKET TOOL, CHAIN WHIP, AND WRENCH ARE NEEDED TO REMOVE A CASETTE.

Beyond this basic set, some riders accumulate still-more-specialized tools. Jigs, headset presses, wheel-building stands (also known as trueing stands), spoke tensiometers . . . When the Revolution comes, they'll be ready.

There is some other stuff you can get, depending on what specific parts you run, and hardly anyone will agree with the order above. Just owning the tools does not automatically give the owner the knowledge to fix the bike. For that there are many other fine books and knowledgeable mechanics who can help.

Experience, of course, is the best teacher. Good luck.

CABLE STUFF

WITH AN ACCURATE PRESSURE GAUGE AND OTHER USEFUL FEATURES, A FLOOR PUMP, OR "TRACK PUMP," SHOULD GET PLENTY OF USE.

CLOTHING

Many people believe, even some relatively experienced riders believe, that certain clothing items are absolutely necessary for cycling. For instance, it is often stated that skintight cycling shorts are almost mandatory. While these shorts do have substantial advantages that many riders appreciate—superior aerodynamics, padding, and enhanced package disclosure, to name a few—a necessity they are not. And as far as the storied comfort of padded cycling shorts goes, you won't have to look too hard to find experienced riders who find these shorts to be less comfortable than regular shorts, even for long rides. These riders don't appreciate the bike shorts' extra, er, grip. Millions of riders, on the other hand, swear by them and can't imagine riding in anything else. The issue of cycling clothing, you see, just like most of the other equipment concerns, in large part boils down to cultural norms and personal bias. This is true even for some of the sacred cows of cycling equipment, shorts included.

Especially if the rider is making a short trip to the office or store or somewhere like that, the practical benefits of special shorts or jerseys may be canceled by the extra time spent changing into them. Everyday trips through the city can be accomplished in just about any garb within reason. Lots of riders have great success wearing jeans and T-shirts, for instance. Some women even wear long skirts.

Really the only clothing items that might approach the grand mantle of necessity are gloves and a helmet, and cleated cycling shoes for those with clipless pedals. Out in the cold rain and snow, of course, jackets and other items become very important, even for the shortest trips.

For longer rides, clothing choice becomes much more important, especially so when bad weather threatens. One of the most unpleasant sensations in cycling is getting sweaty, or otherwise wet, on a cold day. A base layer composed of a wicking fiber—polyester, for instance—will keep the skin dry and prevent the rider from going hypothermic. A synthetic undershirt or a nice wool-blend jersey could be the difference between the perfect ride and a slimy hell.

Beyond the wicking layer, the cold-weather cyclist does well to carry something warm for the top half, like a wool sweater; a decent waterproof breathable jacket, preferably with side zippers; waterproof, insulated gloves; waterproof pants; thermal tights; two pairs of nice wool-blend socks; and a hat of wool or fleece. Polyester skullcaps and balaclavas work well under helmets. This getup will fend off pretty much anything the Lower 48 can dish out. The trick is not so much to stay warm but to balance the outer cold with the inner warmth. This is one of the most difficult tricks in cycling.

Commuters who hope to arrive at work in clean, nonsweaty clothes have special equipment needs. Fenders are key for keeping greasy road splatter and black puddle splash away from the Dockers. Whenever riding in long pants, roll up the right pant leg (the one next to the drivetrain) far enough that any contact with the drivetrain will only soil the inside of the garment; alternatively, lash it firmly around the calf and ankle using a reflective band. It doesn't hurt to roll and/or lash the left pant leg, too. The most devoted fans of cleanliness should consider using a bicycle with a chain case, which completely encloses the drivetrain.

Unfortunately, keeping one's clothes clean while riding is not a simple matter of slapping on some fenders and rolling up a pant leg. On well-used bicycles there are multiple sources of grunge. Bike seats, for instance, often will transfer some of their pigment onto the pants or shorts of the rider—one of the best arguments in favor of black cycling shorts. This problem is greatly exacerbated by moisture. The cables, especially near where they disappear into the housing, are often the culprits for mysterious stains around the thighs and crotch. The bike frame itself can cause the same problem if it's dirty. Bicycle tires are some of the dirtiest things within reach of you at any given time, which becomes evident every time you have to repair a flat. Touch your tire or rim to your khakis as you wheel the bike out of the house in the morning, and you might have a nasty spot staring at you all day long.

Then, of course, there's the drivetrain, which must be avoided like the dark pestilence that it is. A greasy drivetrain is almost as good a reason to wear shorts as any other. Your bike hates pants.

Cyclists can mitigate stains by keeping their bikes very clean, by wearing dark clothing, or clothes that can be terminally dirtied with an easy mind, and by keeping some fresh shirts and pants at the office, if possible.

If we can forget about the problem of greasy stains for a moment, the thought of cyclists pedaling around in their standard everyday garb is heartening. The more riders who do this, the more obvious it will be to the general public that cycling is about straight utility in addition to recreation and exercise, an important point that has yet to penetrate the thick skull of American society.

MESSENGER BAGS, BACKPACKS, AND PANNIERS

So you've got some stuff. How do you carry it?

Well hopefully you won't have to carry it in your hand as you ride along. This maverick hauling method is a traditional wreck causer for bicyclists, often because the rider is unable to properly operate the brake levers and carry at the same time. Other times, a rider will attempt to haul a bag in one hand while holding onto the handlebar with the same hand; the bag inevitably tries to swing into the spokes and cause a wreck. If you find yourself hauling something, keep one hand on the front brake lever, usually the left hand. Carry the bag or object in the other hand, and prepare yourself for the possibility that you may have to jettison the cargo. Obviously, to carry lattes and sacks of tacos and things like this, one must possess a solid command of front-brake modulation and an ability to maneuver the bicycle with one hand on the bars. Some riders have enough trouble using two hands.

Any city rider will eventually have to haul enough stuff around to necessitate the acquisition of a backpack or set of rear panniers—saddlebags that hang over a rack, commonly used by cycle tourists. In deciding what type of system to go with, the rider will have to make a fateful decision: to haul the goods on the body or on the bike.

For decades the conventional wisdom has been in favor of racks and panniers. Putting the weight on the bike is said to be physically easier on the rider, who puts all energy into powering the bike and is not fatigued by weight hanging on the upper body. Panniers also allow the rider to avoid the slimy, sweaty back that often comes from wearing a pack and lower the center of gravity of bicycle and rider.

But not everything is wonderful over in pannier land. Some riders try panniers and detest the new handling characteristics of their weighted bicycle. With a loaded backpack, though the rider's neck and shoulder muscles may be struggling mightily, the quick road bike still feels like a quick road bike. Another problem with panniers is mobility. Let's say you just purchased some expensive new chichi bike parts at the local shop, and you're carrying them home in the panniers. But you want to stop at the grocery store on the way home. Are you going to detach the panniers from the rack and carry them into the store with you to protect those expensive parts from being lifted? Some types of panniers are quite difficult to deal with in these situations. The backpack solves this dilemma. Also, it can be difficult to install racks on the racing-type bikes that many riders prefer. The fastest bikes don't have rack mounts.

MESSENGERS AND HIPSTERS BOTH LIKE WATERPROOF MESSENGER BACKPACKS.

Bicycling-specific backpacks are designed to hold the pack away from the rider's back. This helps with the sweat problem, although it does not solve it completely. The panniers and cargo bikes still own that point.

Among commuters, the popularity of messenger bags probably has more to do with fashion than anything else. Traditional messenger bags, with a strap slung over one shoulder, are designed so the wearer can remove packages from or place packages in the bag without actually removing the bag. It's a nifty feature if you need it. The messenger swings the bag into the front to deal with deliveries, then throws the bag around onto the back and rides. The messenger bag's versatility is also its big problem, though. When well-loaded, the bag has a tendency to swing uncomfortably around the rider's neck any time the rider stands out of the saddle. Many working couriers replaced their traditional single-strap bags with special messenger backpacks with large openings at the top. In turn, the traditional messenger bag's status has declined among the hipsters as well.

There are a few other methods of carrying substantial amounts of loot. Among these, the large seat-mounted bag is promising for small loads. Some riders use a rack, but instead of panniers, they simply lash their backpack or a gym bag to the rack using bungee cords. And don't forget the ever-trusty milk crate. One problem with the milk-crate-on-rack system is that rider's stuff will fly out in a wreck. And it can be hard to find good milk crates these days.

DRIVETRAIN MAINTENANCE

Drivetrain maintenance is a crucial safety matter for cycling.

A chain skip can be disastrous if it occurs, as it often does, when the rider is pushing heavily on the cranks. Standing up to accelerate across an intersection, trying to make it through a gap in traffic, and *ker-chunk!* Even a minor mechanical blip can create an immediate emergency situation if the rider's forward progress is delayed at that critical moment. The sudden disconnect of a slipping chain can also throw the rider violently into the stem and handlebars. These impacts are usually absorbed by the knees, thighs, groin, or chest, where they are known to cause broken ribs. Such an event could also lead to

THE FUNCTION OF YOUR BICYCLE PRETTY MUCH DEPENDS ON KEEPING THE CABLES WELL LUBED—UNLESS YOUR BIKE DOESN'T HAVE CABLES.

a heinous secondary collision with the city surface or a motor vehicle, a possibility that should not be taken lightly.

A very dirty, gooped-up drivetrain can cause the chain to skip, as can a poorly adjusted or bent derailleur or a stiff link in the chain. Another common cause of a skipping chain is excessive wear. With use, bicycle chains elongate slightly as the plate holes and rivets wear.

All new bicycle chains have a half-inch distance from pin center to pin center. Ideally the chain should be replaced when twenty-four pins' worth becomes noticeably longer than 1 foot, but before it reaches 12$\frac{1}{8}$ inches. (Check by holding a ruler up to a chain under tension or using a special chain wear device.) Beyond this point the cog teeth begin to change shape to match the worn chain—the worn-out teeth assume a distinctive shark-fin appearance—and a new chain will not mesh properly with your old gears. This means you will have to replace the cassette and chain rings in addition to the chain. Replacing a worn out drivetrain is expensive but worth it. Take it from any cyclist who's ever wiped out after smashing a knee into the stem.

In the meantime, keep the chain and the rest of the drivetrain, especially the cables, clean of excess buildup and lubricated. There is an ongoing argument about what is the best method for cleaning a chain, if any, and what sort of lube works best, if any—"dry" lube, Teflon, motor oil, chain saw oil, wax. In the nineteenth century, mechanics bathed chains in buckets of hot beef fat.

Many cyclists are insistent that a chain should never be oiled on the bike. They believe this casual lubing washes fine grit into the workings of the chain and accelerates wear. So they remove the chain, submerge it in solvent, and give it a good bath before applying any lube. Others use a special cleaning tool that clamps around the chain and cleans it with brushes as the crank is rotated. Yet others think deep chain cleaning is a silly overreaction to chain wear. These arguments are based largely on superstition and won't be solved here.

THAT'S NOT RIGHT.

OF BICYCLES AND CITIES

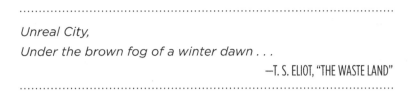

Unreal City,
Under the brown fog of a winter dawn . . .

—T. S. ELIOT, "THE WASTE LAND"

When I tell people that I ride my bike on weekends, for fun and fitness—in addition to riding all week at work and using a bicycle for almost all my transportation needs—they tend to give me a funny look. They want to know: "Don't you get tired of it?"

The answer is no. More precisely, the answer is hell no. And I think I know why not.

Riding a bike allows a person to pack more life into a day. As Americans, we know all too well that the car driver often finds him- herself caught in a void, a void of dead space and time. The time spent driving to the store, to work, caught in traffic—attention vaguely drifting from the road ahead to the radio and back—is so nondescript, so forgettable, it is lost forever. Did the driver really live these minutes spent in motorized transit? Technically. On the bike, it is vastly different. This is actual living. Blood and oxygen pumping, muscles straining. There is a sense of being a true part of the world, a participant in one's own life, rather than simply watching it pass by on a big screen.

If bicycling makes us happier, it's not because bicycling is easy. Biycling requires a high level of engagement, mental and physical. Cyclists have much that they must attend to out there, starting with the constant scanning of the road surface itself, watching for potholes, sand, expansion joints—things that drivers don't have to notice. And negotiating traffic is a whole different ballgame for cyclists. In contrast to motorists, who are enclosed, cyclists are exposed. Completely exposed in a stream of heavy machinery, and exposed to the sky above, feeling whatever weather is coming down. The bicyclist's exposure, although it is a source of fear and trouble, turns out to be an even greater source of joy, as it makes the experience that much more colorful and intense. Even the most ordinary errand becomes a memory maker. Although the trip may take longer, time spent on the bike is never wasted. The journey becomes an end in itself. That, my friends, is what life is all about.

There are many other important reasons, of course, why bicycling is an attractive mode of travel. It's nearly pollution- and petroleum-free, cost-effective in many ways, and all that. You've heard it all before. *Yawn!* These are not the reasons that cause me to stare lovingly at my bikes at night when they're leaning against the wall in the living room. These bicycles, I swear, are possessed of an indescribable magic.

Bicycling is better. Life is too precious to spend it in a car.

It's more than likely that you, reading this book, already know this. I'm preaching to the choir here, and, as a firm believer in the different-strokes-for-different-folks philosophy—whatever turns your crank—I try to resist pros-elytizing to noncyclists. Who am I to tell someone who doesn't ride a bike that he or she should ride a bike? I possess no desire to be the pied piper of cycling, leading fat American motorists down the wide curb lane to freedom. This is a book for folks who are already aware of the bicycle's magic.

But even those of us who understand and appreciate bicycles have trou-ble understanding the cities and suburbs in which we ride them. All that is obvious about these places is that they are imperfect and, from a cyclist's perspective, could be improved. So we bang up against our cities, clash with them, flail about, and try to change what might not be changeable, wasting precious riding time. Today's Real American City, in all its grungy glory, is already rockable on two wheels. Though it is not nearly as hospitable to bicy-clists as the emerald cities in our utopian fantasies, the Real American City can be dealt with in style. Sure it takes awareness, intelligence, a modicum of skill. It requires a healthy dose of compromise. Perhaps above all else, it takes patience. With patient observation the truths of the city are revealed and pathways, literal and figurative, are opened.

As the layers of paint and mystery are pulled away, it becomes apparent that unpredictability, chaos, and madness are some of the most important cogs in the city's machinery. The deck is stacked with jokers. There is a ghost in this machine, and it appears to be stupid and/or drunk. This situation will not change, because the human condition is its source. Accepting this reality is the first requirement of the bicyclist in traffic.

The patient observer will not fail to notice that the messy reality of the Real American City does not coincide with the tidy vision of it that has been offered over the decades by some of the grand, old wise men of cycling.

Theirs is a city governed by order: white lines, laws, and foregone conclusions. In their city, cyclists need only obey a few simple principles to get along successfully. Theirs is just another dream city, and not a very exciting one at that.

The Real American City marches to the crazy beats of millions of different drummers. The masterful urban cyclist finds him- or herself in a strange sort of dance, moving to all those drummers. There is no single principle that will see us through. But we have much more powerful tools at our disposal: timing, flexibility, and flow. Freedom. A successful, safe ride through American traffic is not an exercise in rule following alone, but a beautiful piece of interactive performance art.

Good luck out there, fellow cyclists. Keep your eyes open, your heads up, and the rubber side down. Be considerate to other road users, especially the noncyclists, poor fellows. Ride with fear and joy.

CHAPTER NOTES

CHAPTER ONE: FRANKENSTEIN'S MONSTER

1. Augusto Marinoni, "The Bicycle," in Ladislau Reti, ed., *The Unknown Leonardo* (New York: McGraw-Hill Book Company, 1974), pp. 288–91.

2. The arguments against Marinoni's claim are summarized in Jonathan Knight, "On Yer Bike, Leonardo," *New Scientist,* October 18, 1997, p. 28.

3. The drawing of the chain link can be seen in Reti, ed., *The Unknown Leonardo,* p. 291. See also Vernard Foley, "Leonardo and the Invention of the Wheellock," *Scientific American,* January 1998, pp. 96–100.

4. The account of the draisienne, boneshaker, and high-wheeler eras is a meld of information found in a wide range of sources. Particularly helpful were James McGurn, *On Your Bicycle: An Illustrated History of Cycling* (New York: Facts On File Publications, 1987), pp. 14–50; and Robert Smith, *A Social History of the Bicycle* (New York: McGraw-Hill, 1972), pp. 3–6.

5. McGurn, *On Your Bicycle,* pp. 51–73; and Smith, *A Social History of the Bicycle,* pp. 7–13.

6. McGurn, *On Your Bicycle,* pp. 86–100; and Smith, *A Social History of the Bicycle,* pp. 13–14.

7. McGurn, *On Your Bicycle,* pp. 89–90.

8. Ibid., p. 130; Smith, *A Social History of the Bicycle,* p. 33.

9. Cyclists' role in the smoothing and paving of American roads, prior to the arrival of large numbers of automobiles, is well appreciated by historians of automobility. For example, see James Flink, *The Automobile Age* (Cambridge: MIT Press, 1988), p. 5. Flink notes: "At the national level, a petition to Congress drafted by the LAW [League of American Wheelmen] resulted in 1893 in the creation of the Office of Road Inquiry in the Department of Agriculture." See also Ashleigh Brilliant, *The Great Car Craze* (Santa Barbara: Woodbridge Press, 1989), p. 15. Brilliant includes a quote, dated 1895, from a surveyor of the newly formed California State Bureau of Highways: "The influence of the bicycle upon this agitation for improved highways cannot be overestimated. Millions of dollars have been invested in the manufacture of

these easy and graceful machines of locomotion and this agitation for better roads is due more directly to the efforts of the wheelmen than to any other one cause . . ."

10. Smith, *A Social History of the Bicycle,* pp. 215–19.

11. Ibid., p. 13.

12. Ibid., p. 61.

13. John B. Rae, *The Road and the Car in American Life* (Cambridge: MIT Press, 1971), p. 28. In 1971 Rae called the bicycle "a device whose significance in the history of transportation has never been properly appreciated."

14. Flink, *The Automobile Age,* p. 5.

15. Ibid., pp. 5–6.

16. Peter Nye, *Hearts of Lions* (New York: W.W. Norton & Company, 1988), pp. 42–73.

17. ". . . an engine on four wheels, a machine in which brute strength and a disregard for nearly all the essentials of modern automobile construction are embodied." "How It Feels to Drive Under the Minute on a Circular Track," *The Automobile,* August 1, 1903, p. 116.

18. Ibid.

19. Flink, *The Automobile Age,* pp. 6–10.

20. Barney Oldfield, as reported to William Sturm, "Wide Open All the Way, Part One," *Saturday Evening Post,* September 19, 1925, p. 54.

21. *Horseless Age,* an early auto-booster publication, described the typical crowd reaction to Oldfield in their edition of July 29, 1903: ". . . he could be seen skidding around the curve at the quarter in a manner so obviously dangerous as to draw a spontaneous groan from the crowd." "The Races at the Empire City Track," *Horseless Age,* July 29, 1903, p. 124.

22. "A Carnival of Sport at Yonkers Track," *The Automobile,* August 1, 1903, p. 99.

23. Barney Oldfield as reported to William Sturm, "Wide Open All the Way, Part One," *Saturday Evening Post,* September 19, 1925, pp. 56, 61.

24. Ibid.; also Barney Oldfield as reported to William Sturm, "Wide Open All the Way, Part Two," *Saturday Evening Post,* September 26, 1925, pp. 20–21, 129–134, 137, 140.

25. Barney Oldfield as reported to William Sturm, "Wide Open All the Way, Part One," *Saturday Evening Post,* September 19, 1925, p. 56.

26. Wilson was then president of Princeton. Rae, *The Road and the Car in American Life,* p. 43.

27. Henry Ford's letter to *The Automobile,* January 11, 1906, p. 107. Cited in Rae, *The Road and the Car in American Life,* p. 55.

28. Rae, *The Road and the Car in American Life,* p. 41.

29. Flink, *The Automobile Age,* pp. 24–38.

30. Ibid, pp. 129–30.
31. Rae, *The Road and the Car in American Life,* pp. 73–74.
32. Flink, *The Automobile Age,* p. 359.
33. Ibid., pp. 140, 300.
34. Matthew Wald, "One Vehicle on the Road, Two Others in the Garage," *New York Times,* August 29, 2003.
35. Flink, *The Automobile Age,* pp. 326–27.
36. Ibid., p. 250.
37. National Bicycle Dealers' Association.
38. National Bicycle Dealers' Association.
39. League of American Bicyclists. https://public.sheet.zoho.com/public/bikeleague/2000-to-2010-bike-commuters-largest-70-2-1.
40. Toby Barlow, "Bike Among the Ruins," *New York Times,* July 4, 2009.
41. League of American Bicyclists. https://a/public.sheet.zoho.com/public/bikeleague/2000-to-2010-bike-commuters-largest-70-2-1.
42. Michael Hugo-Brunt, *The History of City Planning* (Montreal: Harvest House, Ltd., 1972), p. 34.
43. Flink, *The Automobile Age,* p. 3.
44. Joel Garreau, *Edge City* (New York: Doubleday, 1991), pp. 120–21.
45. This view is borrowed from Garreau, *Edge City.*
46. Kenneth Jackson, *Crabgrass Frontier* (New York: Oxford University Press, 1985), p. 170.
47. Scott Bottles, *L.A. and the Automobile* (Berkely: University of California Press, 1987), pp. 3–17.
48. As Kenneth Jackson puts it, "Americans taxed and harassed public transportation, even while subsidizing the automobile like a pampered child." *Crabgrass Frontier,* p. 170.
49. Le Corbusier, *The City of Tomorrow and Its Planning* (London: J. Rodker, 1929), pp. 116–18.
50. Congressional Budget Office, "Spending and Funding for Highways," January 2011, p. 4.
51. Rem Koolhaas, *S, M, L, XL* (New York: The Monacelli Press, 1994), p. 961.
52. "Urban Mobility Report," Texas A & M University, 2012, p. 24.
53. Ibid., p. 1.
54. Lewis Mumford, *The City in History* (New York: Harcourt, Brace and World, 1968), pp. 218–19.
55. Jane Jacobs, *The Death and Life of Great American Cities* (New York: Random House, 1961), p. 351.
56. Steven Johnson, *Emergence* (New York: Scribner and Sons, 2001), p. 74.
57. Art Buchwald, "How Un-American Is That," *Have I Ever Lied to You?* (New York: Putnam Press, 1968).

CHAPTER TWO: THE CITY SURFACE

1. Clay McShane, "Transforming the Use of Urban Space: A Look at the Revolution in Street Pavements, 1880–1924," *Journal of Urban History,* May 1979, pp. 282–83.
2. Alessandra Ram, "A Method to the Madness: A Day With York City's Pothole Crew," *The Atlantic,* January 8, 2013. www.theatlantic.com/video/archive/2013/01/potholes/266928/.
3. Nai C. Yang, *Design of Functional Pavements* (New York: McGraw-Hill, 1972), p. 17.
4. E. J. Yoder, *Principles of Pavement Design* (New York: John Wiley and Sons, 1959), p. 506. New York Times, February 23, 2003.
5. Any ranking of surface hazards suggested here is based on circumstantial evidence alone, and there exists no study to confirm or deny it.
6. Correspondence with the author's cousin, July 1, 2003.
7. Yang, *Design of Functional Pavements,* pp. 159–60.
8. See Peter Blake, *The Master Builders* (New York: Alfred A. Knopf, 1960), for a discussion of both Le Corbusier and Mies van der Rohe and the close relationship between the two men.

CHAPTER THREE: IN TRAFFIC

1. Ambrose Bierce, *The Devil's Dictionary* (New York: Dover Publications, Inc., 1993), p. 106. Originally published in 1911 as part of Volume VII of *The Collected Works of Ambrose Bierce* (New York: Neale Publishing Company).
2. This version of the statement actually comes from *Forester's Bicycle Transportation: A Handbook for Cycling Transportation Engineers* (Cambridge: MIT Press, 1994), p. 3.
3. While the vast majority of car-bike crashes occur in urban areas at relatively low speeds, the vast majority of deadly crashes occur on roads with speed limits of forty miles per hour or higher. See, for instance, "North Carolina Bicycle Crash Facts, 2005–2009," University of North Carolina Highway Safety Research Center, August 2011, p. 27: "In all, 76% of bicyclists killed were struck on roadways of 40 mph limits and higher, the majority on 50–55 mph roadways."
4. Most of the research on "conspicuity" involves motorcyclists. For instance see Helman, Weare, Palmer, and Fernandez-Medina, "Literature Review of Interventions to Improve the Conspicuity of Motorcyclists and Help Avoid 'Looked But Failed to See' Accidents." Transport Research Laboratory, 2012.

5. *The Analects of Confucius,* translated and annotated by Arthur Waley (New York: Random House, 1938), Book IV, no. 12, p. 104.

6. "It gives the motorist superior rights and status over the cyclist . . ." writes Forester. Forester, *Effective Cycling* (Cambridge: MIT Press, 1984), p. 154.

7. North Carolina Pedestrian and Bicycle Crash Data Tool, North Carolina Department of Transportation. www.pedbikeinfo.org/pbcat/_bikequery.cfm. Ralph Wessels, "Bicycle Collisions in Washington State: A Six-Year Perspective, 1988–1993," Transportation Research Record 1538, pp. 81–90. On the relative deadliness of different crash types, see the standby "Cross-Fisher" study prepared for the US Department of Transportation in the 1970s: Kenneth D. Cross and Gary Fisher, "A Study of Bicycle/Motor-Vehicle Accidents: Identification of Problem Types and Countermeasure Approaches," Volume One, September 1977, pp. 230–37. Roughly one in every four fatal car-bike crashes was caused by a motorist failing to notice the bicyclist traveling the same direction in front of him or her.

8. Jack Dennerlein and John Meeker, "Injuries Among Boston Bicycle Messengers," *American Journal of Industrial Medicine,* 2002. www.hsph.harvard .edu/ergonomics/bike/index.html.

9. William H. Whyte, City: *Rediscovering the Center.* (Philadelphia: University of Penssylvania Press, 2009), pp. 56–62.

10. Charles Komanoff, "Killed by Automobile: Death in the Streets in New York City 1994–1997," 1999, www.rightofway.org/research/kba_text.pdf. "Bicyclist Fatalities and Serious Injuries in New York City: 1996–2005," A Joint Report from the Departments of Health and Mental Hygiene, Parks and Recreation, and the New York City Police Department, p. 20.

11. http://cityroom.blogs.nytimes.com/2011/09/19/ study-finds-higher-number-of-pedestrians-hurt-by-bikes/

12. Brilliant, *The Great Car Craze,* pp. 89–90.

13. There is a smattering of statistical evidence to suggest that bike lane stripes are somewhat effective traffic-calming devices. For instance, see William Moritz, "Adult Bicyclists in the United States," a survey of League of American Bicyclists members from 1996.

14. Seattle Municipal Code.

15. Exact wording from the municipal codes of Portland, Oregon, and Madison, Wisconsin.

16. Insurance Institute for Highway Safety.

CHAPTER FOUR: BICYCLE ACCIDENTS AND INJURIES

1. These numbers are estimations from the US Consumer Product Safety Commission (CPSC) and are based on the CPSC's National Electronic Injury Surveillance System, a statistical sampling from multiple emergency rooms around the country.

2. The numbers in this section are approximations derived from numerous studies of bicycle accident rates. The studies include Chlapecka, Schupack, Planek, Klecker, and Driessen, "Bicycle Accidents and Usage Among Elementary School Children in the United States," National Highway Traffic Safety Administration, 1975; Kenneth Cross, "Causal Factors of Non-Motor Vehicle Related Accidents," Santa Barbara Bicycle Safety Project, Santa Barbara, 1980; Kenneth Cross and Gary Fisher, "A Study of Bicycle/Motor-Vehicle Accidents: Identification of Problem Types and Countermeasure Approaches," National Highway Traffic Safety Administration, 1977; Jerrold Kaplan, "Characteristics of the Regular Adult Bicycle User," National Technical Information Service, 1976; Schupack and Driessen, "Bicycle Accidents and Usage Among Young Adults: Preliminary Study," National Safety Council, 1976; and Watkins's survey of the British Cyclists' Touring Club (1984). All of the above are cited by Forester, *Bicycle Transportation: A Handbook for Cycling Transportation Engineers,* pp. 41–61. The studies are all more than a bit long in the tooth. Various additional publications from the National Highway Traffic Safety Administration and the US Consumer Products Safety Commission were also used.

3. North Carolina Pedestrian and Bicycle Crash Data Tool, www.pedbikeinfo.org/pbcat/_bikequery.cfm. "Safe Streets Boulder: A Study of Motor Vehicle Collisions Involving Bicyclists and Pedestrians," City of Boulder, February 2012. Neither the Crash Data Tool nor the Boulder study distinguished between deliberate and inadvertent law breaking.

4. Decent data on fatality rates are virtually impossible to come by. The well-known chart from the risk analysis firm Failure Analysis Associates, which first appeared in an article about car fires in *Design News* magazine ("Comparative Risk of Different Activities," *Design News,* October 4, 1993), is effectively useless, because no methodology is provided, and therefore there is no way to check the work. The chart made the claim that cyclists suffered 0.26 death for every one million hours of riding.

5. Based on known fatality statistics and the US Consumer Products Safety Commission's National Electronic Injury Surveillance System.

6. This number is necessarily an estimation, based on the US Consumer Products Safety Commission's National Electronic Injury Surveillance System,

which estimates about five hundred thousand cycling-related emergency room visits each year, which about half are related to head injuries. The total annual number of cycling injuries, as stated earlier, is unknown and unknowable, but five million is a conservative estimate.

7. Forester has been especially exasperated on this point. He devotes much of his energy to debunking the popular fear of this type of accident. Forester, *Bicycle Transportation: A Handbook for Cycling Transportation Engineers,* pp. 9–13, 46–47.

8. Ibid., p. 41.

9. Jack Dennerlein and John Meeker, "Injuries Among Boston Bicycle Messengers," *American Journal of Industrial Medicine,* 2002. www.hsph.harvard.edu/ergonomics/bike/index.html. Compare with William Moritz, "Adult Bicyclists in the United States—Characteristics and Riding Experience in 1996," Transportation Research Record 1636. Moritz studied survey responses from a large number of members of the League of American Bicyclists, who averaged about fifteen years of cycling experience, and came up with the lowest accident rate ever recorded in a serious study. When reasonable assumptions about the messengers' daily mileage are plugged into Dennerlein's paper, their accident rate compares nicely to that tallied by Moritz.

10. Burke, *Serious Cycling,* p. 88.

11. Conversations with Christie M., Winter 2002–2003.

12. John Carey, ed., *Eyewitness to History* (New York: Avon Books, 1987), p. 435. Mr. Bride's account originally appeared in the *New York Times,* April 19, 1912. The *Titanic* went down on April 15.

13. Thompson, Nunn, Thompson, and Rivara, "Effectiveness of Bicycle Safety Helmets in Preventing Serious Facial Injury," *JAMA,* 1996, vol. 276, pp. 1974–75. The researchers conclude, "Helmets do not appear to offer any protection for the lower face."

14. National Safety Council.

15. Robert Berkow M.D., Mark H. Beers M.D., and Andrew J. Fletcher, eds., *The Merck Manual of Medical Information* (Whitehouse Station, N.J., Merck and Co., Inc., 1997), p. 357.

16. Ibid., p. 359.

17. Richard Cherry, *EMT-Basic Exam Review* (Upper Saddle River, N.J.: Prentice Hall, 1999), p. 195.

18. Paine's essay "Old Testament Prophecies of Jesus Christ Proven False (Part 2)," which can be found in Daniel Wheeler, ed., *Life and Writings of Thomas Paine* (New York: Vincent Parke and Company, 1908).

19. Nationwide among adult cycling enthusiasts, 60 to 80 percent helmet use is a safe estimate. The estimate is similarly high for young children. Commuter cyclists seem to hover at around 40 percent.

20. The latest of the Seattle studies is summarized in Thompson, Nunn, Thompson, and Rivara, "Effectiveness of Bicycle Safety Helmets in Preventing Head Injuries: A Case Control Study," *JAMA,* 1996, vol. 276, pp. 1968–73.

21. Ibid. It was one of the very interesting results of this study that helmet wearers were found to be far more well off than their bareheaded counterparts.

22. National Highway Traffic Safety Administration, "2002 Annual Assessment of Motor Vehicle Crashes." www-nrd.nhtsa.dot.gov/2002annual_assessment/non-occupants.htm.

23. Bruce Robinson, "Is There Any Reliable Evidence That Australian Helmet Legislation Works?" Proceedings of Velo Australia, Fremantle, Australia, October 30, 1996.

24. Paul Scuffham and John Langley, "Trends in Cycle Injuries in New Zealand Under Voluntary Helmet Use," *Accident Analysis and Prevention,* vol. 29, no. 1, 1997.

25. "Helmet Help Ahead," *Consumer Reports,* July 2002, pp. 22–24. The article mentions that some helmet models are effective at speeds close to twenty miles per hour.

26. Conversations with Robert R., Spring 2003.

27. Wording taken directly from the website of Giro Sport Design (www.giro.com).

CHAPTER FIVE: AIR POLLUTION AND THE CYCLIST

1. Flink, *The Automobile Age,* p. 136. Jacobs, *The Death and Life of Great American Cities,* p. 341. Jacobs cites a 1958 *Architectural Review* article by H. B. Creswell.

2. Stephen Blewett and Mary Embree, *What's in the Air* (Ventura, Calif.: Seaview Publishing, 1998), p. 103.

3. Dietrich Schwela and Olivier Zali, eds., *Urban Traffic Pollution* (London: E & FN Spon, 1998), pp. 151–52. For a pointed discussion of the long, painful process of Washington's push for environmental regulations on automobiles, and the industry's gambits in response, see Jack Doyle, *Taken for a Ride* (New York: Four Walls Eight Windows, 2000).

4. Many municipalities switched their diesel-fueled fleets to "biodiesel," a 20 percent vegetable oil mixture made from genetically modified soybeans. In 2003 engineering students at the University of Colorado in Boulder proved that buses could be run on a mixture including 100 percent recycled cooking

oil, with no retrofitting of conventional diesel engines. Engines burning these new diesel formulations will still pollute far more than regular gasoline engines, it should be noted. Katy Human, "Running on Vegetable Oil," *Boulder Daily Camera,* March 16, 2003.

5. M. P. Walsh writes that "in 1990 there were 50 million more cars on USA highways than there were in 1970." Walsh, in Schwela and Zali, eds., *Urban Traffic Pollution.* According to the US Department of Transportation, total vehicle miles traveled increased like clockwork through November 2007, then began to fall. In 2012 Americans drove fewer miles than they did in 2007, but more than two and half times as many total miles as they did in 1970. www.fhwa.dot.gov/policyinformation/travel_monitoring/historicvmt.pdf.

6. Schwela and Zali, eds., *Urban Traffic Pollution,* pp. 92–96.

7. One of the only available studies that specifically attempted to quantify bicyclists' exposure to pollutants measured their CO exposure in Southampton, England, in 1991, between 7.9 and 13 parts-per-million. Ibid., p. 96.

8. Ibid., pp. 45–46.

9. "In summary, in spite of decades of laboratory, clinical and epidemiological research, the human health effects of NO_2 exposure have not been fully characterized," writes Isabelle Romieu. Ibid., p. 13.

10. Blewett and Embree, *What's in the Air,* p. 82. The authors quote a strongly worded EPA warning on ozone.

11. Schwela and Zali, eds., *Urban Traffic Pollution,* pp. 14–23.

12. Ibid., p. 161. National Ambient Air Quality Standards (NAAQS). www.epa.gov/air/criteria.html.

13. Ibid., pp. 23–33.

14. "Latex Particles from Tires: Are They a Health Hazard?," *Journal of Allergy and Clinical Immunology,* September 2000, part one, vol. 106, no. 3, p. 573. Hugh Westrop, "Breathing Lessons," *Current Science,* April 20, 2001.

15. Ann Watson, Richard Bates, and Donald Kennedy, eds., *Air Pollution, the Automobile, and Public Health* (Washington, D.C.: National Academy Press, 1988), p. 325.

16. Ibid., p. 326.

17. Information for this paragraph was compiled from a comprehensive survey, by P. G. Flachsbart, of more than ninety different scientific studies: P. G. Flachsbart, "Exposure to Exhaust and Evaporative Emissions From Motor Vehicles," in Schwela and Zali, eds., *Urban Traffic Pollution,* pp. 89–126.

CHAPTER SIX: PUNCTURES AND FLATS

1. Charles Cohen, "All That Glitters Is Not Road," *City Paper* (Baltimore), March 1–March 7, 2000.
2. Technical information on puncture vine is derived from multiple sources, such as the University of California Statewide Integrated Pest Management Program.
3. Brilliant, *The Great Car Craze,* pp. 126–27. The irony is not lost on Brilliant: "The remarkable thing was that the Puncture Vine had not been at all common in California until the advent of the Mass Automobile."

CHAPTER SEVEN: EQUIPMENT

1. "Helmet Help Ahead," *Consumer Reports,* July 2002, pp. 22–24.

BIBLIOGRAPHY

Allen, Frederick Lewis. *The Big Change.* New York: Bantam Books, 1952.

Allen, John. *Street Smarts.* Emmaus, PA.: Rodale Press, 1988.

Berkow, Robert, MD, Mark H. Beers, MD, and Andrew J. Fletcher, eds. *The Merck Manual of Medical Information.* Whitehouse Station, NJ: Merck and Co. Inc., 1997.

Blake, Peter. *The Master Builders.* New York: Alfred A. Knopf, 1960.

Blewett, Stephen, and Mary Embree. *What's in the Air.* Ventura, CA: Seaview Publishing, 1998.

Bottles, Scott. *L.A. and the Automobile.* Berkely: University of California Press, 1987.

Brandt, Jobst. *The Bicycle Wheel.* Menlo Park, CA: Avocet, 1981.

Brilliant, Ashleigh. *The Great Car Craze.* Santa Barbara: Woodbridge Press, 1989.

Burke, Ed. *Serious Cycling.* Champaign, IL: Human Kinetics, 2002.

Campbell, Colin. *The Coming Oil Crisis.* Brentwood: Multi-Science Publishing Company, 1997.

Cherry, Richard. *EMT-Basic Exam Review.* Upper Saddle River, NJ: Prentice Hall, 1999.

Davis, Mike. *City of Quartz: Excavating the Future in Los Angeles.* New York: Vintage, 1992.

Dodge, Pryor. *The Bicycle.* Paris: Flammerion, 1996.

Doyle, Jack. *Taken for a Ride.* New York: Four Walls Eight Windows, 2000.

Flink, James. *The Automobile Age.* Cambridge: MIT Press, 1988.

Ford, Larry. *The Spaces Between Buildings.* Baltimore: Johns Hopkins University Press, 2000.

Forester, John. *Bicycle Transportation: A Handbook for Cycling Transportation Engineers.* Cambridge: MIT Press, 1994.

——. *Effective Cycling.* Cambridge: MIT Press, 1984.

Furness, Zack. *One Less Car: Bicycling and the Politics of Automobility.* Philadelphia: Temple University Press, 2010.

Garreau, Joel. *Edge City.* New York: Doubleday, 1991.

Gleick, James. *Chaos.* New York: Penguin, 1987.

Hugo-Brunt, Michael. *The History of City Planning.* Montreal: Harvest House, Ltd., 1972.

Jackson, Kenneth. *Crabgrass Frontier.* New York: Oxford University Press, 1985.

Jacobs, Jane. *The Death and Life of Great American Cities.* New York: Random House, 1961.

Johnson, Steven. *Emergence.* New York: Scribner and Sons, 2001.

Koolhaas, Rem. *S, M, L, XL.* New York: The Monacelli Press, 1994.

Kunstler, James Howard. *The City in Mind: Meditations on the Urban Condition.* New York: Free Press, 2001.

——. *Geography of Nowhere.* New York: Simon and Schuster, 1993.

——. *The Long Emergency.* New York: The Atlantic Monthly Press, 2005.

Lacey, Robert. *Ford: The Men and the Machine.* Boston: Little, Brown and Company, 1986.

Le Corbusier. *The City of Tomorrow and Its Planning.* London: J. Rodker, 1929.

Marshall, Alex. *How Cities Work.* Austin: University of Texas Press, 2001.

McGurn, James. *On Your Bicycle: An Illustrated History of Cycling.* New York: Facts On File Publications, 1987.

McShane, Clay. *Down the Asphalt Path.* New York: Columbia University Press, 1995.

Mumford, Lewis. *The City in History.* New York: Harcourt, Brace and World, 1968.

Nye, Peter. *Hearts of Lions.* New York: W. W. Norton & Company, 1988.

Rae, John B. *The Road and the Car in American Life.* Cambridge: MIT Press, 1971.

Reti, Ladislau, ed. *The Unknown Leonardo.* New York: McGraw-Hill Book Company, 1974.

Robinson, Bruce. "Is There Any Reliable Evidence That Australian Helmet Legislation Works?" Proceedings of Velo Australia. Fremantle, Australia, October 30, 1996.

Rowland Whitt, Frank, and David Wilson. *Bicycling Science.* Cambridge: MIT Press, 1982.

Safdie, Moshe. *The City After the Automobile.* New York: Harper-Collins, 1997.

Schwela, Dietrich, and Olivier Zali, eds. *Urban Traffic Pollution.* London: E & FN Spon, 1998.

Scuffham, Paul, and John Langley. "Trends in Cycle Injuries in New Zealand Under Voluntary Helmet Use." In *Accident Analysis and Prevention.* Vol. 29, no. 1 (1997).

Smith, Robert. *A Social History of the Bicycle.* New York: McGraw-Hill, 1972.

Thompson, D. C., F. P. Rivara, and R. S. Thompson. "Effectiveness of Bicycle Safety Helmets in Preventing Head Injuries: A Case Control Study." In *JAMA.* Vol. 276, (1996): pp. 1968–73.

Walden, Russell, ed. *The Open Hand: Essays on Le Corbusier.* Cambridge: MIT Press, 1977.

Watson, Ann, Richard Bates, and Donald Kennedy, eds. *Air Pollution, the Automobile, and Public Health.* Washington, D.C.: National Academy Press, 1988.

Whyte, William H. *City: Rediscovering the Center.* Philadelphia: University of Pennsylvania Press, 2009.

Wilson, James Q., ed. *The Metropolitan Enigma.* New York: Doubleday, 1968.

Yang, Nai C. *Design of Functional Pavements.* New York: McGraw-Hill, 1972.

Yoder, E. J. *Principles of Pavement Design.* New York: John Wiley and Sons, 1959.

Zinn, Lennard. *Zinn and the Art of Road Bike Maintenance.* Boulder: Velo Press, 2000.

INDEX

ABOUT THE AUTHOR

Robert Hurst safely completed over 80,000 deliveries as a bicycle messenger in Denver, where he now resides. Robert is also the author of *The Art of Mountain Biking, The Cyclist's Manifesto, Best Bike Rides Denver and Boulder, Road Biking Colorado's Front Range,* and other cycling books, all published by FalconGuides.